D1553050

# THE HEART OF
# JOHN MUIR'S WORLD

Cover photo: John Muir walking along the Merced River in Yosemite Valley at the Royal Arches.
Photo courtesy of Charles Bradley.

JOHN MUIR

# THE HEART OF JOHN MUIR'S WORLD

## Wisconsin, Family, and Wilderness Discovery

### Millie Stanley

PRAIRIE OAK PRESS
Madison, Wisconsin

First edition, first printing

Prairie Oak Press
821 Prospect Place
Madison, Wisconsin 53703

Cover and text design by Caroline Beckett, Flying Fish Graphics,
Blue Mounds, Wisconsin

Typeset by KC Graphics, Inc., Madison, Wisconsin

Printed in the United States of America by BookCrafters, Chelsea, Michigan

Library of Congress Cataloging-in-Publication Data

Stanley, Millie.
    The heart of John Muir's world: Wisconsin, family, and wilderness
discovery / Millie Stanley.—1st ed.
        p.      cm.
    Includes bibliographical references (p.    ) and index.
    ISBN 1-879483-22-X: $16.95
    1. Muir, John, 1838–1914. 2. Muir, John, 1838–1914—Family.
3. Conservationists—United States—Biography. 4. Naturalists—United
States—Biography. 5. Muir family. I. Title.
QH31.M78S88  1994
508.775'092—dc20
[B]                                                                    94-32445
                                                                         CIP

For my son Bob and his family

# CONTENTS

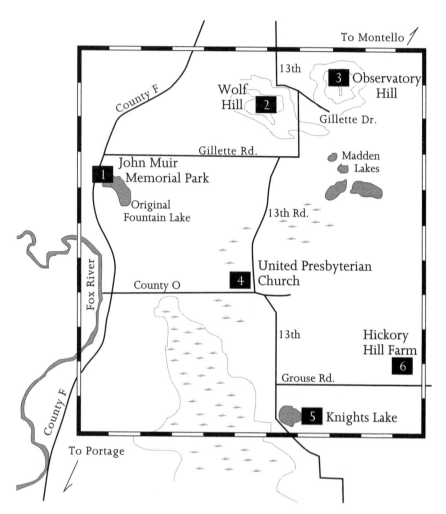

JOHN MUIR'S BOYHOOD LANDSCAPE
Town of Buffalo, Marquette County, Wisconsin

1. JOHN MUIR MEMORIAL PARK—Designated as a National Historic Landmark by the National Park System. FOUNTAIN LAKE FARM settled by the Muirs in 1849 totaled 160 acres. Some sixty acres of the original farm lying along the eastern shore of the lake are within the park.

2. WOLF HILL—Scene of early adventure.

3. OBSERVATORY HILL—The future naturalist was inspired by the view from

atop this "cloud-capped mountain of his child's imagination"—the glacial land-scape of gently rolling hills, rivers, streams, and wetlands.

4. UNITED PRESBYTERIAN CHURCH—Built after Muir left the area. The pioneer UP cemetery holds graves of family members and friends.

5. KNIGHTS LAKE—Where Daniel Muir baptized his son John and the rest of the family.

6. HICKORY HILL FARM—The Muirs moved to this farm in 1856. John left home in 1860 at the age of twenty-two.

"The preservation of specimen sections of natural flora—bits of pure wildness—was a fond, favorite notion of mine long before I heard of national parks. When my father came from Scotland, he settled in a fine wild region of Wisconsin, beside a small glacier lake bordered with white pond-lilies. . . . And when I was about to wander away on my long rambles I was sorry to leave that precious meadow unprotected; therefore, I said to my brother-in-law, who then owned it, 'sell me the forty acres of lake meadow and keep it fenced, and never allow cattle or hogs to break into it, and I will gladly pay you whatever you say. I want to keep it untrampled for the sake of its ferns and flowers; and even if I should never see it again, the beauty of its lilies and orchids are so pressed into my mind I shall always enjoy looking back at them in imagination, even across seas and continents, and perhaps after I am dead.'

"But he regarded my plan as a sentimental dream wholly impracti-cable. The fence he said would surely be broken down sooner or later, and all the work would be in vain. Eighteen years later I found the deep-water pond-lilies in fresh bloom, but the delicate garden-sod of the meadow was broken up and trampled into black mire."

John Muir, November 23, 1895

# FOREWORD

This book is for the kind of reader who likes to get to roots, to causes, to influences, to the core. By examining John Muir's connections with his family and friends, Millie Stanley takes us inside the heart and mind of America's most important Naturalist. In her biography, she approaches Muir's life with the same scrupulous scholarly care he used to describe the natural world.

But like Muir, Stanley always reaches beyond the surface, searching for "the heart," a word which appears frequently in Muir's letters and Journals. When Muir wrote about plants or animals or a geological structure, he wrote not only accurately, but with a need to know, to understand. Millie Stanley takes the same kind of loving care with the details of Muir's life, and she reveals the same kind of need to know.

Using innumerable illustrations from his correspondence, his journals, and from the accounts of others, Stanley documents and brings to life Muir's love affair with nature, and she shows us that his heart first opened at Fountain Lake in the company of his brothers, sisters, and mother. Even his father with whom he had many conflicts, helped initiate him to the wonders of the physical world. Stanley shows us that, though he explored and lived in other inspiring and natural areas, his family and their life in Wisconsin remain at the center (the heart!) of his connections with natural spaces.

We learn from Ms. Stanley's book that John Muir clearly understood the centrality of his family in his life. He was fond of describing his family as trees with intertwining roots. Even when they were living great distances apart, he saw them drawing on the same sources of nourishment, with interwoven origins and affections.

Remembering his arrival in Wisconsin at age eleven, Muir wrote in *The Story of My Boyhood and Youth*, "This sudden plash into pure wildness—

baptism in Nature's warm heart—how utterly happy it made us!" and to conclude the same paragraph, he wrote, "Young hearts, young leaves, flowers, animals, the winds and the streams and the sparkling lake, all wildly, gladly rejoicing together!" At this young age Muir had the sense of the interrelatedness of everything within the natural world. There in Marquette County, Wisconsin, the heart of "Nature" and the heart of the boy came together to forge a life-time connection. Later in his life Muir became the national and international champion of national parks, but Stanley reminds us that his first preservation efforts were for a portion of the Fountain Lake Farm of his childhood.

In this intimate portrait of Muir, Stanley shows us why and how he determined to discover his own center. When Muir was 29 years old, he had an accident which clarified for him the steps he wanted to follow in his life. He pierced his right eye with a file, and as the aqueous humor flowed out, he said aloud, "My right eye is gone, closed forever on all God's beauty." As he healed from the injury, he determined to spend the rest of his life taking in everything he could, and he did not return to industrial engineering. Instead, as he said, he set out to "get as near to the heart of the world" as he could. Though the accident endangered his physical vision, his strength as a visionary naturalist grew more clear and deep.

Reading Stanley's book provides us innumerable glimpses into Muir's own spiritual life. The affection and concern he shows for friends and family in his letters, and the fondness they show for him bring him boldly to life. In Millie Stanley's book, you will hear the beating of John Muir's heart with a clarity and power nowhere else available.

Professor Tim Hirsch
Department of English
University of Wisconsin, Eau Claire

# PREFACE

John Muir once said, "In my walks through the forests of humanity I find no family clump more interwoven in root or branch than our own. . . . As a family we are pretty firmly united. One tree in a close clump cannot very well fall."

The father of our national parks was a prolific writer in behalf of wilderness and many books and articles have been written concerning his life and work. The literature well describes the pioneer ecologist's experiences as adventurer, explorer, discoverer, scientist, and environmental lobbyist.

*The Heart of John Muir's World* shows what an important part a strong sense of family played in John's life and achievements. I have focused on the Muir family story and to a great extent have portrayed his career from this perspective. Close family relationships spanned Muir's lifetime and gave him a strong personal base.

In my search for a better understanding of this man, I read hundreds of Muir family letters housed at the University of the Pacific, Stockton, California. The correspondence casts light on Muir's nature and that of his parents, Anne and Daniel Muir, and his siblings. It illumines their relationships. Many of John's letters contain the exquisite poetic prose for which he became noted in his published works.

An exchange of letters that ensued when Muir first left home in 1860 offers the earliest personal glimpse into the individual lives of the Muirs. John's correspondence with his family continued for many years and provided ever deepening insight into his personality and his mission. His family's constant interest in his experiences and well-being sustained him though he was far afield.

In 1849 Anne and Daniel Muir and their seven children emigrated to America from Dunbar, Scotland, just one year after Wisconsin achieved statehood. They settled 160 acres of virgin land on a glacially created lake in Marquette County and called it Fountain Lake Farm. There were the two oldest girls, Margaret (Maggie), who was born in 1834, and Sarah, born in 1836. Then came John, born in 1838, David, in 1840, and Daniel (Dan), in 1843. The twins, Mary and Anna (Annie), were born in 1846. Joanna, the eighth child, was born at the farm in 1850.

My narrative expands on the early influences that helped shape Muir's nature. It tells of his youthful years on Fountain Lake and Hickory Hill Farms and shows that his Wisconsin inspiration and experience paved the way for his later accomplishments in preserving the national landscape.

*The Heart of John Muir's World* describes the Wisconsin countryside so beloved by Muir. The diverse glacial landscape of pioneer Fountain Lake Farm and the surrounding area provided an excellent place for the young Scottish lad to explore nature and discover interrelationships within the natural world.

In researching this book I gained insight and knowledge in many ways. For over twenty years I have lived in the heart of John Muir country—the Town (township) of Buffalo, Marquette County. In all seasons I have roamed the landscape Muir loved. With the help of local residents, I tramped the fields and woods—occasionally climbing barbed wire fences—to locate the sites of Muir's early experiences as described in his autobiograpical *The Story of My Boyhood and Youth*. To trace farm boundaries, I consulted early land records in Register of Deeds offices and poured over atlases and plat books.

I conducted over fifty interviews, many in Marquette County. Muir stories have been handed down through the generations, a number only one generation removed from the time of the Muirs.

Information was garnered from the State Historical Society of Wisconsin archives, and those at the University of Wisconsin, as well as local libraries and historical societies. Study trips in Wisconsin and Canada were fruitful.

As well as reading the Muir correspondence in Stockton, I spent momentous days with Sherry Hanna roaming the area around Martinez,

California, where the Strentzel-Muir ranch was located and where Muir spent thirty-four productive years. I spent time at the John Muir National Historic Site in Martinez and at the Yosemite Park Library in the Sierra Nevada. John Muir Hanna, grandson of Muir, introduced me to the Sierra Nevada high country where his namesake explored more than a century ago.

John Muir was part of the pioneer growth of Wisconsin. He helped build a pioneer farm; worked on a pioneer corduroy road; attended early district school and home church services; displayed his inventions at the state fair; traveled on the earliest state railroad; and attended the fledgling Wisconsin State University (now called the University of Wisconsin).

Muir's land preservation idea began to take shape in Marquette County. When he was about to leave Wisconsin for a sojourn in Canada in 1864, his first attempt to preserve a treasured bit of Fountain Lake land for its beauty alone was the seed that grew into his major contribution to the formation of the national park system. Muir later explored and studied amid spectacular scenery, but he always carried a bit of Wisconsin with him.

In December, 1856, his sister Sarah married David Galloway and the couple took over the Fountain Lake home and 120 acres. The rest of the family moved to their new farm, Hickory Hill. Young John left Hickory Hill Farm in September, 1860, to show his whittled hickory inventions at the State Fair in Madison, about sixty miles away. This was his introduction to the outside world.

As the years went on, John, in the role of elder brother, was always concerned about the welfare of his mother, brothers, and sisters. He took an active interest in their affairs and helped them over many a hurdle. They counted on him when they needed a hand.

He didn't have much money in the early years when he was filling his "wheat bins" as well as his "wisdom bins," as his friend Bradley Brown once called making a living and going to school, but he shared what he could. As his three younger sisters grew up, he gave them much brotherly advice and aided them financially. Unfortunately, Daniel Muir did little to help his children.

After his 1880 marriage to Louisiana Strentzel, John became wealthy through his management of the Strentzel-Muir orchards in the Alhambra Valley at Martinez. He was then in a better position to help his sisters and brothers further.

Daniel Muir was a stern, restless man of fanatic religious zeal, and when he left to do missionary work in Canada, John told his mother and sisters at home that they need have no concern for bread. As they had done in times past, John, his mother, brothers, and sisters provided affection and stability for each other.

Letters to his family marked the beginning of Muir's prolific writings. He began early to keep journals on his foot journeys through the wilderness. He labeled his first known journal "Earth-Planet, Universe" and hung it on his belt as he started off on his thousand-mile walk through the southeastern states to the Gulf of Mexico. In it he described his diverse impressions—from his pleasure at seeing his first mountain stream to the desolate post-Civil War conditions in the South. In later journals he continued to note everything from his joy at a sunset to meticulous measurements of the movement of a glacier. These journals became a main source for his published articles and books covering a myriad of subjects—natural history, glaciers, plants, animals, mountains, and natural processes. He devoted much of his later writing to efforts to preserve the national landscape.

In his wilderness quest, he eventually traveled and studied all over the globe—the United States, Canada, Europe, South America, and Africa. In 1879 he made the first of seven trips to Alaska, then virtually unexplored.

Wherever he went, this man of personal magnetism made lasting friendships with people from all walks of life. He carried on a voluminous correspondence with his legions of friends, colleagues, fellow scientists, fellow activists, and his family.

At Muir's death in 1914, there were five living brothers and sisters —David, Dan, Sarah, Mary, and Joanna. Margaret and Anna had preceded him in death.

My account of the family continues till the end of Muir's life, for their bond remained strong. At his death the outpouring of sentiment from the remaining sisters and brothers was significant, for their tributes told of their brother's life and brought it full circle. They had loved and respected him, applauded his career, and basked in his limelight. They had played an important role in his life as he had in theirs.

The comment Muir made when his father died held true at the time of his own death: "Through all our devious ways and wandering we have loved one another."

As I was led from one bit of knowledge to another in my research, I realized how true is Muir's famous quote: "When we try to pick out anything by itself we find it is hitched to everything else in the universe."

# ACKNOWLEDGMENTS

On a sunny October day, Allan and Phyllis Turner and I sat at the dining room table, in their home at the base of Observatory Hill, pouring over Marquette County, Wisconsin, platbooks to define for a sketch the sites of John Muir's youthful haunts. I soon found myself in Allan's plane flying over our own beloved landscape with its hills and shining waters—the land where John Muir spent his boyhood and youth—and where I began my search for his roots.

Many people have helped me along the way as I researched this book. It is impossible to adequately express my gratitude to each one in this space, but I would like to mention a number of people who were of special help.

First on the list is Harry Kearns, the venerable Irishman with the friendly twinkle in his eye and engaging way of speaking. Harry, who lived to be a hundred, grew up on Hickory Hill Farm, the second Wisconsin farm settled by the Muirs. It has been in the Kearns family since 1873.

When I was a newcomer to the relatively unspoiled Marquette County countryside, Harry and his wife Lorena, who died some years before, were the first people to answer my questions about Muir's background. They encouraged me in my endeavors.

I wandered Hickory Hill fields with Harry many times over the years, at the growing season or at harvest—fields the Muirs used to work. He would tell fine stories of the farm during Muir times, or from his own rich heritage. His father, Thomas, who remembered Daniel Muir, had passed along tales from the Muir era. When we stood at the door of the original Muir barn filled with hay, and he described how it was built, I imagined I could see young John working with his adz on the timbers, the marks still visible. When we sat in the tiny original parlor of the farmhouse, I could believe Daniel Muir was in the adjacent bedroom translating his Bible and looking out over the fields where his children worked. Not only did we roam Hickory Hill, but we explored the Fountain Lake environs and other places that were part of John Muir's youth in our Town of Buffalo.

Hickory Hill is a working farm, but since Harry was retired, he had time to reminisce. He bridged the gap between Muir times and our own. I did thank him sometimes, but today I wish I could tell this wonderful man one more time how deeply I appreciated him.

For some years Hickory Hill has been farmed by Harry's son Maurice, his wife Mary, and their son Paul. Although they are all exceedingly busy, they have been unfailingly hospitable and have often taken time to share a bit of knowledge with me.

The many local people I interviewed were a rich source of information and insight and are noted in the text and endnotes. Bessie Eggleston, who owns a portion of the orginal Fountain Lake Farm, was especially generous with her time and knowledge.

Over the years, the Turners shared with me and others, their corner of the world at Observatory Hill, that was so inspirational to Muir in his youth.

The present owners of Mound Hill Farm, George and Amy Horton, showed me the remnant of Fern Lake, the glacial pond that Muir tried in 1871 to protect from the trampling hooves of cattle.

In my quest for information, the Portage Public Library librarians were consistently helpful. Librarian Edwynna Curry was of special help. I obtained basic land information from the offices of the registers of deeds of Marquette and Columbia counties.

I sometimes counted on my own Marquette County Historical Society and Columbia County Historical Society, particularly Frances Sprain and Jean Jerred.

My long-time friend, local historian Rita Fredrick, supported and encouraged me from the start. She helped me in many ways and I valued her advice. Her husband Leo offered many a practical tip, especially with maps and site locations. The three of us often trudged around the countryside in search of significant places and usually found what we were seeking.

The historical collections of the State Historical Society of Wisconsin, Madison, were of great importance. The staff in the archives department and the reference library with its newspaper collections provided competent assistance. Of particular note is Myrna Williamson in the iconography department who ably guided me through the fine photographic collection.

The University of Wisconsin archives in the Memorial Library provided good information on their famous alumnus.

In researching background material on Muir's stay in Prairie du Chien at the confluence of the Wisconsin and Mississippi Rivers, and his later walk, I received help from Michael Douglass, director of the Villa Louis, operated by the State Historical Society of Wisconsin. Mary Antoine de Julio, curator of collections there, critiqued chapters pertaining to the Praire du Chien area. Historian and writer Griff Williams provided information on the Prairie du Chien of the 1860s.

Across the Mississippi, Mrs. Mae Huebsch of the McGregor (Iowa) Historical Society and the McGregor Museum shared information.

I procured information from the archives at Effigy Mounds National Monument at Harpers Ferry, Iowa, James David, superintendent, and from materials collected by staff member Timothy Mason.

My travels took me to Meaford, Canada, where Muir spent two years exploring the Canadian wilderness and working at the Trout sawmill and broom and rake handle factory. Meaford historian Frank Dougherty took me to the sawmill site on a stream a mile or so from the Georgian Bay of Lake Huron. Although the timberlands have largely disappeared, I could envision John and his brother David arriving at the Trout home that winter of 1864-65 to "den up."

Acting on Muir biographer Fred Turner's timely suggestion, my John Muir trail naturally took me to California and to the John Muir Papers housed in the Holt-Atherton Center for Western Studies at the

University of the Pacific at Stockton. Dr. Ronald Limbaugh, Professor of History, and Kirsten Lewis were then in the process of organizing them for the subsequent publication of *The Guide and Index to the Microform Edition of the John Muir Papers.* I appreciate Dr. Limbaugh's patience in finding a corner for me in their limited space where I could read the Muir letters.

Librarian Daryl Morrison, Special Collections librarian of the University of the Pacific Libraries, gave me able guidance in my further use of the Muir papers in their present fine facilities, as did manuscripts librarian and archivist Cynthia E. Stevenson and Janene Ford.

During one California sojourn, I found myself on the doorstep of William and Maymie Kimes, authors of *John Muir: A Reading Bibliography.* I considered it a rare privilege to visit the John Muir room in their home containing the precious volumes, magazines, and other materials they have collected throughout years of devotion to John Muir's life and legacy. I used their intriquing bibliography extensively to keep me on the right course in tracing Muir's career and published writings.

My friend, fellow Wisconsinite Mary Vocelka, gave me fine assistance in her capacity as librarian of the Yosemite National Park Library. I am grateful to her for her for critiquing the manuscript. I will always remember my joy in sitting quietly on her patio savoring for hours the changing granite face of Half Dome across the Yosemite meadow. I experienced at least a bit of the feeling John Muir had for this remarkable formation.

I thank Director Phyllis Shaw and the fine staff of the John Muir National Historic Site at Martinez for the many courtesies they showed me during several visits to the mansion on the hill. The home, where Muir lived for twenty-four years, overlooks a portion of the original ranchlands. Staff member Pat Thomas was especially helpful in guiding me through the archives there and verifying information.

As a climax to the whole research adventure, I wandered the Martinez area, Yosemite National Park environs, and the California desert with Muir descendents who are carrying on the Muir tradition in their own way.

I cherish the time I spent with Sherry Hanna, wife of John Muir's grandson, Strentzel Hanna. Sherry lived on a garden acre in the Alhambra Valley at Martinez, California, one of twenty that John and Louisiana Strentzel gave their daughter Louisiana (Louie) and John Muir as a wedding gift in 1880. She lived just down the road from the original ranch house built by the Strentzels in 1853 when they settled vast acreage in the valley and beyond and began extensive fruit growing.

I am pleased that Sherry cared so well for Muir family treasures for so many years and took such interest in the Muir family heritage. Wandering the Alhambra Valley and Martinez area on Suisun Bay with her gave me a fine idea of the setting where Muir lived from 1880 till his death in 1914. I enjoyed the beautiful valley, the creek, and the splendid sunrises and sunsets over the hills that frame the valley as I know Muir did.

John and Louie raised their two daughters, Wanda and Helen, on the ranch, first living in the old ranch house and then the mansion on the hill. Successfully managing the ranch, Muir made exploratory trips from there to Yosemite, the Sierra mountains, the western forests, Alaska, and the rest of the world. Here he wrote articles and books in behalf of wilderness and lobbied for its preservation.

One day when Sherry and I crossed the flooded ancient pear orchard to the tiny cemetery by Alhambra Creek and stood by Muir's grave, I thought of his sister Sarah Galloway's comment, "His work is done and now he is resting."

When we visited the picturesque Martinez City Cemetery atop the hill overlooking the bay where Sarah, another sister, Maggie Reid, and his brother David are buried, I reflected on how close he had been to his Wisconsin family. Four of the eight brothers and sisters eventually lived on the ranchlands.

I am grateful to Muir's grandson John Muir Hanna and his wife Virginia for their kindness. John is now raising grapes in the Napa Valley, and my visits to his vineyards gave me added understanding of what the Muir-Strentzel ranch in the Alhambra Valley might have been like. John had much to tell of his adventurous youth when he lived in the original ranch house there with his parents, Tom and Wanda Muir Hanna, and his sister and four brothers. A memorable trip with John and Virginia and Sherry Hanna to the Sierra high country expanded my mountain horizons. John Hanna's tales gave me the grand feeling of reliving both his and his grandfather's adventures. I value this great experience.

It was a privilege to visit John Muir's grandson, Walter Muir, and his wife Margaret in their California home in its beautiful desert setting. I experienced a sense of the wonder of the Mojave Desert as Walter and I trudged through the sands in the warmth of the bright sun in search of remnants of an old aqueduct. His parents had built this ingenious plank-covered cement waterway many years ago to carry water over the surface five miles to their alfalfa fields near Daggett, California. Walter's mother, Helen Muir Funk, who eventually returned to her family name of Muir, lived at Daggett for a number of years. Muir was visiting his daughter there during the Christmas season in 1914 when he became so very ill and died the day before Christmas at California Hospital in Los Angeles. I felt once more the sadness of that day.

I owe my thanks to Elizabeth Durbin, author, editor, and teacher for her early encouragement and practical suggestions, and to writer and editor Constance Conrader. I am grateful to Charlotte Johnston, high school teacher of Wisconsin writers; Dr. Tim Hirsch, professor of English, University of Wisconsin—Eau Claire; and Gwen Schultz, professor of geography University of Wisconsin—Madison, for critiquing the manuscript.

On the technical side of the project, my son Bob deserves a thank-you for his guidance in keeping me on the right track in the world of word processors and printers, and Linda Ornes has helped as well. I thank Jane Ziehmke for helping me in many ways—at one point typing an entire earlier manuscript into the new processor so I could proceed with the work.

This, then, is at least a partial list of people who have been so helpful and supportive.

# CHRONOLOGY

April 21, 1838—John Muir is born in Dunbar, Scotland to Anne and Daniel Muir. Begins classical education. Love of nature awakens in early childhood.

1849—Family emigrates to America and settles land on Fountain Lake, Town (township) of Buffalo, Marquette County, Wisconsin. Hard work of developing pioneer farm mingles with inspiration of native Wisconsin landscape. Whittles hickory inventions.

1856—Moves to Hickory Hill Farm nearby. Continues to whittle and briefly attends district school. Exchanges youthful thoughts in 1858 correspondence with neighborhood farm boys. Harsh methods of father Daniel Muir, a self-styled minister. Encouragement of neighbors William and Jean Duncan.

Sept. 1860  Takes inventions to Wisconsin State Agricultural Fair. Accompanies Norman Wiard, inventor of an iceboat, to Prairie du Chien, Wis. Stays with Pelton family and forms long-lasting friendship with Emily Pelton. Family letters offer earliest insight into natures of John and his family.

Feb. 1861—Enrolls at Wisconsin State University, Madison. Irregular attendance for about two years. Learns about "nature's basement rooms" from Dr. Ezra S. Carr. Is consumed with interest in botany. Carr's wife, Jeanne, becomes his mentor. Feels heavy burden of Civil War.

Dec. 1861—Muir family moves to Portage. John's sister Margaret and her husband John Reid take over Hickory Hill Farm.

July 1863—His first foot journey of discovery is along the Wisconsin River to the Mississippi. Returns to Marquette County. Stays with sister

Sarah and her husband David Galloway who now own Fountain Lake Farm until March, 1864.

March 1864—Before leaving for Canada to join his brother Dan, Muir's attempt to save a portion of Fountain Lake Farm for its beauty alone is the seed of his major contribution to the formation of the national park system. Botanizes in Ontario. Works at Trout's sawmill, using inventive abilities to improve the broom and rake handles factory.

Jan. 1865—By Jan. 1, 1865 the Muirs returned to Hickory Hill Farm.

March 1866—Fire about the first of March at Trouts destroys this career. Takes job at Osgood & Smith carriage parts factory in Indianapolis, Indiana where he improves operations in an early version of time-study.

March 5, 1867—Accident to his eye destroys second industrial career. Decides to leave industry to get close to nature.

Sept. 1, 1867—After recuperation and extended visit at home, begins thousand-mile walk to the Gulf of Mexico ending at Cedar Keys (sic), Florida Oct. 23, 1867. Sends botanical specimens home to sister Sarah.

Jan. 1868—March 28, 1868—Makes way to San Francisco. Begins a ten-year career, living, working, studying, and making scientific observations in the Yosemite Valley and the Sierras.

1869—Helps young sister Mary financially, enabling her to attend Wisconsin State University. Encourages Dan to attend medical school and Annie and Joanna in their teaching careers. Gives business advice to David, now a partner in a Portage dry goods store.

1871—From California, makes a second attempt, through David Galloway, to buy a portion of Fountain Lake Farm for preservation. The attempt fails.

1874—Father Daniel Muir sells Hickory Hill Farm, moves family to Portage, Wis. A self-styled preacher, he moves to Hamilton, Ontario, Canada to preach. His wife Anne and the rest of the family do not follow.

1878—Begins writing mountain articles for *Scribner's Monthly*.

1879—Makes the first of seven journeys to Alaska.

April 14, 1880—Marries Louie (Louisiana) Strentzel, daughter of Dr. John and Louisiana Strentzel. Begins work on the Strentzels' extensive fruit ranch at Martinez, California.

March 24, 1881—Birth of Annie Wanda Muir.

May, 1881—Begins cruise aboard the "Corwin" into Arctic waters.

1882-1887—Devotes his time to family matters and managing the ranch.

1884—Sarah's husband, David Galloway, dies.

1885—Muir has premonition of the death of his father, now living with daughter Joanna in Kansas City, Mo. Goes east and visits Portage family and sister Mary Hand in Nebraska. Visits old friends and scenes of childhood. Daniel dies Oct. 6, 1885. John's sister Annie returns to California with him for extended stay.

January 23, 1886—Birth of Helen Lillian Muir.

1889—Writes two articles for *Century Magazine* urging that the lands surrounding Yosemite Valley be made into a national park.

1891—Muir's sister Margaret and John Reid move to the California ranch, giving Muir more time to pursue wilderness causes.

Spring, 1892—David moves to the ranch from Portage and relieves his brother of the burden of ranch management. Muir is completely free to return to the wilderness and his efforts to save it.

June, 1892—Instrumental in organizing Sierra Club to support preservation of western lands and forests. Is president for the rest of his life.

1893—During extensive European travels, he visits Dunbar, Scotland, the scene of his early childhood.

1894—First book, Mountains of California, is published.

1896—His mother Anne Muir dies in Portage. While visiting her, Muir makes third attempt to buy land at Fountain Lake, this time acreage adjoining the original Muir farm. Receives MA degree from Harvard.

1897—University of Wisconsin awards him Doctor of Laws Degree.

1899—Sarah Galloway moves to California.

1903—His sister Annie Muir dies in Portage, the last of the Muir family there.

1903—Camps with President Teddy Roosevelt in the Sierras and enlists his help to save western lands and forests.

1905—Yosemite Valley receded to federal government.

Aug. 6, 1905—Louie Muir dies.

June, 1911—Publishes My First Summer in the Sierra.

March, 1913—Publishes The Story of My Boyhood and Youth.

December 24, 1914—John Muir becomes ill with pneumonia while visiting his daughter Helen in the desert at Daggett, California. He dies the morning before Christmas at California Hospital in Los Angeles with a manuscript on his travels to Alaska spread before him on the bed.

After his death—The outpouring of letters from his family and many, many others and the outpouring from the press bring Muir's life and legacy into focus. John Muir's life comes full circle.

# MUIR FAMILY AND FRIENDS

Blake, James A.—Muir's student companion on his first wilderness walk

Branch, George—Muir's district school teacher

Brown, Alfred Bradley, Muir's boyhood friend

Brown, Walter—husband of Joanna Muir

Butler, James Davie—Muir's revered classics professor at Wisconsin State University

Cairns, Catherine—first wife of David Muir, b. July, 1839, d. March 27, 1885

Carr, Ezra Slocum—professor of chemistry and natural history at Wisconsin State University

Carr, Jeanne, wife of Ezra, Muir's longtime mentor

Delaney, Don—Muir tended his sheep when he first explored the Sierras

Duncan, Jessie—daughter of William and Jean, b. 1859, d. 1955; Jessie's foster daughter, Annie Duncan Waite

Duncan, William b. 1806, d. August 18, 1895, and Jean, b. 1814, d. June 11, 1903—Hickory Hill Farm neighbors who were Muir's benefactors

Funk, Buel—husband of Muir's daughter Helen who later returned to the family name of Muir

Galloway, David—husband of Sarah Muir, b. January 28, 1828, d. September 28, 1884
> Galloway children: Anna, Cecelia, George, b. June 8, 1860, d., June 8, 1879, and Grace

Galloway, George, b. February 26, 1801, d. January 12, 1893 and Jean Millar d. December 22, 1876—parents of David. Jean, an avid supporter of Muir

Gilrye, David and Margaret—Muir's maternal grandparents of Dunbar, Scotland

Gray, Alexander and Jane—early pioneers who befriended the Muir family in 1849

Gray, David—Fountain Lake neighbor, one of the "twa Davies" who inspired Muir to further learning

Gray, Philip C.—father of David, member of the Body of the Disciples of Christ

Gray, William—uncle of David, member of the Body of the Disciples of Christ

Griswold, Milton—fellow North Dormitory resident who gave Muir his first lesson in botany

Hand, Willis—husband of Mary Muir

Hanna, Thomas—husband of Muir's daughter Wanda

McKay, Alexander and George—previous owners of Hickory Hill lands.

McReath, James—b. 1801, d. 1869. His descendants handed down Muir stories through the generations

Moores, Merrill—Muir's young Indianapolis, Indiana friend

Muir, Daniel—b. 1804, d. October 6, 1885, and Anne Gilrye, b. March 17, 1813, d. June 22, 1896—John Muir's parents
> Muir children:
> Anna (Annie), twin to Mary, b. October 5, 1846, d. January 15, 1903
> Daniel (Dan), b. 1843
>> Mabel—daughter of Dan and his first wife, Emma

David, b. July 11, 1840, d. October 28, 1916
> Children of David and Catherine Muir: Anna, Carrie, John, b. September, 1868, d. June 15, 1886, and Wilberforce

Joanna (Brown)—b. 1850

John, b. April 21, 1838, d. Dec. 24, 1914
> Children of John and Louie Strentzel Muir: Annie Wanda, b. March 25, 1881 and Helen Lillian, b. January 23, 1886

Maggie (Reid)—b. 1834, d. 1910

Mary (Hand), twin to Annie, b. October 5, 1846

Sarah (Galloway)—b. February 19, 1836, d. April 11, 1932

Muir, Emma—first wife of Dan

Muir, John—of Crawfordjohn, Scotland and Sarah Higgs Muir, from England, John Muir's paternal grandparents

Parry, William T.—David Muir's partner at Parry & Muir store.

Osgood, Judson—partner at carriage wheel parts factory where Muir suffered an industrial accident

Pelton
> Edward—owner of Prairie du Chien hotel where John Muir stayed and worked
> Emily, Edward's niece—lifelong friend of Muir
> Frances, wife of Edward

Reid, John—husband of Maggie Muir, b. 1835, d. 1926
> Reid children: Harry, Jessie, b. January 29, 1863, d. Dec. 8, 1944, John, Jr., b. 1874, d. 1954, and May

Rice, M. M., student companion of Muir on first wilderness walk

Smith, William—partner at carriage wheel parts factory where Muir suffered an industrial accident.

Sterling, John, Dean of Faculty, Wisconsin State University

Strentzel, John—Muir's father-in-law, Martinez, California rancher and doctor

Strentzel, Louisiana—Muir's mother-in-law

Strentzel, Louisiana (Louie)—Muir's wife, d. August 6, 1905

Taylor, David—one of the "twa Davies" who inspired Muir to further learning

Treadway, Juliaette—b. December 25, 1844, d. March 8, 1906, second wife of David Muir

Trout, William—owner of Meaford, Canada sawmill and factory where Muir worked

Vroman, Charles—roomed with Muir in the North Dormitory

Waite, Annie Duncan—foster daughter of Jessie Duncan and wife of Frank Waite, farm worker for the Duncan family

Whitehead, Charlie—the "child man," d. August 17, 1859, age 38, cared for by his brother Benjamin, blacksmith and self-styled minister

Whitehead, James—son of Benjamin and friend of Muir

Wiard, Norman, inventor of ice boat

# THE HEART OF
# JOHN MUIR'S WORLD

# I

# SOME OF THE HAPPIEST DAYS
# OF MY LIFE

> Oh, that glorious Wisconsin wilderness!
> Everything new and pure in the very prime
> of spring when Nature's pulses were
> beating highest and mysteriously keeping
> time with our own! Young hearts, young
> leaves, flowers, animals, the winds and
> the streams and the sparkling lake, all
> wildly, gladly rejoicing together!
> —John Muir

"The happiest days and scrap portions of my life were [spent] in that old slant-walled garret and among the smooth creeks that trickled among the sedges of Fountain Lake meadow." So wrote John Muir to his brother David on March 20, 1870. "You stirred a happy budget of memories in speaking of my work-shop and laboratory," he continued, recalling the mechanical achievements of his early days in Wisconsin. He then added, "The only sounds that strike me to-night are the ticking of the clock, the flickering of the fire and the love songs of a host of peaceful frogs that sing out in the meadow up to their throats in slush, and the deep waving roar of the falls like breakers on a rocky coast."[1]

The man who became the father of our national park system wrote this letter from a sugar pine shanty he had built at the base of Yosemite Falls in California's magnificent Yosemite Valley. He was there to explore the Sierra Nevada, the mountains he called the range of light. Though living almost in the shadow of the granite formation Half Dome that

Muir called the queen of all the valley rocks, his thoughts turned to his first home in America and the green, rolling landscape of Wisconsin.

He first saw that landscape in 1849 when he was eleven years old. His father Daniel had brought him, his thirteen-year-old sister Sarah, and nine-year-old brother David to America to find land and prepare a home for the rest of the family. Waiting in Dunbar, Scotland were his mother, Anne Gilrye Muir, and the other children, Margaret (Maggie), fifteen, Daniel (Dan), six, and the twins, Mary and Anna (Annie), almost three. They would come to the new world when their farmstead was ready.

It was early May when the wagon, drawn by oxen and loaded with household goods and tools, rumbled onto the land Daniel had chosen on the northeast side of Fountain Lake in the Town (township) of Buffalo, Marquette County. John and David jumped from the wagon eager to explore. Finding a bluejay's nest was John's first discovery at Fountain Lake and one of many more he would make in his lifetime.

John was thrilled with the landscape. "Oh, that glorious Wisconsin wilderness! Everything new and pure in the very prime of spring when Nature's pulses were beating highest and mysteriously keeping time with our own! Young hearts, young leaves, flowers, animals, the winds and the streams and the sparkling lake, all wildly, gladly rejoicing together!"[2]

That first spring and summer, as he explored the farmland and nearby countryside, John soon began to realize that in nature "when we try to pick out anything by itself we find it is hitched to everything else in the universe."[3] His boyhood explorations in the Fountain Lake environs foreshadowed his later discoveries in the mountains of California and other wilderness regions in North America. He early recognized that there are interrelationships in the natural world, the basic principle of ecology today. Though that term would not come into use until more than a century later, Muir was truly a pioneer ecologist.

John Muir was born April 21, 1838, in Dunbar, Scotland, on the North Sea, to Daniel and Anne Gilrye Muir. The oldest boy in the family of eight children, he was named for his grandfather, John Muir, who probably lived on a small tenant farm in the Lowland country near Craw-fordjohn in the county of Lanarkshire.

Daniel Muir's obituary, written by his son John and published in the (Portage) *Wisconsin State Register*, October 31, 1885, provides biograph-ical information. John's grandfather, John Muir, was a British soldier. When stationed in Manchester, England, he married Sarah Higgs, an Eng-lish girl. John's father Daniel was born to them there in 1804. Daniel was only six months old when his mother died, and, with his father's death a few months later, he and his eleven-year-old sister Mary were left alone. The two children then went to Scotland to live with relatives near Crawfordjohn. When Mary became the wife of Hamilton Blakely, a sheepherder, she took her brother with her to her new home. Until he was twenty-one years old, Daniel toiled on his brother-in-law's farm.

He had little opportunity for an education. Eager to excel, young Daniel liked athletic games. The handsome boy had an artistic side to him as well. He enjoyed music, and with his fine voice he took a lead-ing part in the "merry song-singing gatherings" of the neighborhood. He loved the violin and so wished to own an instrument that he carved one with his skilled hands. "One night he ran ten miles through mud and rain to a nearby village to get strings for it."[4]

His son John recognized Daniel's poetic streak. Years later in a letter to his sister Mary he wrote that ". . . we have all at some time been guilty of poetry. . . . Mother made poetry when first acquainted with Father and I think that Father must have made some verses too, for he must have been musical when he made the fiddle, and imaginative when he made carts and horses out of turnips."[5]

At the age of fourteen, Daniel was converted to a sect of Chris-tianity. From then on his nature changed to one of religious fervor, and he pushed aside any spontaneous feeling for the joy of life. An enthu-siastic believer, he joined one Protestant sect after another, always seek-ing a warmer, more active enthusiasm among the membership of his current group. "His religious beliefs [now] formed the basis of his nature,"[6] but despite constant searching in his quest, he didn't achieve a measure of contentment until late in life.

One day, when Daniel was twenty-one, he disappeared from his sister's home without telling anyone. Mary frantically searched the ponds and streams, frightened that her brother might have drowned on the moors. It turned out that he had ". . . left home to seek his fortune with only a few shillings in his pocket . . . his head full of romantic schemes for the benefit of his sister and all the world besides."[7] He wanted to see more of the world than was possible on the farm and in the little village of Crawfordjohn. He had gone to Glasgow, and after drifting about that city for a time, joined the British Army.

He was sent to Dunbar as a recruiting sergeant, and there he married a girl who had inherited a food and grain store. Daniel purchased his discharge from the army and devoted himself to managing the store where he earned a reputation for fair dealing. When his wife died a short time later, the business became his. In their brief marriage the couple had a child who also died.

On November 28, 1833, at the age of twenty-nine, Daniel married twenty-year old Anne Gilrye, daughter of David and Margaret Hay Gilrye who lived across High Street from his store and lodgings. David Gilrye was a wealthy flesher, or meat seller. Anne's mother was a member of the distinguished Hay clan. Fond of painting and poetry, she had spent a more privileged youth than had her husband.

Under the code of the times, the husband was the master of the house and, accordingly, when Anne moved across High Street to Daniel Muir's home, she always went along with his wishes in their daily lives. Their manner of living became so austere that he did not even allow her to hang the pictures she had painted.

In contrast to her husband's religious discontent, Anne's religion was a personal one of deep abiding faith. She early found peace and comfort in her beliefs and an inner strength that enabled her to weather many a disappointment in her life. Throughout the years she constantly referred to her blessings. John described his mother as a representative Scotch woman, quiet, conservative, of pious, affectionate character.

All her life Anne Muir remembered with joy ". . . the old church I attended in the happiest days of my life." She remembered ". . . the bell ringing and the family so large that we occupied two long pews," and the "songs we used to sing and the sermons we used to hear." She later told her son John that his Grandfather Gilrye had been an elder of the church for fifty years. It ". . . stands in the graveyard where the precious dust of my parents and brothers and sisters and friends are laid away till the resurrection morn."[8] Out of ten Gilrye children, eight had died, six victims of the white plague. Only Margaret, the eldest, and Anne, the youngest of the seven daughters, survived past young adulthood. Anne bore seven of the Muirs' eight children in Dunbar. Their youngest daughter, Joanna, was born in Wisconsin.

John Muir spent his first eleven years in Dunbar. In *The Story of My Boyhood and Youth* he wrote eloquently about his childhood adventures there, his schooling, and church studies. But no amount of regimen from parent, school, or church could keep down his irrepressible spirits. He described the fine walks he took as a small boy with his Grandfather Gilrye who introduced him to nature. He told of rough and tumble exploits as he and his companions played war games or explored the countryside.

One of his lasting memories was of daring excursions among the ruins of Dunbar Castle by the sea, destroyed almost three hundred years before. Built upon basaltic rock, the castle had briefly sheltered Mary Queen of Scots. For centuries it had stood guard near the entrance to the Firth of Forth, the large body of water where the River Forth meets the North Sea. John and his friends defied danger in the face of incoming tides as they scrambled into the remains of the castle dungeon at sea level.

But Daniel Muir was becoming restless—the restlessness that would keep him from ever staying long in one place. A sense of religious mission now drove him to leave Scotland and move his family to America. He wanted to convert people to his brand of Christianity—to save souls. In contrast to many others who left their homeland penniless, Daniel had accumulated enough money to help him settle in the new land.

He and three of the children set sail from Glasgow in early February, 1849. John had anticipated the voyage with great excitement, but he carried with him vivid recollections of his life in Dunbar. He never forgot the sea view from Dunbar, and the Bass Rock, a dark basaltic formation a mile around that rose from the sea. And sometimes, when he would later feel the touch of a sea breeze, he would think of the "Firth of Forth, the Bass Rock, Dunbar Castle, and the winds and rocks and hills [that came] upon that wind and stood in clear and sudden light as a landscape flashed upon the view by a blaze of lightning on a dark night."[9]

After weeks of travel, the little family finally arrived in Milwaukee, Wisconsin, on Lake Michigan. A farmer took them across the prairies to the tiny village of Kingston. There Daniel rented a room at the Kingston Inn, built in 1846 near a sawmill on the banks of the Grand River.

At Kingston, Daniel Muir was given the name of Alexander Gray as someone who could assist him in locating farmland in the region. He left the children at the inn and made his way to Gray's home, ten miles away on the southern border of Marquette County.

Alexander Gray, called Sandy by his neighbors, was well known in the area for his aid to new settlers. Hauling a load of rye by ox team to Milwaukee where Lake Michigan steamers docked and where the nearest railroad station and post office were located, he would then return with supplies and mail for his neighbors. Sometimes he would bring back new settlers and their goods as well. Gray, accompanied by Daniel Muir, drove his ox team and wagon through the oak woods to Kingston to bring Sarah, John, and David and their heavy load of supplies to the Grays.

Although he used oxen for farm work and to transport people and goods, Sandy and another pioneer neighbor, John Turner, held the distinction of being the only area farmers to own horse teams. Sandy owned a good deal of land, at least 360 acres, mostly located in the Town of Buffalo, Marquette County. Gray received deeds to his lands dated September 1 and November 1, 1847, signed by President Zachary Taylor under the terms of an act of Congress, February 11, 1847, "to raise for a limited time an additional military force." United States government land was granted to men who would serve. Sandy and his wife Jane built their home on eighty acres on the Marquette County side of the county-line road that was well rutted by turning wagon wheels. The other eighty acre parcel of their home farm lay directly across the roadway in Columbia County.

The Grays had also come from Scotland—the sheep country of Parish Davitt, Aberdeenshire. Sandy and his family originally migrated to Glengarry, Ontario, Canada. From there, one by one, he and his brother George and sister Elizabeth came to Wisconsin and settled on farms within one mile of each other. Their homes were all strung along that same countyline road.[10]

So it was at the home of Sandy and Jane Gray that John Muir was introduced to the region where he would live during his youth. With unaccustomed freedom, he and his brother David raced exuberantly down the road that cut through the gentle hills covered by large oaks and woodland shrubs. They ran through the fields and down to the creek meandering through the extensive marshland near the house.

In the spring when the snow melted and the rains came, the marsh became a large, shallow lake. Now, in early May, the shiny yellow marsh marigolds were past their prime, but the deep purple violets and early yellow buttercups were just starting to bloom. It was the beginning of a profusion of wetland flowers that would flourish from early spring, through the warmth of summer, and into fall. When young John came to know well all the area plants, he especially loved those of the wetlands.

Sandy and Daniel soon located a farm for the Muirs six miles away on the northern shore of a lake on the other side of the Town of Buffalo from the Gray farm. The paths of the Muirs and the Grays would cross for years to come, both while the Muir family lived at Fountain Lake and when they later moved to a farm closer to their benefactors.

The young boy had a wonderful place to begin exploring his new world. The Muir farm was located on a sparkling spring-fed lake with a little outlet creek wending its way westward a short distance through the grasses and sedges to the Fox River. This area of south-central Wisconsin was beautiful and diverse. Thousands of years before, a lobe of the mile-deep continental glacier, scouring its way southward and west-ward, advancing and retreating, had sculptured the landscape into low, rolling hills, glacial lakes, marshes, and kettle holes. An occasional out-crop of bedrock marked the terrain.

The farmland and immediate lake area was also varied. There were the prairie, the oak openings, and oak woods. There were the marshes and the fens, and the many springs bubbling up like gentle fountains in the wet sedge meadow by the lake. Daniel well described his land on the northern shore when he called it Fountain Lake Farm.

During that first spring and summer, Daniel and the three children lived in a bur oak shanty on a rise by the lake. Sarah called that period their shack experience. With the help of hired men, Daniel broke ground, planted crops, and built a fine frame house. He worked hard and could not always keep an eye on his sons. He often traveled to Kingston to get lumber for the house leaving John and David free to indulge in many an escapade. Never before had they had such freedom to play, and they made the most of the opportunity. Occasionally, after their most daring exploits, Daniel dealt harshly with them.

All too soon the fun gave way to backbreaking drudgery. Daniel set the boys to work feeding the great fires of oak brush as he cleared the land for planting. When most of the farm work was done and the house completed, Sarah and her father planted lilacs by the dooryard; they were at last ready to welcome the rest of the family.

Every year thereafter Anne Muir would recall the date when she and the other four children arrived from Scotland. "The ninth of this month is the anniversary of my arrival at Fountain Lake twenty years ago," she wrote John on November 11, 1869. "How happy I was to meet you and the others after such a long journey."[11] After nine months of separation the family circle was complete once more.

That day Daniel proudly showed his wife the results of their months of labor—the crops, the fine two-story frame house, the barn, and the shack they had lived in during the summer, now turned into a shelter for the pony Jack.

The lake shone golden in the autumn sun, and the surrounding fields had turned brown after harvest. In the woods, bright colored leaves had fallen to earth. Some leaves would remain on the oak trees till warm spring breezes would bring an end to winter.

As season followed season the Muir family set about cultivating their farm in earnest. John thought that "farming was a grim, material, debasing pursuit under father's generalship . . ."[12] but all the family members were expected to do their share from sunup to sundown each day.

As John went about his farm chores, he developed the physical skills that would prove useful to him in his later wilderness explorations. In odd moments he would read a bit from the few books in the Muir household or whittle on his wooden mechanical inventions.

Daniel allowed no time for recreation. He saw no need for any activity beyond work and religious pursuits. He was strict about the early bedtime hour, but he once gave John permission to get up in the morning as early as he liked. One of the first uses John made of these golden blocks of time was to carve self-setting sawmills out of shagbark hickory, using them to dam up little streams that ran among the sedges near the lake. He also whittled other inventions. Many of these creations worked, but John was secretly glad that the least successful one was that horrid guillotine of a thing slicing off gophers' heads.

All the while John was growing up on the farm, he closely examined the natural world around him. Deep feelings began to stir within him.

Once, in a letter to his young sister Mary, he declared, "You and I, Mary, began to sing at the same time in life, and our song was stimulated by the same causes and objects . . . a shade of imagination, and lakes, birds, thunderclouds and rabbits."[13]

It was well known in the neighborhood that Daniel Muir was a severe task master, harsh with his children, especially his high-spirited eldest son. James Whitehead, a boy nine years younger than John, son of Benjamin Whitehead, a blacksmith and self-styled minister, lived on a farm adjacent to the Muir land. The Whitehead family had come to Wisconsin in 1855 from the Leeds area of England.

In 1913, the year before John Muir's death, there was an exchange of letters between Muir and James Whitehead who had known each other for more than fifty years. Whitehead recalled what a rigid disciplinarian Daniel Muir had been.

"That your father was rigorous and exacting was known to his neighbors. This with his dignified and gentlemanly appearance begat among the younger class a sort of respectful awe when in his presence. To the credit of his children be it said no murmur or complaint escaped their lips as to the harsh and strict discipline to which they were subjected."[14]

In an article in the *Emporia Gazette* (Kansas), January 21, 1915, Whitehead described Daniel Muir "as a man of soldierly bearing" who "ruled his household as a general would a camp." He said Muir was a man of "deeply religious nature, [who] possessed the unbending will, abhorrence of sin, disobedience and wrongdoing with the intolerance characteristic of those who had been reared under the uncompromising theology of his time and country." He said too that Daniel "had a splendid physique and was the soul of truthfulness and honor and that he was esteemed by his neighbors and all who knew him."[15]

Whitehead's central purpose for writing Muir in 1913 was to correct what he considered to be a misconception about his own father.

The *Atlantic Monthly* had just published an excerpt from Muir's book, *The Story of My Boyhood and Youth*, then in the process of publication. It was a sketch about Whitehead's Uncle Charlie, the child man, and Charlie's callous treatment at the hands of his brother Benjamin with whom he lived. James felt strongly that Muir had put his father in a bad light. Although Muir had not used the blacksmith-minister's name, James was sure he would be recognized.

Muir's narrative dealt with Charlie Whitehead's life and death as he understood it from the Muir family and neighbors. It showed the extent of Muir's sympathy for others.

In *The Story of My Boyhood and Youth*, he wrote:

"One of the saddest deaths from other causes than consumption was that of a poor feebleminded man whose brother, a sturdy devout, severe puritan, was a very hard taskmaster. Poor half-witted Charlie was kept steadily at work—although he was not able to do much, for his body was about as feeble as his mind.

"He never could be taught the right use of an axe, and when he set to chopping down trees for firewood he feebly hacked and chipped round and round them, sometimes spending several days in nibbling down a tree that a beaver might have gnawed down in half the time. Occasionally when he had an extra large tree to chop, he would go home and report that the tree was too tough and strong for him and that he could never make it fall. Then his brother calling him a useless creature, would fell it with a few well-directed strokes, and leave Charlie to nibble away at it for weeks trying to make it into stovewood."[16] The neighbors had sympathy for the child man. The McReaths in particular warmly welcomed him into their home. When Charlie was thirty-eight years old, he became discouraged and told his friends he was going to drown himself in Fountain Lake. "My heart's gone and I want to die," he said.

"The next day, when Mr. Anderson, a carpenter whose house was on the west shore of our lake, was going to a spring he saw a man wade out through the rushes and lily-pads and throw himself forward into deep water. This was poor Charlie." Mr. Anderson saved him, but Charlie lived only a few days longer.

Charlie's brother went to Mr. Anderson and "after talking on ordinary affairs, . . . said, 'I have a little job of carpenter work for you. I want you to make a coffin.' 'Who is dead?' 'Charlie,' was the cool reply."

The first copies of *The Story of My Boyhood and Youth* that rolled off the presses in 1913 then went on:

"All the neighbors were in tears over the poor child man's fate. But, strange to say, in all that excessively law-abiding neighborhood none was bold enough or kind enough to break the blacksmith's jaw."[17]

Whitehead claimed that the stories of Charlie's treatment were exaggerated.

"My Uncle Charlie's troubles were prenatal," he explained in his March 10, 1913, letter to Muir. "His mother became frightened at some wild animals while attending a menagerie and he was born crooked. His limbs had to be broken and straightened."[18]

In an earlier letter to Muir, Whitehead had recorded his perceptions of his uncle and his father. "My Uncle possessed a certain ready wit, was deemed by many a good singer, was acquainted with a number of old country songs and ballads, was gifted as a rhymer and to the McReaths [the neighbors who befriended Charlie] was not all together the simple minded person he appeared to others.

"During the latter years of his life he became somewhat proficient in the use of the axe and found immeasurable delight in piling the stove wood into oval shaped piles that would shed rain like an umbrella. He was never driven or forced to work by my father.

"My Mother was a tender hearted, sympathetic woman and spared no effort to make it as comfortable for him as our limited means and accommodations would permit. In this she was assisted by us children.

"For sometime preceding his death he became weak and poorly, the trouble being Bright's Disease. The doctor was consulted but was unable to help or relieve him and though able to be about he did no chopping, did not take an axe in his hand or perform any work for four months preceding his death."

Whitehead's account of his Uncle Charlie's death differed from Muir's.

"In the month of August, 1858, while sitting in his chair, he breathed his last, my brother Ben being with him at the time. The doctor had told us we might expect his death at any time. This condition was known to the immediate neighbors, to the McReaths and Walter Sanderson (your 'Anderson', I doubt not) especially. The direct and abrupt manner in which my father (if correctly given) asked Mr. Sanderson to make a coffin was simply characteristic of the man and his country, but in its relation to [your] Narrative and setting given it is made the climax to a painful . . . tragedy. I have no remembrance of his attempted suicide and never heard of it till I read of it in your printed article."

Whitehead went on to describe father's bitterly hard life: ". . . he was compelled from childhood to the most arduous toil. . . . Rough, toiling, uncultured men had been his associates. He had never crossed threshold of a school room, knew nothing of [children's] natures and their needs and was seemingly incapable of entering into our thoughts and feeling and adapting himself to the requirements and cravings of our childish natures."

Whitehead said that his father was "a strict disciplinarian so deeply imbued with the wisdom of Solomon's conclusions as to the training of a child that he spared not the rod when in his opinion the exigencies of the case required its application."[19]

In another letter Whitehead declared, "With the fortunate and intelligent there is a craving for sympathy when in pain and trouble. With my Uncle Charlie it was a mania. While my father was not insensible to this feeling, he religiously abstained from expressing it in words. To him it would have been an exhibition of weakness as unmanly as tears. To win . . . words of condolence and pity, Charlie would tell of neglect and cruelty which had no foundation save in the characteristic treatment shared by us children."[20]

Despite his explanation of these childhood events, James Whitehead obviously did not realize the extent of his Uncle Charlie's problems. Benjamin Whitehead's young brother needed the compassion and sensitivity that Benjamin did not provide. The story does indeed evoke a vision of cruelty.

Muir's reply to his old friend's painful letter contained much of the philosophy he lived by all his life. In their exchange of letters about their fathers, he showed his deep feeling about the way Daniel Muir had treated him when he was a boy.

"I have good reason, as you know," he wrote February 13, 1913, "to hate the habit of child beating having seen and felt its affects in some of their worse forms in my father's house, and all my life have spoken out against the habit.

"Your father, like my own, was, I devoutly believe, a sincere Christian, abounding in noble qualities, preaching the gospel without money or price while working hard for a living, clearing land, blacksmithing, able for anything, and from youth to death never abating one jot of his glorious foundational religious enthusiasm. I revere his memory with that of my father and the New England Puritans, types of the best American pioneers whose unwavering faith in God's eternal righteousness forms the basis of our country's greatness.

"I never did intentional injustice to any human being or animal and I have directed my publishers to cancel all that has so grievously hurt you."[21]

However, Muir was able to change only a few lines in the next printing of the 1913 autobiography. Instead of wishing the neighbors to break the blacksmith's jaw, he wrote, "Strange to say, the brother who had faithfully cared for him controlled and concealed all his natural affection as incompatible with sound faith."[22]

Through this exchange of letters and Whitehead's further writings after Muir's death, a picture emerges of the severe treatment of children in the pioneer homes of two stern religious men. Despite the Christian evangelistic work done by both men within their community, a great deal of rationalization took place to excuse the harsh methods used by Benjamin Whitehead and Daniel Muir.

Despite his severity, Daniel was never able to break his son's spirit, for John lived his life with optimism and determination. Somehow he managed to get around his father when he needed to and accomplished what he wanted to do. Daniel must have had a grudging admiration for the boy.

A turning point in John Muir's life occurred about the year 1855. He and two other Fountain Lake Farm boys, Davie Taylor and Davie Gray, were assigned to work on a Town of Buffalo corduroy road together. Taylor and Gray, both nineteen, were known as the twa Davies. Intimate friends, they spent many exciting hours reciting poetry and pursuing the classics together. It is remarkable that three such talented young men lived in an area only a little over a square mile in size. The Grays, from Edinburgh, Scotland, lived on the south side of the lake, while the Taylors, also from Scotland, lived on the north, adjacent to land owned by Daniel Muir.

In the few years before and immediately following Wisconsin state-hood in 1848, county and town governments were organized to provide services to township residents. The Town of Buffalo, Marquette County, established road districts, naming an "overseer of highway" for each district in the township. At one time Daniel Muir was listed in the town records as overseer for district six. Road building began in earnest in 1850, and became an annual event that provided an opportunity for the men of the township to discuss the news of the day as they worked.

A major project was building corduroy roads across the marshlands. The road builders laid lengths of tamarack trees in criss-cross fashion, then filled the space between with brush and dirt. Tamaracks growing straight and tall in the nearby swamps provided resinous, virtually inde-structible wood. Their bright green clusters of needle-like leaves turned yellow in late summer and dropped off in October. In the winter the trees stood leafless as the dark swamp waters froze around them.

County residents say John Muir helped build the road from the pioneer cemetery, down the slope, and across the marsh. This section could be the one he worked on with Davie Taylor and Davie Gray more than a century and a quarter ago. John set about the task of cutting the tamaracks to lay, using his special method, while Taylor and Gray discussed literary works as they usually did when they were together.

That day the twa Davies discussed and quoted Charles Dickens while they labored. The younger boy was enthralled with the Dickens works and characters. And just as Davie Gray's inflammable imagination had flashed a year earlier at contact with the fiery soul of Davie Taylor, so now did John Muir catch the spirit of the inner fires of them both.

Years later Muir told David Gray's biographer, his brother, John Gray, that the thrilling discussion of Dickens that day filled him with such envious delight that it spurred him on to read and learn from books, something he had not done since his early schooling in Dunbar. In the five or six years since coming to America John had worked diligently on the farm, but had been unable to fulfill his hunger for learning. The few books in the Muir home were mostly of a religious nature. Daniel

Muir felt that the Bible was the only companion and guide that anyone needed.

The rekindling of his desire for learning inspired Muir to begin again a never-ending search for knowledge. That summer, in spare moments, he gave himself an education in mathematics and also managed to read the classical novels his father had strictly forbidden. His life had changed direction and he owed it to the inspiration of Davie Gray and Davie Taylor.

The three young men had much in common. They lived on nearby farms sharing the same natural environment and knowing the same people. Each had similar yearnings as he searched for his niche in life and each expressed himself eloquently in his own style through the written word. Muir and Taylor had an added bond: both were sensitive to the natural beauty around them—to the plants and wildlife.

In 1888, when the Muir family read aloud Davie Gray's biography written by his brother John, Anne Muir was pleased, for the book described the life, the people, and the land as she had known them in the early Fountain Lake days. It told the fascinating story of the remarkable friendship between the twa Davies who influenced John Muir so profoundly.[23]

After plowing in the field one summer morning in 1854, David Gray and David Taylor sat together to eat their "plowman's dinner." Gray's was wrapped in a scrap of newspaper, perhaps the *New York Tribune*, which his family read regularly. In this fragment they read an item about the British poet, Gerald Massey. Taylor went on to quote from Moore and other poets. In that moment the twa Davies found a wakening love of literature which drew them together.

"From that day forth," Taylor later wrote, "we were bound together like a team of wild horses which no barrier could stop."

John Gray described how the two found a common ideal world into which they were rapt, where they lived together, feeling themselves apart from other men. For three seasons after their farm work was done the two young men would walk the misty fields night after night engrossed in their own exciting world. They would sit on the rail fences and quote literature to one another, or share original verses they pulled out of their pockets. One night there was such a splendid display of northern lights they didn't get home till dawn.

Those were "fiery nights when two minds burst into volcanic action," wrote John Gray. "It takes actual contact to strike fire like what was wont to blaze o' nights."

The biography sketched David Gray's early life. Born in Edinburgh in 1836, he attended three different schools in that historic city. He made his mark by his "quickness in learning. . . . He kept in advance of appointed work and was first in all his forms." As a young boy, David was as competitive as John Muir had been. He played "goff" (golf) and running games, which he consistently won, and was marble champion as well.

David's father, Philip C. Gray, was a stationer. A religious man, he had come to believe as Daniel Muir had once concluded in Dunbar, that the Bible was the all-sufficient guide to faith. In 1839 Gray was active in starting The Body of the Disciples in Christ.

Philip's brother William was active in the Dunbar Disciples' group. Daniel Muir must have known him there, for Daniel had finally found his spiritual home with the Disciples. William Gray eventually settled in Buffalo, New York, where Muir contacted him when he first arrived in America.

The Philip Gray family were strict adherents to their faith, but they were friendly people as well who took pleasure in life and literature. They treated their children tenderly, and the sociable atmosphere in their home was far different from that in the Muir household when Daniel Muir present.

When the Grays left Edinburgh to come to America the same year the Muirs did, there were "several scores of old friends gathered at the station to see [their] party of over a score off."

They too settled in Wisconsin, first buying a farm at Waupun, about twenty-five or thirty miles east of Fountain Lake.

In his diary, thirteen-year-old David Gray described the landscape when he saw it for the first time: "Far to the westward, nothing was visible but the waving line of prairie, the horizon as smooth and unbroken as the ocean."

In 1850 Philip Gray purchased land on the banks of the Fox River near the south edge of Fountain Lake. It took three days to drive the cattle across the prairie to the new farm. The family set to work clearing and cultivating their land as the Muirs had done the year before on the other side of the lake. At last, with enough land under cultivation, David was able to attend high school at Waupun during the winter of 1853-54. In the spring he returned home to the family farm. That summer marked the beginning of his intense friendship with David Taylor.

For over two years, Taylor and Gray shared a consuming passion for classical writers. They pooled their funds to provide themselves with books. Though there was "a scarcity of capital," Taylor managed to buy Byron, his favorite poet, "complete for a dollar and a half," while Gray obtained Moore, "a splendid book." When they discovered Edgar Allen Poe and obtained three volumes by him, they felt they made a great gain. All the while they were composing their own verses.

One day Gray confided a problem to his friend. His sister was reading his compositions and making fun of them. He believed he had solved the dilemma by purchasing in Portage a leather folio with a lock and key for "ten wretched shillings," but Taylor thought a better idea would have been to make a box and use a little brass padlock he owned. Gray's sister managed to get into the leather folio with her deft fingers despite the lock and continued to read the precious documents.

In the summer of 1854 the Grays moved from the log house close to the Fox river into a new house on the hill, buying some of the lumber from a raftsman going by on the Fox River.

That winter Davie Gray spent three months teaching school ten miles north of his home. He received a salary of $15.50 a month. The following winter he briefly attended Britain's school in Portage before again teaching, this time at a school only four miles east of his home.

He was given an exciting task to perform when the Buffalo town board voted funds for a town library and he and his brother-in-law,

Walter Sanderson, were chosen to select the books. Gray "enjoyed a feast beyond description in the selection and reading of the books got together for this little library, which remained for a time in his custody in his father's house." Perhaps John Muir read some of these volumes.

In August, 1856, Gray, then twenty, left Marquette County to become secretary and librarian for the Young Men's Christian Union in Buffalo, New York, where he eventually became editor of the *Buffalo Courier*. He lived in Buffalo for thirty-two years, a popular, public figure, who moved in high social circles.

Although Davie Gray saw Davie Taylor only once after he left the farm, his friend remained important to him. The memory of their early days together provided a haven for him when he felt under pressure.

"I yearn for those enchanted nights," Gray wrote to Taylor, "to watch sunsets from your house or moonsets from John Mahaffy's fence." And continuing this thought in another letter he said, "We would start from the riverside about gloaming and sit a half-hour on every fence as we came up . . . the moon would be large and white ere we reached the swamp where the mist used to meet us and the tamaracks [would] whisper and shudder where they listened. We would mount the knoll and look down into those round basins of mist, which I often see in my dreams."

Only scattered fragments are known about Davie Taylor's background. Also from Scotland, he and his mother, grandmother, and two uncles settled on a quarter section adjacent to land owned by Daniel Muir. It was located north and east of the Muirs' original homestead.

One Fountain Lake neighbor, George B. Mair, recalled in a letter to the *Montello Express* that Davie Taylor had a marvelous memory, and was a walking encyclopedia of historical dates and events. Mair said that Taylor had "come from a family of remarkable literary taste" and that in his early youth he developed a passion for reading which became almost his sole source of enjoyment. "Poetry was his favorite. Byron, Moore, Shelley, Coleridge, and Tennyson were his constant companions."[24]

A local resident, Harry Kearns, who remembered Taylor, once said, "He was a man of good education. The neighbors all said that. He could talk about any subject you could name. At night he wrote poetry and in the morning he tore it all up."[25]

After the death of his mother and uncles, Davie Taylor lived out his later years alone on the Taylors' original quarter section, growing, among other crops, the apples people remember to this day. He kept domestic animals and bees and took care of the usual farm matters. And he continued to write poetry.

In Buffalo, New York, Davie Gray wanted the world to know about his friend's ability to both write and read poetry. He explained to Taylor that during the literary evenings he and his wife held in their home, he read poetry to their guests "after your own style and tune, and with all the rhetorical tremor I learned at your feet."

About Davie Taylor's poetry, Gray declared, "The lyrical element exists in your mind as it does in no other mind in the country."

There are virtually no remnants of Taylor's poetry in existence today; Gray once quoted two lines where the lyrical quality shows through:

Every leaf of the soundless oak
Lent its voice as the melody broke.[26]

As well as Davie Gray and George Mair, other area people appreciated this eloquent, sensitive man. One was James Whitehead, who was only eight years old when he met the much older Taylor. Upon Taylor's death, Whitehead portrayed his friend with sensitivity in a letter to the *Montello Express*, April 7, 1900.

"His companionship was a source of pleasure and delight. . . . He was the Gamaliel at whose feet I sat a willing pupil, delighted, charmed, electrified by the magnetism of his wonderful personality. He possessed a poet's fervid fancy and was passionately fond of paintings, flowers and music. In his wanderings among the woodlands that surrounded his home he would turn aside from the beaten path lest his presence might disturb the sweet carol of birds. . . . [Taylor] would transport you on wings of thoughts into other ideal realms, peopled by beings and surrounded by images, such as his own fertile imagination could alone produce."

Whitehead felt that Taylor's letters to him were "veritable mines of wealth, gems of thoughts, rich in poetic sentiment."[27]

Sometimes during central Wisconsin winters, thick, white snows cover the countryside and the winds pile high drifts around buildings, and across fields and roads. During these times Taylor would stay by his hearth, studying and writing.

Once he wrote Whitehead that he "put in a happy winter studying many things in heaven and earth and had caught glimpses of the dim waters under it." But another winter he wrote, "My seclusion is almost without parallel. I have seen no living soul for many days. I am very tired, nobody to care for, nothing to see but snow and sky, nothing to look forward to but death. I do not remember the time I was so heart hungry for someone to talk to."[28]

And in a letter written during "a night of exceeding darkness," he said, "And now there is a pale tinge of light in the east and the old house and the trees are cloudless in the light of early morning. I must to bed, and may a brighter dawn be on our faces when we have passed through the night of death."[29]

When Whitehead visited him the year before he died, Taylor prophesied, "I feel I am being hurried forward by flight of time, till soon I shall be placed in the little row over there in the graveyard."[30]

Davie Taylor died alone in the windowless attic reached only by a ladder. He had lived in the home near Fountain Lake for over forty years. Several of his neighbors lowered his body down to the ground floor by ropes and buried him in the graveyard as he had predicted. His grave is marked only by a few glacial stones protruding slightly through the grass.

Of the two youths who inspired John Muir that day they worked on the corduroy road together, Davie Taylor was the more profound and eloquent, the one who provided the original spark. Like the pebble thrown into the water causing it to ripple in everwidening circles, Taylor's influence had more effect on others than he would ever realize. He may have died unsung and unheard as Gray once thought, but he did not die unremembered.

The thick white mists still rise from the lowland basins as the night air cools after a hot day—the kind of night Davie Taylor and Davie Gray walked the fields reciting poetry together. It was the kind of night John Muir remembered.

In 1849 the Muirs were the first Scottish people to settle the Fountain Lake area of the Town of Buffalo. The following year the James McReath family arrived from Scotland and settled a farm on the west side of the lake where the outlet creek flowed through their lands.

In recent years, McReath descendants and others have related anecdotes which shed light on Muir's early Wisconsin experiences with his neighbors and friends and what the countryside was like.

Allen McReath, grandson of James who grew up in the neighborhood of his ancestors and is still farming in the area, recounted an adventure one of his forebears named John McReath shared with young John Muir. When Allen was six or seven years old he noticed an old gun leaning against the wall in the corner of the machine shed on the family farm at the base of Wolf Hill. Located about a mile northeast of Fountain Lake, this hill is a rather steep, flattopped sandstone outcrop rising about a hundred feet above the surrounding countryside.

Allen's father told him the story of the gun: One day the two boys, John Muir and John McReath, took the gun along when they hiked up Wolf Hill, carrying only one shell with them. They planned to hunt and possibly pick some berries. When a wolf crossed their path, they wounded it with the one shell, then hit the animal over the head with the butt end of the gun to finish him off.[31] This adventure with his friend gave Muir one escape from what he called the grim and Gad-grind of early days and undoubtedly was among his happy budget of memories.

Ben and Mary McReath Hull once reminisced about the days when the McReaths and the Muirs lived on nearby farms at Fountain Lake. When Mary, James McReath's daughter, married Ben Hull, the neighboring farm boy, the young couple lived with her parents for a time on the original farm.

Ben recalled the time he and his father-in-law had worked in the fields together. When John Muir's name came up in their conversation, Ben said, "You knew John Muir very well?"

McReath answered, "Yes, I did. John was quite a lot older than I, but I knew the mon real well."

"What was your opinion of him?" Ben asked.

His father-in-law replied, "He was a fine mon, but I thought that he was a wee bit crack-ed." The last word of this reply was spoken in two syllables.

John Muir had many friends and neighbors who admired his creative abilities, but there were others who felt as McReath did.

Mary Hull declared that John was a great nature lover who put his life into it. Ben added that "Mary's father wasn't particularly interested in nature because he mainly wanted to get his work done and make a living, while Muir's work was secondary because of his study of nature."

Hull described the creek that flowed from Fountain Lake past the old McReath home. "It never had a name. It was a beautiful little creek that ran through the farm, a clear stream that had good fish in it. The banks were high and it was narrow enough that you could jump it. We used to bridge it for the farm wagons."[32]

Within half a mile of Wolf Hill is a somewhat higher companion hill, Observatory Hill, the "great cloud-capped mountain of our child's imagination"[33] as Muir later recalled. Sometimes John and his friends would climb the Observatory, as they called it, on the Fourth of July or New Year's Day, the two days each year other than Sundays that Daniel Muir allowed off from farm work. John explored the volcanic-created rhyolite outcrop with its fern-filled rocky ravines. Glacial ice riding atop the pinkish rock rounded and polished it to a high gloss, while the striations scratched onto its surface showed the direction of the ice flow thousands of years before.

In 1906 John Cairns, a local resident who was the son of Muir's friend, John Cairns, was hiking on Observatory Hill with a companion one day when he found a cedar tree with the words "J. Muir 1856" cut into an eight-inch-thick limb. Upon Muir's death in 1914, Cairns went back to retrieve the limb as a memento, but although cedar is a tough, longlasting wood, the limb had disappeared.[34]

The Observatory was a talisman to John during his childhood. On a summer day, the young explorer could climb to the top and sit upon the rock watching billowy white clouds floating across the vivid blue sky or viewing the panorama of the glacier-sculpted landscape stretching out for miles in front of him. The chain of lakes and the hills in varied shades of blues and greens were a familiar part of the landscape he roamed as a youth.

Muir's local explorations and observations foretold the time to come when, as a glaciologist, he would study the action of mountain glaciers of California's Sierra Nevada and would proclaim glaciers responsible for creating the magnificent Yosemite Valley. It foretold the many days he would spend on Alaskan glaciers discovering their icy secrets. The Observatory may not compare to a lofty Sierra peak, but it remained the great cloud-capped mountain of John Muir's childhood and surely must have inspired him to a lifetime of discovery.

# II

# HICKORY HILL FARM

*And just by that great oak is where in the*
*moonlight evenings I used to spend hours*
*with my head up in the sky*
*and soared among the planets.*
                    —John Muir

After coming to the United States in 1849, Daniel Muir "first settled on a half section of land near the Fox River about twelve miles north of Portage and remained there eight years or until it was brought under thorough cultivation. Then feeling the need of more work he purchased half a section of wild land about four miles to the eastward of the farm and began building, breaking, fencing and planting anew."[1]

That first 160 acres located on the shore of Fountain Lake in Marquette County was owned by the Fox and Wisconsin River Improvement Corporation. The United States Congress had passed an act on August 8, 1846, "to grant a certain quantity of land to aid in the improvement of the Fox and Wisconsin Rivers and to connect to the same by a canal in the Territory of Wisconsin." The corporation was charged with the task of digging a canal between the Fox and Wisconsin near Portage City, where the two rivers were located within about a mile and a half from each other. The Fox River flowed northeastward to become part of the Great Lakes and St. Lawrence River system emptying into the Atlantic Ocean; the Wisconsin River flowed southwestward to its confluence with the Mississippi to become part of the Gulf of Mexico.

The small area between the two rivers at the present city of Portage was a crossroad of history. For centuries the Indians had shouldered their dugout canoes at the Fox River and hiked across the wetland to put them into the Wisconsin. Later, the French explorers, Father Jacques Marquette and Louis Jolliet, searching for a route to the Pacific Ocean, heard from the Indians about the great sea to the west. In 1673, with five companions, they set out from Green Bay in two canoes. They made their way southwestward up the Fox River to find this great sea and to determine where it flowed. It was a historic moment when the two famous explorers transferred their gear overland at le portage and set sail down the Wisconsin River toward the Mississippi. This single event helped to open up the western continent.

After the time of the explorers came a century of European and Indian fur trading. There were many journeys over the "carrying place," as the English called the area between the Fox and the Wisconsin.[2] The French voyageurs traded blankets, guns and whiskey for valuable stacks of furs. In the 1800s the American Fur Company, under John Jacob Astor, established a trading post at the portage. The legendary Pierre Pauquette, who was noted for his feats of strength, managed the post and transported many a fur-laden boat between the rivers by oxteam and wagon.

Astor wanted the United States government to build a fort at the Fox River to protect his lucrative fur business from the Winnebago Indians. In 1828, the army, recognizing the strategic importance of the portage for the movement of military men and equipment, began the construction of Fort Winnebago's seven barracks and other buildings. For seventeen years the soldiers provided protection for the fur trade as well as for new settlers.

With the signing of a treaty in 1829 in Prairie du Chien between the United States and the Winnebago Nation, the United States began the systematic process of dispossessing the Winnebagoes from this region. The United States government would buy their lands in Illinois and the Michigan Territory, which included the present state of Wisconsin, and the Indians would be moved westward across the Mississippi River.[3]

That year John Kinzie, sub-agent for Indian affairs who had a command of thirteen Indian dialects, was assigned to Fort Winnebago to expedite the terms of this treaty. From a sturdy chest, he annually paid each Indian man, woman and child a stipend of three dollars in silver. Respected by the Winnebagoes, Kinzie and his wife Juliette ministered to them for three years. During these times of hardship, the Kinzies gave them food and other supplies—corn, salt, tobacco, charcoal, and cloth; they befriended them and occasionally bestowed them with gifts. During the last months of their tenure the Kinzies lived in a fine new home across the Fox River from the fort.

The idea of building a canal between the Fox and Wisconsin Rivers had surfaced by the year 1837. Such a canal would complete an inland waterway from the Atlantic Ocean to the Gulf of Mexico, and the need to transport goods overland would be eliminated. However, in 1838, the first effort to dig a canal ended in failure. A second attempt in 1849, the year the Muirs arrived, eventually failed as well.[4]

The canal had been a factor in Daniel's decision to settle in Wisconsin instead of Canada. Hearing about the project while enroute to the new land, he recognized its potential for transporting farm produce to market. When the Muirs first journeyed into Portage City from the lake farm for supplies, they crossed the Fox River on the wooden bridge at Fort Winnebago recently vacated by the military. The barracks were now occupied by, among others, Irish immigrants working on the canal. The home where the Kinzies had lived stood on the bank of what was now little more than a plank-lined ditch. Throughout the ensuing years of struggle to finish the waterway, there was some traffic on it despite the problems.

In 1855, the Fox and Wisconsin River Improvement Company started the third attempt to finish construction, but not until the Army Corps of Engineers worked on it between 1874 and 1876 was it finally completed. The canal was used for a comparatively short time before the railroads came into prominence.

Today, canal waters move slowly past the still-standing house where the Kinzies lived; the banks are still shored up by the original huge planks of Douglas fir, three inches thick, twelve to fourteen inches wide and up to twenty-four feet long. A short distance away stands the surgeon's quarters, all that remains of Fort Winnebago.

Daniel Muir purchased the land he first settled in 1849 from the Fox and Wisconsin River Improvement Corporation, although the transaction was not finalized until six years later. On January 8, 1855, the corporation gave Daniel a land payment receipt that read:

"Received of Daniel Muir of Marquette County the sum of two hundred dollars being in full for the east half of the northeast quarter and east half of the southeast quarter section no. 14, north of range 9 east containing 160 acres at the rate of $1.25 per acre. . . ."

When Daniel bought another parcel of Fountain Lake land the following year, he doubled his first farm to a total of 320 acres—or half a section. His deed to the northwest quarter of Section 13 showed that he bought the land directly from the State of Wisconsin May 8, 1850 for $1.25 an acre.

After Wisconsin became a state in 1848, the United States Government conveyed canal grants, and at the same time deeded certain lands to the state, which was then empowered to sell them. The quarter section Daniel bought in 1850 was originally listed as U.S. Patent No. 420. This second 160 acre parcel adjoined an original eighty that lay on the north side of the road.

Sandy Gray had helped Daniel locate Fountain Lake Farm in 1849, and in 1855 he was instrumental in persuading Daniel to buy a new farm in Marquette County. This half section was adjacent to some of Gray's holdings.

In January, 1855, Daniel paid George and Alexander McKay from Racine, Wisconsin $1.25 an acre for lands in sections 28 and 29 in the Town of Buffalo. The McKays each held a United States patent to 160 acres, dated July 1, 1848. This farm of 320 acres was located a little over four miles to the southeast of Fountain Lake. On May 30, 1855, Daniel's deed to Hickory Hill Farm was recorded with the Marquette County Register of Deeds along with the Fountain Lake lands. No matter when Daniel acquired the various parcels, he took apparently care of all the paper work and recording at one time.

It has been said that Daniel Muir bought Hickory Hill Farm because the sandy soil of the first farm was worn out after intensive wheat farming. However, the move to Hickory Hill was only one of many Daniel would make in the new world and exemplified his restless habit of constantly moving on.

The glacier molded the new farmland a bit differently than Fountain Lake farm. There was no lake, but there were ponds and marshland nearby. A low ridge of glacial moraine material extended westward on a line with the future site of the Muirs' farm buildings. The land was gently rolling and virtually all tillable.

For two growing seasons John walked from Fountain lake to Hickory Hill to bring it under cultivation. Once again trees were grubbed out—some bur oaks that had survived fires once caused by lightning or started by Indians to clear the brush for driving animals in the hunt. When the pioneers planted crops the practice of burning was stopped, and, unless cultivated, the land eventually returned to trees.

The Muirs put up a log house and stable for temporary shelter for themselves and their animals until they could build a permanent house and barn. These log buildings, built near a ravine about fifty feet west of the well site, still existed in 1873 when Thomas Kearns purchased Hickory Hill.

The family moved to their new farm about the time of Sarah's marriage to David Galloway in December, 1856. A member of the Royal Stewart clan from Fifeshire, Scotland, Sarah's new husband had come to Wisconsin earlier to scout out land for himself, his parents, and other relatives in his large family who were all anxious to depart for America.[5]

David's father, George, born February 26, 1801, the son of John and Ann Watson Galloway, married Jean Millar Gibb who had a daughter, Ann. Jean's family, the Millars, lived at Kirkcaldy on the Firth of Forth across the water from where the Muirs had lived in Scotland. They were members of the Gordon clan to which the Muirs belonged.

David's father and his Uncle David farmed together in Fifeshire, first leasing a farm called Finmont. Then George Galloway leased one named Bankhead at Inchdarnie about five miles from Kirkcaldy where he devised advanced farming methods. When the Bankhead farm lease was about to expire the Galloways decided to try their fortunes in America. As well as leaving Scotland for religious reasons they longed to own their own land.

David eventually came to the Town of Buffalo, Marquette County where the Philip Grays had settled near Fountain Lake in 1850. The Galloways and Grays shared a religious bond, for in Scotland they had belonged to the Body of the Disciples in Christ as had Daniel Muir. At Fountain Lake David met Sarah Muir, and they became friends.

David selected land for his family several miles northward in the Town of Packwaukee and spent three years breaking and clearing it and building a house. He then returned to Scotland for about a year to help the Galloways complete preparations for the long-awaited trip to America.

Finally, in 1856, the Galloways set sail from Scotland. Besides David's parents, seven sisters joined the exodus, some of them with families. Only his Aunt Cecilia stayed behind; his brother John had died when he was a small child.

In America, David and his family took the train from New York to Milwaukee where they boarded a stagecoach for Packwaukee.

Soon after David returned to Marquette County, he and Sarah planned their marriage. Since David bought eighty acres adjacent to Hickory Hill in April, 1856, the young couple may have planned to live near the Muir family, but by October, 1856, the housing plans seem to have changed. On the 16th of that month, David Galloway deeded his Town of Buffalo parcel in section 29 to Daniel Muir for $1,200. Two days later Daniel signed over the deed to 120 acres of the original Fountain Lake property to Galloway for $2,000. So Sarah and David became proprietors of much of the original acreage the Muirs had settled in 1849 and lived in the two-story home where Sarah and her father had planted lilac bushes in the doorway seven years before. The Muir family circle was broken for the first time.

In 1857 the Muirs built a fine new frame home at Hickory Hill on a high slope where it commanded a panoramic view of the rolling countryside. The T-shaped house had an upright two-story section from which a lower wing extended; the cellar below the upright was reached by an outside cellar stairway as well as from a trap door inside.

John helped build a barn with structural pine beams forty and fifty feet long and ten inches in diameter that had been rafted down the Wisconsin River from the northern pineries at Stevens Point. Oak timbers from the farm were also used in its construction. Nearby Dates Mill provided waterpower for sawing the wooden shingles for the barn roof.

A well behind the house supplied the water. Muir's *The Story of My Boyhood and Youth* relates the famous story of the time he almost lost his life while digging the one-hundred-foot well. Working in a space only three feet in diameter, John dug through forty feet of gravel and clay and chiseled through sixty feet of bedrock sandstone before he reached water. Each day his father lowered him into the hole in a bucket. One day while he was chipping away at the sandstone he started to lose consciousness from the deadly choke damp, an accumulation of carbonic acid gasses which collected at the bottom. His father, alarmed that he could get no response from his son, shouted for him to get in the bucket. John barely managed to do so and Daniel hauled him up to the air just in time.[6]

Harry Kearns, son of Thomas Kearns who bought the farm in 1873, added to the story. He heard that the Muirs' neighbor, William Duncan, came to the Muir farm that day.

"Where's Johnny?," William asked Daniel.

"He's digging the well," Daniel replied, "and I haven't heard from him in awhile." Kearns said that the two men looked into the pit to find the boy barely conscious. They managed to haul him up to the surface. Accordingly, William Duncan would have been responsible for saving John's life.[7]

Duncan, an iron worker and stone mason from Lanarkshire, Scotland, was familiar with the problem of lack of oxygen in the mines. He showed Daniel how to maintain an adequate oxygen level by stirring the air at the bottom of the pit with a branch to bring the gases to the surface.

William, who later played a pivotal role in John's career, and his wife Jean lived about half a mile down the road west of the Muir farm. Always interested in their young neighbor, the Duncans befriended him in many ways. Since the day the two Davies so inspired him when they worked on the corduroy road over the swamp together, Muir had been reading everything he could get his hands on. After working so long at physical labor, he needed to satisfy his burning desire to read and learn. William loaned him several books and John would read the precious volumes in the cellar or whatever corner of the house he could find to keep out of the way of his father's watchful eye. One book he took home under his coat was a volume of *Scott's Waverly Novels* which included "The Bride of the Lammermuir."

The Duncans also befriended John on one occasion when they noticed that he was not well. Eva Turner, a local resident who had roots in Marquette and Columbia Counties, remembered a story her friend Jessie Duncan told her.[8] Jessie, the daughter of Jean and William, said her parents were invited up to Hickory Hill for supper one evening with the Muir family. They were surprised when they were served only mush and milk.

Referring to his son John, Daniel Muir said, "I don't know what's the matter with that boy. He's so thin. He's not a bit well and I don't know why it is. I give him mush three times a day."

"What else do you give him?" William Duncan asked Daniel.

"Why, I don't give him anything. That's all he has."

"That's not enough," Duncan insisted. "He needs meat and plenty of it. You'd better take him in to Doctor Meacher."

When Daniel did so, the doctor told him that John had no nutrition. He said that if Daniel didn't start to feed his son better he wouldn't have him. Daniel then added meat to the family diet to correct the nutritional deficiency and later informed Duncan he hadn't realized how lacking the diet had been.

The Duncans had three children, William, Robert, and Jessie. Annie Williams Duncan was Jessie's foster daughter who became a member of the household just four years before Jean Duncan's death. Annie's memories and those of her husband, Frank Waite, gave a picture of her foster grandparents who were so important in Muir's life. Waite grew up on an adjoining farm and worked for the Duncans as a youth. When he came of age he moved into the Duncan home.

Annie told about the Duncans' background:[9] Jean Duncan was born in 1814 in Linlithgowshire, Scotland, the daughter of the Duke of Hamilton's chief forester. She grew up on the duke's estate in a "house made of stone." Jean was "a typical pioneer woman who believed in helping people. There wasn't a better hearted woman in all the Town of Buffalo. Everyone was welcome in her house. She was a midwife who brought most of the children of the settlers in this area of the county into the world."

Annie explained that Jean spun wool from her own sheep on her spinning wheel. An accomplished seamstress, she made up a whole bolt of cotton cloth into sheets the year before her death. Annie remembered how her foster grandmother looked sitting in the chair as "she laid the hems and stitched them by hand. She was a thin, angular woman who always wore a cap."

Born in 1823, William Duncan worked as a spool boy in a textile mill when he was eight years old. He and some other boys were befriended by a woman who invited them to read the books in her home. At seventeen he became an apprentice to a stone mason. Later, he was employed in an iron works where he eventually rose to the position of foreman.

William and Jean were married in 1839, and eleven years later they set sail for America. One of their twelve sea chests contained the books they lent to "Johnnie Moore."

Frank Waite recalled that Duncan raised oats, corn and rye. "William Duncan raised some tobacco in his garden just for his own use. He was a great hand to set to smoke his clay pipe," he said.

Annie Duncan and Frank Waite were married later in life and lived for many years on the Duncan place they called Century Farm in Century Valley.

Muir began to mature during the Hickory Hill farm years. As he went about his chores, he constantly reached out for something beyond the drudgery of his daily life. He was eager to learn, to stretch his imagination, and to have new experiences. A series of letters between him and three of his friends provides the earliest known glimpse into his innermost thoughts and hopes as he expressed them at the time.

During the cold, snowy winter of 1858 when John was almost twenty, he began to correspond with his friends, Alfred Bradley Brown and Charles and William Reid, though they all lived within a few miles of each other. Winter chores kept the young farmers busy, but since they could not work the fields till spring, they did have some time to write letters, allowing their thoughts and imagination to wander as they exchanged confidences. Although the letters John received are still in existence, those he himself wrote are lost. However, because Bradley and the Reids made direct references to their friend's comments, his thoughts are clear.

That winter John walked a little more than a mile from Hickory Hill to attend a term at the log school nestled in the oak woods on a rise of land near the same marsh he and his brother David explored when they first arrived in Wisconsin and stayed with Sandy Gray on the county-line road. In a few short months the schoolmaster, George Branch, made a lasting impression on his students. After the term was over in March, Bradley Brown, who also attended the school, wrote nostalgically how he "should like first rate to meet over to the Old *school house* and speak pieces and sing our Old *Press onward* song as we used to last winter. I wonder where our *teacher* has gone and if he . . . thinks how his schollers [sic] are getting along, and of the mary [merry] *times* we used to have last winter and I wish we might meet him again in the Old school house and hear him call us to order again and hear some of his wonderful speeches."[10] It was easy for Bradley to attend for he only needed to walk across the field to the schoolhouse.

In early February, 1858, John invited Charles Reid to attend a school function. The roads were bad and the weather bleak. The blacks, browns, and dark grays of leafless trees were silhouetted against the snow. Arriving late at the schoolhouse, Charles had been having trouble with his horses and also had to repair the shoe on his sledge. Afterwards, he wrote to John that he did drive by the little log school on his way home that day but did not stop, although the scholars told him John was still there. John had gone to the schoolhouse door just in time to see Charles and his team disappearing down the road. Charles explained that when he looked back he thought he saw David Muir in the doorway, not John. He wrote that he did not stop because he was in a hurry and not because he was bashful as John implied in his letter.

On February 22 Charles quoted John: "I can only use myself as a wisdom bin a week longer." He had to return to full time work on the farm. Charles advised his friend not to lose anything out of his wisdom bin, for "they are precious bins. I hope your wisdom bin is as large as the wheat bin you talk of making."[11] In his letter of March 10, 1858, Charles quoted John as saying that time to stock wisdom bins was precious.

Whether or not John would be able to continue his schooling, he would never stop filling his wisdom bins, and, symbolically, he would always manage to fill his wheat bins.

Years later John would make his mark in literature, but even at this age, his friends respected his literary ability. Charles wrote about the poems John sent and how much he thought John's poetry had improved from his earlier efforts. He said he liked John's letter that was so neat and complete. Bradley Brown was glad to get a poem from John but didn't feel he could reciprocate. "I am't so used to writing poetry as you be,"[12] he explained.

Although their attendance in school was sketchy, the boys found other ways to satisfy their hunger for knowledge. As was the custom in early communities, neighbor loaned books to neighbor. John loaned Charles Reid the first of a two volume set of history books. Fascinated with the accounts of the generals, the battles, and the rise and fall of empires, Reid said he wanted to borrow the second volume when John was through reading it so he could continue the story.

In one letter to John, Bradley touched on another activity that was popular in the neighborhood. During the fall or winter months a teacher or someone interested in singing would lead people in regular evening song sessions. Bradley had just attended one such school and felt wistful that it was over.

"Our singing school was out last Tuesday evening. Had a very good sing and was sorry it was out so soon, but I suppose it was just as well seeing that the roads are so bad and the evenings are getting rather short."[13]

John and his friends were at an age when they were thinking about girls. Although they didn't express their feelings to the girls themselves, they did confide in each other. Charles spun romantic notions as he commented on a poem John had written "against the sweet little creatures," and believed the reason John wrote such a poem was unrequited love. Expanding on the subject of romance, Charles said he wished he had stopped in at the schoolhouse that day he was in such a hurry for he "might have seen the face of a young female of eighteen with blue eyes and fair hair flowing in lines of beauty . . . with eyes full of love that could have had its ideal only in the refined and passionate imaginations of the poet, John Muir, esq." He then asked John when he "would ever get married."[14] Muir immediately dispelled all such romantic notions, stating that the young female of eighteen was only an imaginary maid. He certainly did not plan to marry.

Despite the friends' literary outlets for their feelings, their lives were filled with hard work. In February of 1858, Charles cut down a great oak tree four feet in diameter and fantasized about Indians wearing beads making peace under its huge branches in years gone by. Taking a long time to finish the task, he was relieved when the tree was finally cut down and hauled out of the way. John's reaction to cutting down the giant tree was quite different—he seemed to "mourn its death,"[15] and wrote an elegy to the magnificent oak.

February came to an end and March weather was borne in on blustery winds. Swirling snowstorms dumped the winter's last deep snows on the woods and fields. The occasional rise in temperature began to melt the snow, and the Canada geese filled the air on their northern migration.

In April the snow melted away, the earth warmed, and according to William Reid, "it is music to the ears of man to hear the birds sing in the spring after a long, cold, dreary winter."[16] In May he commented that the "grass, bushes and trees are beginning to look green again. It is a time of reviving of everything." And placing an added value on the natural progression of the seasons, he said that "Things temporal and spiritual seem to bud out together."[17]

As for Daniel Muir, regardless of the season, he was always interested in things spiritual. Within his family, he was the guardian of the faith. He began to spend more and more time these days in his tiny Hickory Hill bedroom studying and translating his Bible while his children worked in the fields. A self-styled minister, he often preached at meetings around the countryside.

Jessie Duncan said that her father told her how Daniel Muir baptized his children in Knights Lake about a mile and a half from the Hickory Hill farmhouse. William Duncan recalled that he was out in his yard one warm Sunday morning when Daniel Muir came by with his team pulling the lumber wagon with all his children in it. Daniel told William that he was going to baptize them in the nearby lake.

"All of your children have been baptized," William said.

"No," replied Daniel. "That wasn't the right kind of baptism. I'm going to baptize them in a different way."[18]

And spurring the horses on, he continued on down the road and across the field to the wooded shore of the small lake sparkling in the sunshine.

However the baptismal ceremony had been carried out before, this time Daniel baptized his children by immersion. He could now be satisfied in his own mind that the ceremony was done right.

During this period Sarah and David Galloway were working hard to make a go of Fountain Lake Farm. Soon after Sarah's marriage to David Galloway, John found a good friend in David's mother, Jean, and their friendship continued twenty years until her death in 1876. A great favorite in the neighborhood, she was one of his earliest and staunchest supporters. John said that "she was one of the finest examples I ever knew of a great-hearted Scotch woman."[19] He said that everyone who knew her loved her. The children, especially, were fond of this affectionate woman whose generous-sized hands and rather large facial features matched her generosity and big heart.

Many years later, Sarah and David's daughter, Anna Galloway, remembered that her grandmother slipped her a big cookie when she was a wee girl going to a religious meeting in the old log schoolhouse near the Galloway farm at Fountain Lake. In later life Mrs. Galloway became blind, yet still gave the children sweets, bits of "sugar elly," (licorice) from the little bag she carried in her pocket. She had made the bag with fine, even stitches after she lost her sight.[20]

When John pursued his career in California, Grandma Galloway always looked forward to hearing about him and cherished the greenery and pressed flowers he enclosed in his letters.

Finding her greatest satisfaction in the happiness of her children, Anne Muir was also a staunch supporter of her son, and always encouraged him in his endeavors. Daniel's attitude was in direct contrast to his wife's. Yet, somehow, during his youthful years, John managed to pursue his interests despite his father's constant discouragement.

As time passed, Hickory Hill Farm was becoming too small for John. All the while he did his farm chores his mind and imagination were busy elsewhere. He was restless and anxious to see something of the world.

As he continued to whittle hickory inventions, his reputation grew among his friends and neighbors. Bradley Brown showed an interest in his friend's construction of clocks and sawmills. William Duncan, of course, was always interested, often driving over to Hickory Hill in his buggy to see what new contraption John was working on. In late summer of 1860 Duncan suggested that John take some of his inventions down to the Wisconsin Agricultural State Fair in Madison.

After much agonizing, John decided to act on William's suggestion. Leaving Hickory Hill and his family was an important milestone, for it put him on the road to his lifetime quest of learning and discovery in the world of nature. When he boarded the train at Pardeeville for Madison, he must have realized he was really striking out on his own.

A portion of him always remained at home. Two years later he shared memories of Hickory Hill and his family in a letter to his friend, Mrs. Edward Pelton of Prairie du Chien, when he took her on an imaginary walk around the farm.

"Down here across the little ravine is the best place. . . . Across this ravine and up the opposite hill a little bit in that thick little grove is where I used to pray. In this great field is where I've sweated and played, worked and rejoiced. There is the garden where Maggie and I have lavished away many happy hours. And away down this slope and over the level prairie is where we have taken hundreds of long walks and talked of earth and heaven . . . Just by that great oak is where in the moonlight evenings I used to spend hours with my head up in the sky and soared among the planets."[21]

# III

# ADRIFT IN THIS BIG
# SUNNY WORLD

*I am now adrift in this big sunny world. Jumping
out of the woods I was at once led and pushed and
whirled about by new everythings everywhere.*
—John Muir

"The aching parting from my mother and my sisters was,
of course, hard to bear,"[1] John related in his autobiography when he left home in September, 1860. It
had been an agonizing decision to leave Hickory Hill farm to take a few
hickory inventions to the Wisconsin State Agricultural Society Fair in
Madison, but his feeling of sadness was coupled with the excitement
of new adventure.

He had about fifteen dollars in his pocket—the gold sovereign his
Grandfather Gilrye had given him when he left Scotland—and perhaps
ten dollars he had made by raising a few bushels of grain on a little patch
of sandy abandoned ground. When he asked his father if he would send
him some money if he needed a little, Daniel refused. "No; depend
entirely upon yourself," he advised his son.

David hitched the horses to the wagon and got ready to drive his
brother to Pardeeville to take the train. John placed his meager baggage
in the wagon. It consisted only of a "package made up of the two clocks
and a small thermometer made of a piece of old washboard, all three
tied together, with no covering or case of any sort, the whole looking
like one very complicated machine." He climbed onto the seat beside
David and the team and wagon set off down the long farm drive and
along the country roads. Although Hickory Hill was only ten miles from
Pardeeville, this was the first time John had ever traveled to that village.

41

In Pardeeville, David pulled the horses to a stop in front of the inn near the La Crosse Milwaukee railroad station. John jumped down and set his bundle on the platform of the seemingly deserted inn, and the brothers said goodbye. They had been through many an adventure together and would miss each other. John was twenty-two and David twenty.

David reined the horses in a short turn and headed back to Hickory Hill. The grinding noise made by the turning wagon brought the landlord out of the inn. '. . . the first thing that caught his eye was my strange bundle. . . . 'Hello, young man, what's this?' 'Machines,' I said, 'for keeping time and getting up in the morning, and so forth.' 'Well! Well! . . . Where did you get the pattern for such a thing?' 'In my head,' I said.

". . . in fifteen or twenty minutes the greater part of the population of Pardeeville stood gazing in a circle around my strange hickory belongings. . . . Almost every one as he came up would say, 'What's that? What's it for?' 'Who made it?'

"The landlord would answer them all alike, 'Why a young man that lives out in the country somewhere, made it and he says it's a thing for keeping time, getting up in the morning . . .' Someone in the crowd said, 'Mark my words, you'll see all about it in the newspapers some of these days.'"

Finally, the impromptu demonstration ended and John managed to take his inventions into the inn where he stayed overnight to await the arrival of the train the next day.

"In the morning I went to the station, and set my bundle on the platform. Along came the thundering train, a glorious sight, the first train I had ever waited for." When the conductor saw John's bundle, he too was interested in the inventions and suggested that John give them to the baggage master. "If you take them into the car they will draw a crowd and might get broken."

This John did and then he asked the conductor if he might ride on the engine, but the engineer was reluctant to allow it. "I wish you would take this young man on," the conductor urged. "He has the strangest machines in the baggage car I ever saw in my life. I believe he could make a locomotive. He wants to see the engine running. Let him on."

John climbed onto the engine and in a short time the engineer agreed to the young man's request to go outside the cab to see the train's machinery in action.

". . . I went out and walked along the foot-board on the side of the boiler, watching the magnificent machine rushing through the landscape as if glorying in its strength like a living creature. While seated on the cow-catcher platform, I seemed to be fairly flying, and the wonderful display of power and motion was enchanting. This was the first time I had ever been on a train . . . since I had left Scotland."

He described the ride to his sister Mary: "Well I got into the car . . . the car burred and away . . . I went over hills . . . over hollows and marshes and creeks, over bridges and rivers and they all whirled and I came to Madison."[2]

Built on the isthmus between Third Lake and Fourth Lake, Madison, the capital city, hub of state affairs, was busier than ever during fair week. For weeks newspapers throughout the state had been running notices and ads about the Wisconsin State Agricultural Society's Tenth Annual State Fair at their fairgrounds just outside the city.

It was Monday, September 24, when John arrived, the first day for entrants to set up their exhibits. The ticket agent at the gate told him to take his inventions to the Temple of Art on the hill.

He walked through the grounds, described by the Madison Evening Patriot to be a "scene of bustling activity [as] the work on the stands and tents was being hurried to completion."[3] The Temple of Fine Arts, as it was sometimes called, gaily ornamented with flags, was "a building of great size which housed the products of artistic genius."[4] In an amphitheater effect, the grounds sloped down to the fenced-in course where the equestrian events would take place.

According to Muir's autobiography, a dignified gentleman met him at the door of the fine arts building and after examining the two clocks and the thermometer asked, "Did you make these? They look wonderfully beautiful and novel and must, I think, prove the most interesting feature of the fair.

"You can have your pick of all the building, and a carpenter to make the necessary shelving and assist you every way possible."[5]

The young Marquette County farmer quickly had a shelf made large enough for all of his carvings, "went out on the hill and picked up some glacial boulders of the right size for weights, and in fifteen or twenty minutes the clocks were running."

In his opening address on Wednesday, September 26, B. R. Hinkley, president of the Wisconsin State Agricultural Society, spoke to the crowds assembled on the hillside. He noted the scope of the fair entries, 2200 in all: "the horses, the cattle, the sheep and swine; the products of the field, garden and workshop; and the finer products of artistic genius in yonder Hall of Art."[6]

Mr. Hinkley gave an overall view of Wisconsin progress since it achieved statehood:

"We have subdued the native wilderness of territory, and covered it with luxuriant crops; built hundreds of beautiful villages, and one noble commercial city; made costly improvements on our great lakes and navigable streams; banded our domain with railroads, and threaded it with telegraphs; have organized systems of education which are now offering the boon of intelligence to almost every community and neighborhood within our borders which then look to the highest culture of all; and we have increased our population from a few tens of thousands to almost a million people."

Between 11:00A.M. and noon on this opening day, the melodious tones of a calliope were heard all over the grounds, attracting many people toward the Temple of Art. Within that building or one nearby, Norman Wiard was "grinding out the music by turning the calliope handle round and round."[7] He was promoting his ice boat, the Lady Franklin. Advertised as "the most surprising invention of the last quarter century . . . [it was] procured at large expense to the Agricultural Society." It was promised that a visit to the ice boat display "would repay a visit to the fair."[8] Over the next four days 6,000 people paid ten cents each to see the ice craft.

"The ice boat is elegantly got up, and is handsomely ornamented on the inside. It will undoubtedly distinguish itself next winter on the frozen water of the Mississippi river."[9]

All that week reporters from the two Madison newspapers walked the grounds. The *Evening Patriot* described the many exhibits in the Temple of Art. "In this building there are many handsome specimens of fancy work, Paintings, Engravings and elegant Wood Ware. The click of Sewing Machines is constantly heard. . . . Cases of Fuller's Ambrotypes occupied a prominent position."[10] And the young man from Marquette County had set up his unique carvings in the midst of it all.

The front page for the *Wisconsin State Journal* for Tuesday, September 25, 1860, featured an item on "An Ingenious Whittler." "While at the Fair Grounds this morning, we saw some very ingenious specimens in the form of clocks, made by Mr. John Muir, of Buffalo, Marquette County. They were without cases and were whittled out of pine wood [actually, hickory]. The wheels moved with beautiful evenness. [One clock] registered not only the hours, but the minutes, seconds, and days of the month. The other was in the shape of a scythe, the wheels being arranged along the part representing the blade. It was hung in a dwarf bur oak very tastefully ornamented with moss about its roots. We will venture to predict that few articles will attract as much attention as these products of Mr. Muir's ingenuity."[11]

The *Evening Patriot* also described John's exhibit: [In the Temple of Art] "we noticed . . . two great curiosities in the shape of some wooden clock work, which was in motion, and the cog-wheels and all the wood work about it had been cut out of wood by the young man from Marquette County who is with it. One of the pieces is emblematic of Old Time and the design is forcibly and appropriately presented. The work is surprising, and could only have been executed by genuine genius."[12]

And in another edition of the *Patriot*: "Among the novelties we noticed two rustic Wooden Clocks, the result of jack-knife whittling, by John Muir, A Scotchman, of Marquette County. These were prodigies in the art of whittling."[13] A *Wisconsin State Journal* reporter commented that "the wooden clocks of our Marquette County friends were among the objects most surrounded by crowds."[14]

Both Muir and Wiard were creative and imaginative. Since his clocks were housed near the ice boat John had the opportunity to study the craft's intricate mechanisms. They held close kinship with his own inventive designs.

As stated in Norman Wiard's patent of January 24, 1860, the ice boat was "to combine a boat with runners and skates to propel it on the ice by locomotive steam power for the purposes of general travel and transportation during the winter in northern climates." At the same time it would have the buoyant capacity of a boat in case the ice should break.[15]

Muir was interested in the boat's runners, the drive wheel to penetrate the ice, the steam power, the system of air tubes, and the apparatus at the rear to cut fine chips of ice to replenish the water supply in the boiler. Wiard even planned "an arrangement whereby freight could be moved by a locomotive in trains of cars, each a boat, and with but one pair of runners. The freight cars would be "coupled to each other like the cars on a railroad."[16]

According to the Prairie du Chien *Leader*, May 10, 1860, "[The ice boat] is tastefully ornamented; has a beautiful headlight, bell, steam whistles, etc. The boilers are covered with sheet brass, nicely burnished. The nineteen panels on the outside are splendidly painted upon inlaid pearl. Inside the cabin, the seats are upholstered with damask velvet, and the panels over the windows are fixed with gilt mouldings. . . ."[17] The handsome seats were placed in a circle around a table.

In artistic lettering across the top of the twenty-eight foot craft, the words, "Prairie du Chien & St. Paul Mil. and Miss. R R Line," attested to the fact that Wiard was working in conjunction with the railroad. The Lady Franklin was to revolutionize travel during the icebound winter months and would link the riverfront communities from Galena, Illinois to St. Paul, Minnesota.

Originally from Janesville, Wisconsin, Norman Wiard had superintended shops employing as many as 150 machinists and engineers.

The entrepreneur had begun work on his craft in the winter of 1856-1857 at the time the Milwaukee and Mississippi Rail Road was laying track from Milwaukee to Prairie du Chien. Muir's mechanical abilities would gain more notice later when he would design factory machinery and layouts.

During the fair, when John wasn't demonstrating his self-rising bed and other inventions, he wandered the grounds on those warm, sunny days with fresh September breezes blowing. He examined the farm machinery—the harrowing and plowing implements, the grist mills, threshing machines, and windmills. As he walked through the tents and buildings, he saw the stoves, carriages, and churns in the manufacturers' tent; the potatoes, wheat, and monstrous squashes displayed in the vegetable tent; and in the fruit and flower tent, the ruddy apples, purple grapes, and bottles of sparkling wine.

He shared his vivid impressions of the week's experiences in a letter to Sarah.

"But Sarah, I am now adrift in this big sunny world, and I don't know how I feel. Jumping out of the woods I was at once led and pushed and whirled about by new everythings, everywhere. For three or four days my eyes . . . were pleased and teased and wearied with pictures and sewing machines and squashes and reapers and quilts and cheeses and apples and flowers and soldiers and firemen and thousands of all kinds of faces, all of them strange but two."[18]

On Saturday, the 29th of September, the jubilee was over. The exhibitors packed up their displays, returned to their farms and businesses, and looked ahead to the next annual fair in 1861. But the shadows of civil war were darkening over the land. The papers which carried the fair news also carried accounts of the Lincoln-Douglas debates and chronicled the events that widened the rift between the northern and secessionist states. The happy fair goers could not know that by the following September the fair grounds would become Camp Randall, a major staging area for Union troops, and the Temple of Art would be turned into an indoor drill room.

By the close of fair week Muir accepted Norman Wiard's invitation to accompany him and the ice boat back to Prairie du Chien on the Mississippi River and to work in his foundry and machine shop.

John wrote Sarah about his plans. "I am in Madison. Tomorrow morning I suppose I shall seat myself in Mr. Wiard's ice boat to be hurled to Pr[airie] du Chien. Mr. Wiard is an old machinist. I am to have access to his books and tools. I have had many other offers, but stern looking Mr. Wiard is my choice. If I am at all able to lay down any particular plan for myself while at the mercy of so many chances and influences . . . I mean to stay a month or two with this man and then steer eastward."[19]

The boat was again loaded onto a Milwaukee and Mississippi Rail Road flat car for the return trip to Prairie du Chien where, before its sojourn at the fair, it had been taken by flatcar from New York and stored in the river town since May. John settled himself and his bundle of clocks in the elegant cabin of what he called Wiard's droll-looking boat for the memorable one-hundred-mile ride to Prairie du Chien.

The Milwaukee and Mississippi Rail Road stretched across all of Wisconsin from Lake Michigan to the Mississippi River, following the Wisconsin River for many miles. The unusually wide Wisconsin River valley provided a good site for building railroad beds. Framed by tree-covered bluffs, it had been created thousands of years before by torrents of meltwaters from the receding continental glacier. On April 15, 1857, the first train had steamed into Prairie du Chien amid much fanfare and flag waving by the crowds. A new era had begun.

As the train steamed along the Wisconsin River on those same tracks, John may have had some feeling that he was taking part in the great westward movement of the country. When he had boarded the train at Pardeeville the week before, his horizons suddenly expanded, and when he boarded the train for Prairie du Chien, they widened still further.

It was an especially beautiful season of the year. The foliage was changing from the greens of summer to the bright colors of early autumn. Muir could see the vivid reds of the soft floodplain maples; the bright yellow of the birches and willows along the river bank; and the clusters of quaking aspens, their yellow leaves lighting up the land-scape in sunshine or in rain. On the higher ground, the sumacs had turned a brilliant orange-red and the leaves of the white oak were already tinged with reddish pink to dark purple. Nearby on the drier prairie soils, the bright purple asters bloomed in company with yellow goldenrod.

The railroad followed the Wisconsin River where explorers Father Jacques Marquette and Louis Jolliet paddled downriver in 1673, almost two hundred years before, in search of a passage west. The train neared the end of its journey at Bridgeport where the valley narrowed to half a mile between steep bluffs before widening again at the confluence of the Wisconsin and Mississippi rivers. The French explorers had been the first Europeans to view that magnificent sight.

For thousands of years the rivers had been a navigation route. A succession of Indian cultures had inhabited the lands along the river-ways—the food gatherers, the mound builders, and the native peoples of more recent times.

At the junction of the two rivers a gently sloping plain stretched northward for about twelve miles along the Mississippi and extended about two or three miles eastward to spectacular sandstone bluffs. This prairie was the future site of Prairie du Chien. Here, in 1673, a Fox village of about three hundred people was located. In historical times the prairie land was called the neutral or treaty ground. In spring and fall hundreds of Indian families from various tribes came together for celebrations and to exchange furs for goods brought by the fur traders.[20] After the settlers came, a succession of forts was built on the site as the French, British, and Americans vied for control of the region. Eventually the Americans secured it. In 1816 they began construction of the first Fort Crawford in the Main Village at Prairie du Chien on the island in the east channel of the Mississippi. After a few years John Jacob Astor extended his American Fur Company activities to Prairie du Chien, and later, the second Fort Crawford was built in the Lower Town section of that village.

The United States government had begun to deal with the Indians by first convening the famous Great Council of 1825 on the neutral ground attended by two thousand members of nine tribes. United States Commissioners assured the tribes they only wished to establish peace between the nations and had no desire to take their tribal lands. With great ceremony the Indians signed treaties defining tribal boundaries. The government had now taken the first step toward negotiating with individual tribes—toward buying their lands and forcing the Indians from them. In 1829 the Winnebago nation signed a treaty, relinquishing their homelands and agreeing to relocate west of the Mississippi. This was the treaty John Kinzie administered at Fort Winnebago on the banks of the Fox River at the portage.

The 1829 treaty was executed just thirty-one years before John Muir arrived in Prairie du Chien with the ice boat. The western terminus of the Milwaukee and Mississippi Rail Road was located near the vacated buildings of the second Fort Crawford. The ice boat was unloaded at the Holton & Co. warehouse built just three years before on the river across from the newly finished depot. Here, it would stay until the winter cold froze over the Mississippi and Wiard could test it on the ice.

Perhaps Muir understood the railroad's interest in promoting the ice boat. If the device proved successful there would be a continuous flow of people, carts, wagons, animals, grains, and other goods on the Mississippi in all seasons.

River crossings had long been a problem. Early settlers had used pole ferries first, then horse-powered ferries, and later, ferries operated by steam. Finally, when the railroads pushed west, they operated steam-powered railroad packets on the Mississippi to continue the flow of goods and people at the river. The packets were the link between the eastbound and westbound trains that stopped at the river's edge.

On May 10, 1860, soon after the ice boat's arrival in Prairie du Chien, Wiard had given readers of the Prairie du Chien *Leader* a detailed account of the twelve hundred mile trip of the Lady Franklin and its entourage from New York. Relating how the ice boat was loaded onto a railroad flatcar in Jersey City, he wrote that all along the way "I found all the officers and employees of the several roads ready punctually to give me every facility possible . . . It has not cost me one cent to move the Ice Boat and a party of eight persons attending it from New York to Prairie du Chien, or for the return of the party to New York." He commended the people and railroads by name and individually praised their railroad lines.[21]

On that same page, the *Leader* editor had devoted a column of lavish praise to the craft. "Mr. Wiard's Ice Boat, so long expected, arrived on the cars of the M. & M. R. R. on Monday afternoon. . . . Notwithstanding the delays and disappointments attending its arrival, we think Mr. Wiard has exhibited a wonderful skill in its construction, and commendable energy and determination in overcoming the difficulties he has had to encounter since the beginning, without means, to the complete building, equipment and transportation so long a distance, of so elaborate, and if successful, so important a machine. . . . Mr. Wiard intends having the boat on exhibition here during the summer and proposes to visit the river towns with his beautiful working model."[22]

Wiard promoted his craft all that summer, traveling up and down the river, lecturing and showing a model of the ice boat. At the same time, he promoted railroad lines, urging people to take the Prairie du Chien route and "visit this interesting machine, destined to give better facilities for travel in Winter than in Summer . . ."[23] For some months there was a steady stream of news and ads about the creation. According to one ad: "The beautiful ice boat, Lady Franklin, is placed in a Building near the M. & M. R. R. Depot . . . and will remain on Exhibition during the Summer with steam up and engines running. Visitors to Prairie du Chien and Travelers from the North and East can always see it."[24] Many people paid a fee to see the famous craft.

That fall, John found lodging at the elegant Mondell House where he did chores in exchange for room and board. The coming of the railroad to Prairie du Chien had spurred a great deal of commerce and construction in that enterprising pioneer town of two thousand, and the Mondell House was but one of the hotels built to accommodate the influx of people.

The *1884 History of Crawford County and Richland Counties* states that "Another fine hotel was erected in 1856-57 by E. W. Mondell, at a cost

of $40,000. This was known as the Mondell, . . . a very superior house
. . . [it] was a fine three story structure, situated on Bluff Street, the principal street of the city. . . ."[25] Located in the Upper Town section of Prairie
du Chien the L shaped hotel, built of brick, fronted both Minnesota and
Bluff streets with its main entrance facing Bluff Street.

When John moved into the Mondell House, Edward Wright Pelton
was the owner and proprietor, one of those "experienced hotel men
who . . . won the esteem their merit deserved as good landlords."[26] Pelton
had owned and operated the Phoenix Hotel several blocks away on Main
Street in Prairie du Chien's Upper Town section. Fronting the east channel of the Mississippi, it was in danger of occasional flooding. He sold
the Phoenix before coming to the Mondell House, located on higher,
drier land where it was safer from high water.

An advertisement in the Leader that summer claimed that "This
house will be carefully conducted by its proprietor who will make the
comfort of his guests his first endeavor. Day Boarders will be received
at $2.50 per week. An omnibus will convey Passengers and Baggage to
and from Cars and Boats."[27]

From the entrance of Mondell House Muir could look westward
down Bluff Street sloping gradually down to the river. Toward the east
he could see the street rise gently as it crossed the prairies till it reached
the foot of the bluff beyond. There it graded more steeply and disappeared within the coulee, a short v-shaped valley cut by a stream from
the top of the rock formation to the terrace below.

After living on two farms during his youth, surrounded only by
farm buildings, John found town life strange and new. There were several homes and businesses near the Mondell. Down in the next block
on the same side of Bluff Street was a red brick home built in 1842,
owned by Edward Pelton. Across Bluff Street to the west was the story-
and-a-half Prairie House, an inn built in 1834.

It was strange, too, to be living in a different household. When John
joined the Peltons shortly after the first of October, he was introduced
to a home life far different from his own. The warm, gay atmosphere

of the Pelton family was a distinct change from the restrictive atmosphere at Hickory Hill.

Edward Pelton's niece, Emily Ordelia Pelton, lived with them at the Mondell. The friendship that developed between Emily and John during his stay there spanned many years.

Tragedy had befallen Emily, born December 21, 1837, when she was nine years old and her sister Ida Estelle, was twelve. The Pelton genealogy states: "The year 1846 will remain memorable in the annals of the Peltons of Prairie du Chien as the year of death."[28]

Emily's father, Ezra, died on September 11, and her mother, Nancy, died two days later. Both were 39. Ezra's single brother Champion, who lived with them, also died September 13. All were victims of malarial fever.

The scourge felled many others that year. "Not a relative was able to attend either [Nancy or Ezra's] funeral," the genealogy recounted, "six members of their families lying near death's door at the time. There were not enough well persons to care for the sick, and medical attendance was not to be had."[29]

1845 had also been a year of death, for Nancy and Ezra lost three small children to malaria. Their four year old son had died the year before. Upon their parents' death Emily and Ida were the only surviving members of their family.

Edward Pelton became Emily and Ida Pelton's guardian. He and his first wife, Sarah Brunson Pelton, took his little nieces into their home to raise as their own. The genealogy noted Edward's generosity: " . . . he was always ready to contribute liberally to the welfare of relatives and friends and to any worthy object."[30] The genealogy noted that Emily was well cared for and well educated.

Pelton sent both nieces to eastern schools. Ida attended school in Hartford, Connecticut as Emily may have done. When Ida died at the Hartford school at the age of twenty, Emily became the only surviving member of her family.

It is an interesting fact that Emily's father, Ezra Pelton, was the second child in his family to be so named; his parents had named a child who died Ezra, so Emily's father was called Ezra, Jr.

The five Pelton brothers were a commercial force in Prairie du Chien. Edward and Champion ran large mercantile, elevator and milling enterprises, businesses that "extended to adjoining counties, largely among the French and Indians. Later the two, with the help of their brother, Alonzo, commanded the larger share of the business of Prairie du Chien. They built the first elevator and flourmill on the river at that place, the builder having been their brother, Ezra, Jr."[31]

In 1854-55 Edward was president of the company formed to build the toll bridge across the Wisconsin River at Prairie du Chien. It was completed in 1857, the year the railroad arrived. He was also a member and an eventual stockholder of the group promoting the Milwaukee & Mississippi Rail Road.

Almost ten years after the months he spent in Prairie du Chien, John wrote to Emily from the Yosemite Valley in California. He recalled his arrival at the Mondell House when the family gathered to greet him—Emily's Uncle Edward, his second wife Frances Newton Pelton and their tiny daughter Fannie, and Emily, who was "remarkable for tact and ready wit in social circles."[32]

"Something or other jostled a bunch of old Mondell memories. I thought of the days when I came in fresh verdure from the Wisconsin woods, and when I used to hurl very orthodox denunciations at all things morally or religiously amiss in old or young. It appears strange to me that you should all have been so patient with me."[33]

And in a later letter to Emily he wrote, "How you must laugh at the memories of my odd appearance among you all. I remember rebuking you and Mr. Lovewell without mercy for silly chat, old Mr. Newton too for irreverence and all of you for sins of some kind or other. And something else I remember, Emily—your kind words to me the first day I saw you. Kind words are likely to live in any human soil, but planted in the breast of a Scotchman they are absolutely immortal, and whatever Heaven may have in store for you in after years you have at least one friend while John Muir lives."[34]

Years later John reminisced about the evenings they spent together with Emily's cousins singing merrily all the time; about the people he knew and the things he did—"the chores in the brick house and that old horse and cow and Mrs. Grogan."[35]

As he had always done at home, Muir found time to explore the countryside and to continue his avid search for plants. Hiking across farmland and prairie toward the bluffs he could marvel at the carved castle effect of the sandstone outcrops. When he scrambled to the top of the bluff covered with occasional oaks, he got a fine view of the broad Mississippi valley: of the marshes, and islands and lakes within the river; of Prairie du Chien, both Lower Town and Upper Town; and of the second Ft. Crawford.

For thousands of years, the Mississippi has been a major North American flyway for migrating birds. When Muir arrived in Prairie du Chien in early October, 1860, the fall migrations were coming into full swing. During the ensuing weeks vast numbers of ducks, geese, cranes, and hawks flew over the landscape. The valley filled with "flying, squawking hosts [of ducks] beyond counting."[36] Hawks by the thousands roosted in the trees on the bluffs and in the dawn they all rose at once to continue their southward journey. Huge flocks of Canada geese filled the sky in everchanging arrangements—from v-shaped formations to long lines flying in a checkmark pattern. The raucous sound of the huge birds penetrated the valley, and as the multitude passed overhead, Muir heard the rustle of thousands of rapid, powerful wingbeats.

In Muir's time, passenger pigeons, now extinct, still filled the land. He had been fascinated with these birds in Marquette County, and here, at the confluence, great armies of them, "in numbers beyond comparison, visited, now this year, now that."[37]

He also explored the limestone formations in the high land near the town, finding many fine plant specimens for his collection.

"Do you ever find time to botanize?" he asked Emily five years later. "These cold limestone rocks so abundant in your neighborhood [are] an excellent field for ferns and many other interesting plants which will grow nowhere else."[38]

He described his surroundings to Sarah that fall of 1860, and in her reply his sister placed herself in imagination with him in Prairie du Chien.

"I don't know what would give me more pleasure than scrambling with you to the top of the ridge you spoke about . . . Take a sketch of Prairie du Chien if you can and send it to me. Mark the house where you stay and then I can tap at the door every morning and ask for John if I choose."[39]

Missing his home and family on this first time away, John told Sarah and David that the city was a miserable place, but that he was living in a cheery home in polite society. He wrote that he set up his rising bed in his room and that he made a lamplighter to start his fire.

If John felt lonesome for his family and the old familiar surroundings, so too, did his family miss him. As the eldest son, he occupied a special place in the family circle.

As soon as they found out where to send letters, all the Muirs sat down around the table at the Hickory Hill farmhouse to write to John, the first letter since he left. Their combined family letter of October 14, 1860, and his mother's one week later, gave the earliest revelations as to what the Muirs were like.

Anne Gilrye Muir's fine qualities showed through in her concise, well written letter to her son. She was concerned for his well-being and comfort and interested in his goals. Her practical nature was evident as she recounted what she and Daniel had done about sending him a trunk.

"We have received three letters from you," she wrote in her precise handwriting, "two from Madison and one from Prairie du Chien. We were glad to know your health was pretty good in the midst of so much excitement and praise.

"I hope you find yourself comfortable in your new home, and likely to learn some of those things you want to know. I am glad you found so many friends at Madison and hope you will find friends wherever you go. We were rather surprised to know that you had set your face westward and so is everyone that hears of it—however, I hope that will turn out for your good. I always understood that Prairie du Chien was an unhealthy place but perhaps it is healthy in winter.

"Your father went down to Portage on Friday [October] 19th and bought a trunk for you and a suit of clothes and a hat and three pairs of socks and a pair of drawers—and I sent three fine shirts and two common ones and your flannel shirt and your papers and letters and small books. Your father put them all in the trunk together at Portage and then put the key in a paper and took it to the post office.

"I have been particular in telling you of all things as your father left the trunk for the person to send off that he bought it from. However, I hope you have received the key and the trunk too before this comes to hand. I hope you have received the letter we sent off last Sunday night written by so many. They will all be glad to hear from you. We have received the books you sent and those that proposed giving you them were certainly much interested in your welfare.

"Now John, I hope you will write as soon as your trunk comes to hand as I am anxious to know that you received it safe. I hope everything will suit you. Your father intended to send a silk napkin for your neck, but forgot until the key was sent off. Let us know how much the carriage of the trunk cost you. Let us know how many churches there are in Prairie du Chien and which you entered and if there are any Sunday Schools and let us know how you are getting on.

"There is a prayer meeting every Sunday night at Midland School and [it] is pretty well attended. I intend to send this letter with them tonight. We all join in love to you, hoping your health improves. from your affectionate Mother."[40]

His father's letter showed that Daniel Muir was only interested in spiritual and practical matters.

"I am glad you are well in body," he wrote, "[but] I should like to hear of your spiritual health being good [also]. Do not let the vanities of this life possess your soul. I will send a trunk with your things by railway as directed, to the care of Mr. Wiard."[41]

David, perhaps, missed his brother the most since the two boys were close in age and had shared so much in their boyhood years. He gave voice to his loneliness in an understatement: "For awhile after you left home the house looked rather empty especially on Sunday, but now we begin to get used to it."[42]

David had read the Madison newspaper stories of John's inventions with much interest.

"I suppose you begin to feel as though you were a man now standing on your own [feet] when you have produced the greatest curiosity invention of the whole state. The neighbors wherever we go ask about you." He continued his letter with everyday news: "We are busy husking corn."

Sarah's letter had a rather motherly tone. "Tell me all the news, mind. I hear there has been great excitement about your clocks, and I am very glad you are prospering so well and are so comfortable where you are."[43]

John's oldest sister Maggie, putting his happiness above her own, sounded motherly too. "John, I dreamed you and your mills had come back. But John, I would not be so selfish, I hope, as to wish you back when it would be better for you to be far away."[44]

In asking many questions of his older brother, seventeen-year-old Dan showed a bright, inquisitive mind with an early scientific bent. He showed originality when he headed his letter Hickory Dale instead of Hickory Hill as the others called the farm. The younger girls—the twins, Mary and Annie, and Joanna wrote short little notes.

Soon it was Thanksgiving and the Peltons and their guests celebrated the occasion in the great hall of Mondell House.

John, reacting to the fun in a moralistic way, confided his thoughts to Sarah and David Galloway. In his answer David wrote, "John, you seem to have good times among the belles but I guess you have not yet felt that inexpressible something or you would never call [them] sinners who play at 'blindman's buff' or who have so far cast off all natural coldness and sullenness as to kiss each other promiscuously. I will not at this time censure you for your stiffness for I know you are bashful and I spare you."[45]

Although there was a certain excitement in the new scenes and experiences, John continued to miss his family at Hickory Hill. In December he confided his homesickness to Maggie who hadn't expected him to be so homesick. She felt sad for him and wanted to comfort him.

But Maggie was too happy about her own plans to be in low spirits for long, for she was to be married that month to John Reid, a boy from a neighboring farm. Maggie and John's friendship had flourished since their school days. One winter he had pushed the deep snow away before her with a branch as they made their way over the hill to the schoolhouse. Now, there was excitement in the air and much to be done before that certain day, as she called it. Anne and Daniel Muir had already taken her to Portage where they bought a bureau, a bed, a barrel full of dishes, and a great many other things for the young couple to set up housekeeping.

One day Maggie was at the Galloways' house at Fountain Lake taking care of little Anna and George while their parents attended a religious meeting. Feeling sentimental about family ties she sat down to write a letter to her brother. The family was breaking up. Sarah and David had been married four years; John had been away from home for several months; and she would soon be leaving Hickory Hill for a home of her own.

"John, we would very much like to have you with us," she wrote. "Then we would once more be all together . . . Dear John, perhaps we will never all meet around the same fireside at one time again, but 'tis my greatest wish that we'll meet an unbroken family at God's right hand."[46]

Maggie Muir and John Reid were married December 18, 1860, in the Hickory Hill farmhouse, by Elder Almond S. Round. Many friends and relatives gathered for the ceremony, although Maggie wished John had been able to come.

Giving her absent brother a full account of the day, Sarah related that after the ceremony there was singing, and then about four o'clock in the afternoon a group escorted the couple to their cozy log cabin not far from Hickory Hill for more singing. The festivities ended with a wedding supper prepared by John Reid's mother.

According to Sarah's account, Maggie, seated in the rocking chair, looked happy, and when her new husband came near her she looked up in his face and smiled. He too was happy as could be. Their certain day had been a memorable one.

Soon after the wedding, David Galloway, who understood how it felt to be away from home for the first time, shared some thoughts with his brother-in-law in Prairie du Chien. "I remember well when first I left my father's house and fatherland and how I longed and pined for news from [the] old home. . . .I guess you were as verdant now as I was then—tickled with every new thing and, as you say in your letter, 'Seeming all a dream.'

"You say you guess you are happy. John! hear me! I am happy with my Sarah and Anna and George, and you would say so if you saw me with a little one on each knee cozily toasting by the warm fire while the 'guid wife with her needle and shears gars auld class look amaist as well as new.'"[47]

In that same letter Galloway painted another side to his picture of domestic bliss. He said he was not content to grub with his nose in the dirt from daylight to dark from January to January and not have time for leisure and reflection and social friendly intercourse with kindred spirits. He yearned for something more in life beyond hard work and love for his family.

He wrote, "While cutting stove wood this afternoon and being tired pounding at these old, twisted, gnarled, knotty, thrawsy, crop contendre, ugly sticks, I sat down a few minutes, [and] my eyes instinctively turned toward Prairie du Chien to John and his contrivances. You would be a philanthropist in the highest sense of the word if you could invent some kind of battering ram to split wood. You would indeed bestow a priceless boon on the present after generation, but especially on your humble servant Dave."

David Muir missed his older brother, and began to have thoughts of leaving home too. As he went about the monotonous routine of winter farm chores, he imagined the interesting time John was surely having in Prairie du Chien. "I feel as though I would like to come down and spend the winter with you for I have the prospect of a pretty tough one here," he wrote. "We have got through with our folks work and have commenced chopping. I guess we are going to break another 'dad' [sic] next year."[48]

In Prairie du Chien John wrote Mary that although he was learning something about making machines, he was disappointed in Norman Wiard. He found Wiard was seldom home and that he was not likely to learn much in his small shop.

John stayed in Prairie du Chien only three months and was not present when Wiard finally tested the Lady Franklin on the Mississippi ice. It is known that he was drawn back to Madison by January 1861 since he received a letter there from a Prairie du Chien friend dated January 21 in answer to one he had written earlier from the capital city.

Just about that time Norman Wiard attempted to take the ice boat from its Holton Warehouse berth and put it on the frozen river. The Prairie du Chien *Courier*, January 24, 1861, recounted:

"This greatest invention of the age is fated to meet more obstacles before its practical utility is demonstrated to the world. It was steamed up the other day, removed from its house, and—not tried. One of the shoes or runners came in contact with some resisting force, slightually [sic] broke. Another delay is in the consequence."[49]

Two other newspaper accounts suggest that the ice boat was indeed tried. One reported that the craft made a trial trip upriver with twenty passengers from Prairie du Chien to Lafayette, the round trip of approximately sixty miles being made in four hours and ten minutes. The other commented that it was used a short time in ferry service across the Mississippi River and north to Harpers Ferry.

Prairie du Chien newspapers carried Wiard's last advertisement February 14, 1861, and ran no more stories that winter. The following November 27 the *Dubuque* (Iowa) *Herald* derided the project and indicated that the ice boat was still in Prairie du Chien. Nothing further was heard about the venture. In the end, despite great hopes, the Lady Franklin did not achieve Wiard's dream of revolutionizing winter navigation.

But in Madison, John took a step toward fulfilling his dreams. On February 6, 1861, he enrolled in Wisconsin State University, as the University of Wisconsin was then known, to pursue his quest for learning.

# IV

# WISDOM BINS AND WHEAT BINS

*I thought if I could only join them
it would be the greatest joy in
life. I was desperately hungry and
thirsty for knowledge and willing
to endure anything to get it.*
—John Muir

"No University, it seemed to me, could be more admirably situated," Muir wrote in his autobiography, "and as I sauntered about it, charmed with its fine lawns and trees and beautiful lakes, and saw the students going and coming with their books, and occasionally practicing with a theodolite in measuring distances, I thought that if I could only join them it would be the greatest joy in life. I was desperately hungry and thirsty for knowledge and willing to endure anything to get it."[1]

John yearned to continue filling his wisdom bins and hoped to raise some money to enroll at Wisconsin University. He worked briefly for a Mr. Hasting in his insurance office addressing circulars and stayed with the Hasting family, caring for their horse team and doing errands. He also sold a few bedsteads equipped with his whittled mechanisms that set sleepers on their feet in the morning. He often walked on the nearby campus.

"One day I chanced to meet a student who had noticed my inventions at the Fair and now recognized me. And when I said, 'You are fortunate fellows to be allowed to study in this beautiful place. I wish I could join you.' 'Well, why don't you?' he asked. 'I haven't money enough,' I said. 'Oh as to money,' he reassuringly explained, very little is required. I presume you're able to enter the Freshman class, and you can board yourself as quite a number of us do at a cost of about a dollar a week. The baker and milkman come every day. You can live on bread and milk.' Well, I thought, maybe I have money enough for at least one beginning term. Anyhow I couldn't help trying."

John tried it. He enrolled in the second twenty week term beginning February 6, 1861. John Sterling, professor of mathmatics and natural philosophy, first interviewed him.

"With fear and trembling, overladen with ignorance, I called on Professor Stirling [Sterling], the Dean of the Faculty, who was then Acting President, presented my case, and told him how far I had got on with my studies at home, and that I hadn't been to school since leaving Scotland at the age of eleven years, excepting one short term of a couple of months at a district school, because I could not be spared from the farm work. After hearing my story, the kind professor welcomed me to the glorious University—next, it seemed to me, to the Kingdom of Heaven."

Sterling placed the young Marquette County inventor in the Preparatory Department, and assigned him to North Middle Hall, as North Hall was known at the time. John was now embarked on his educational career.

Muir had been in on a number of historical beginnings since coming to Wisconsin in 1849 just one year after statehood. He was part of the European immigration movement that populated the new state as it emerged from territorial days. When he attended the little log school one winter, the district elementary education system had been in existence only a short time. Wisconsin State University had been established just thirteen years before his enrollment in 1861.

There had been early interest in establishing an institution of higher learning. Even in the days preceding statehood, the idea of a state university to be located near the capitol had been raised in the territorial government. In 1838 the United States Congress granted 46,080 acres of land to support such an institution. The income from the sale of lands was to provide the money to run it. Immediately thereafter, each state house created a Committee of University and University Lands. In June 1848 Governor Nelson Dewey spoke in favor of a public school system in his message to the first state legislature. Wisconsin State University was launched on July 26, 1848, when a bill, passed by both houses, organized a university with four departments. Dewey promptly named a Board of Regents and the work of establishment had begun.

A fifty-acre site was selected—the steep hill on Fourth Lake (now Lake Mendota), called College Hill, looking down toward the capitol a mile away. Committees were named and thrust into the formidable task of raising building and operating funds through land sales. They planned the first buildings, set initial policies and courses of study, and hired professors. In 1849, before there was enough money on hand to erect buildings, the first university classes were held in the Madison Female Academy. By the time John arrived on campus twelve years later, three buildings had been erected on the hill—the North Dormitory in 1851, South Hall in 1855, and University Hall (now Bascom Hall) in 1859. Two additional professorships were established, only now they were called departments.

Muir became well acquainted with early university luminaries. His adviser, John Sterling, became the virtual head of the university when its first chancellor, John H. Lathrop, resigned after serving ten years. Though Henry Barnard was then named chancellor, Sterling, the senior member of the faculty, acted as the administrative officer, performing the functions necessary to keep the institution going. He was not listed officially as Dean of the Faculty until Barnard's departure in January, 1861.

It was the philosophy of the university to provide education for every young man who wanted it. It understood that the district schools did not always prepare students for higher learning and that many youths did not have the prerequisites for the courses of study offered.

Prepared by Sterling, the "Circular of the Wisconsin State University for the Year 1861" stated under the Preparatory Department heading: "Experience in this University . . . has demonstrated the necessity of provision for instruction in branches which are properly preparatory to the different University courses. Young men of mature age often come to the University for instruction in some of its appropriate subjects, who wish also to perfect themselves in more elementary branches. To close the doors of the University upon this class of young men, or not to afford them the facilities of instruction they need, would be greatly to limit the sphere of its usefulness as a State Institution."

Although Muir had done much independent studying, Sterling felt that he required some preliminary work, so he assigned him to the Preparatory Department. Muir didn't stay long in prerequisite work. In a few weeks he entered the freshman class.

"In Latin I found that one of the books in use I had already studied in Scotland," he stated in *The Story of My Boyhood and Youth*. "So, after an interruption of a dozen years, I began my Latin over again where I had left off; and, strange to say, most of it came back to me, especially the grammar which I had committed to memory at the Dunbar Grammar School."[2]

From the time he was fifteen or sixteen and had persuaded his father to buy him a higher arithmetic book, John had done a good job filling in background information he needed to proceed with his education. One summer, in scraps of time during farm chores, he studied arithmetic from the end of the noon meal till the afternoon start of work in the hay fields. That season he studied algebra, geometry, trigonometry, and grammar. Then for the next three or four years he read the classic poets in books he purchased for himself and also read borrowed novels.

In the Wisconsin State University catalogue for the year closing June 26, 1861, John Muir from Midland (the post office serving Hickory Hill) was listed under the heading, "first year undergraduates." The "s" by his name indicated he was taking the scientific course. The student account book credited him with having paid $5.00 in fees.

That same catalogue described the fine new University Hall, just completed at a cost of $50,000. "This building contains commodious public rooms for recitation, lecture, library, cabinets, literary societies &c." Referring to South Hall and the North Dormitory, the catalogue continued: "There are also two large buildings provided with pleasant study and lodging rooms for students, and apartments for boarding clubs, &c. These buildings are warmed, in the winter, by furnaces in the basement . . . rooms are furnished at the expense of the students, who should bring their own bedding, towels, &c. other furniture can be obtained here second-hand or new at moderate prices. . . .Good board in private families can be obtained for from $1.50 to $2.50 per week; in clubs, from $1.00 to $1.50 per week." Tuition for a twenty week term was listed at $6.00, room, $5.00, and fuel, $5.00. "Communications addressed to Prof. J.W. Sterling respecting board, rooms, and other particulars will receive prompt attention."

Of special interest to Muir was the catalogue listing for science showing Dr. Ezra S. Carr, A.M., M.D., to be the professor of science. Carr had presented his own geological specimens to add to the university's scientific collections. The catalogue stated: "In the cabinet of minerals, there are over four thousand specimens, and the whole is of great scientific value. Full suits of specimens, collected in the geological survey of the State, are directed by law to be deposited in the University. The Farwell collection of specimens in natural history, recently donated to the University, is in excellent condition, and is of high scientific and instructional value."

After Muir settled into this northeast corner room on the first floor of the North Dormitory, he was ready to begin his studies in earnest. He wrote home about his struggle to earn his way through the university.

"A body has an extraord.[inary] amount of long faced sober scheming to get butter and bread for their bodies . . . since I began this bachel[or] affair I don't feel so well, but I think if other things run smoothly I would do fine."[3] Despite the difficulties in his scramble to set up housekeeping in the dormitory, take care of his meals, and keep himself going, he still called it an exciting life game. One way Muir added to his diet was buying a barrel of crackers with fellow student Will Fuller.

As John threw himself into university studies and activities, life continued in a normal pattern for the family at Hickory Hill. At the end of March Daniel and the boys, Dan and David, went to Portage for seed wheat and Anne Muir sat down to write her oldest son in time to send the letter along with them to be mailed.

"We received your letter today dated the 20th and were surprised to know you were batchin' at the University," she wrote. She hoped John's health wouldn't suffer because of his "new mode of living" as compared to boarding with a family. She said she expected his father to assist him some financially but didn't know when he could send anything. She wished for a visit from him and wanted him to bring his clothes home so she could mend them. She advised John not to be discouraged, and offered him a bit of the philosophy that she herself lived by:

"If things don't turn out just as you expect, try to make the best of them," she advised. "I hope you will not feel too deeply when you meet with disappointment from the world. You know that prosperity is not always best for us. You know that we are assured that all things will work together for good to those that love and fear God. . . .I hope you will learn what you want to." Anne ended her letter with a note of concern: "You know I am anxious. If you are in any difficulty let us know it. I shall do what I can for you."[4]

The splendid setting of the university on the hill above Fourth Lake was an inspiration for learning. Here, the landscape was more dramatic than that of Fountain Lake and Hickory Hill where the Wisconsin lobe of the continental glacier sculptured the farmland region into rolling hills, lakes, and marshes as it had done over three-quarters of the state. In the Madison area the bulldozing action by the slow-moving ice sheet widened and deepened the Yahara River valley and scooped out the boat-shaped depressions containing the four lake basins. The ice eroded the limestone and sandstone bedrock to form the basin of Fourth Lake. The ice mass stopped just a few miles south of the site of Madison where it melted back, leaving its terminal moraine as it retreated.

The university buildings were located near the top of College Hill. North Dormitory sat close to the bank that descended sharply to the lakeshore below and from his room John could see across the wide expanse of beautiful Fourth Lake. In the wintertime, after the trees had dropped their leaves, there was an especially clear view. When he made his way between buildings, it seemed to him that the snow-covered slopes were Madison's icy mountains.

As the term progressed and became increasingly hard for John to make ends meet, he asked his father for help. Daniel responded that his son should not be going to the university or inventing things, but should do all for the glory of God instead. However, he did send John money from time to time. Soon after the term started he sent $50. He planned to drive to Madison with the money but because the roads were so bad he turned back at Portage. He mailed the money from the local post office instead of visiting his son at the university.

Once Daniel replied to John's request for aid by telling him he was not in a position to help much, that it was getting on toward the spring of the year when times were leanest. "I was startled when I learned you wanted money," he wrote, "as I've got so little of it at present. You got all I had in the bank last time you got some excepting $10. Besides, I have got all in that anybody owes me, and all I have is spent but about $18.00, and I do not want to sell any of my wheat yet. But I have inclosed $10.00 hoping it will serve you till I get something more. Let me know when you are in great distress and I will try what I can do."

He then proceeded to give his son a financial lecture:

"Make all the money you can and save all you can, give away all you can and borrow as little as you can. You will find that it is easier spending money than making it.

"I should like you to be temperate, but would not like you to starve yourself. That is, I should like you to have the real necessaries of life, and if you should want the necessaries of life, I should not feel vexed about it."

Once again Daniel expressed disapproval of his son's avid interest in creating inventions.

"I wish you may be loving your God much more than inventing machines."

Despite this sentiment, Daniel did not hesitate to capitalize on labor saving devices. The next paragraph in the letter described such an implement.

"I have bought a machine for sowing wheat, oats, and all kinds of grass seeds. It is a great help to us. We can now sow 8 or 9 acres per day with it amongst the stumps. The price of it is $85 but there is $65 to pay on it.

Your mother and all the rest of us are well. Thank God for it. Yours affectionately, Dan'l Muir."[5]

Always highly motivated, John was dedicated to getting a university education, although he didn't yet know what he wanted to do with his life. A year or so later he discussed his goals with his old friend and Fountain Lake neighbor, James Whitehead. The friendship of the two men would span over fifty years.

John had been home one winter for the Christmas holidays and was walking back to Madison when Whitehead joined him and walked with him as far as Portage. After Muir's death in December, 1914, Whitehead reminisced in a newspaper article about their foot journey that January 1.

The day was "remembered as the coldest and most disagreeable day in Wisconsin history by the oldest inhabitant. It was distinct from all others in its intensity.

"One bright cold morning I started back to my work," Whitehead continued. "The snow was deep, but the road was well beaten. I had not gone far when I was joined by John who was returning to the university. We met where the road to [his] father's place intersected with . . . the River Road.

"During the twelve mile walk to Portage he told me of his life at the university and what it meant to him as a means of equipment and preparation for his life work, and while he did not seem to have any definite plans for the future, and did not mention anything along the lines in which he has since become famous, he expressed a determination to profit as best he could by the opportunities he then enjoyed. He spoke of the work and labor entailed and emphasized the fact that by persistent, persevering application alone could he hope to win success. He spoke in glowing terms of the university which, at that early date, would, he thought, compare most favorably with older institutions of learning."

Whitehead recalled that Muir felt badly about the students who didn't take advantage of their opportunity. Failing to realize the value and importance of time, they dissipated precious moments. Muir didn't understand how these students could fail to acquire the knowledge and information upon which their future depended. Whitehead added that to do the things he wanted to, Muir always used every minute he could find.

"During twenty years or more of public life, I do not recall a single person that would compare with John as a conversationalist. Easy, fluent and free from all display of superior knowledge, he told what he had in mind in simple, pure Anglo Saxon. He possessed a poet's fervid fancy, and without intent or seeming knowledge his language was richly embellished." Whitehead described John as "a cheerful, optimistic, splendid man, six feet in height, straight as an arrow, with light hair, full beard, clear blue eyes and a skin so smooth and transparent it would satisfy a maiden's dream of attainment."[6]

As the weather mellowed into spring that first year, the campus took on a different aspect. The slopes didn't seem quite so much like icy mountains, and College Hill became green as the weather warmed.

Muir described the scene to Sarah and David Galloway. "The three university buildings are in the middle of a beautiful park of maybe a hundred acres. The trees are close and beautiful in some places, at others [it is] smooth and velvety. Ask David Muir when you see him if he don't think it a fine place for breaking steers. The lake, too, would be so fine for steers."[7]

The young student wrote often to his parents, and his older sisters and brothers, but he never forgot the "little people" as Mary once called the three younger girls—herself, her twin Mary, and Joanna, the youngest in the family. In a letter to the little girls he further described the place where he lived.

"I guess that you would like to go along the lakeshore to gather shells and pebbles. You would have to take care not to fall over the banks for they are so steep every place near our house that you could not go down, or rather if you got started you could do nothing else but go down. There is an old basswood tree hangs way out over the bank. It is a fine shape to sit or lie on. You see the lake far below. It seems as though you would fall right into it if you should roll off. I often go there with a book." He went on to describe the visit of a dazzling little hummingbird among the berry bushes and raspberries.

John was not certain his little sisters would like city living.

"In the morning when you awake instead of hearing two or three roosters crowing, you would hear about a hundred all at once. And then the locomotives whistle so loud you would almost think the end of the whistles were in your ears. And so many [people] are running and walking up and down the lots o' long stairs and hundreds of common and uncommon sounds make city sounds very funny, but the thrushes in that fine grove don't seem to care. They whistle just as they do on the black or bur oaks at Hickory. I always keep my window open so I can hear them fine.

"I guess you would like to go to the top of University Hall but you would be thinking the stairs have no end. You could see the city and far out all around. When it's clear you can see two windmills, great big ones, working. We measured how far it was to one of them a few days ago without going to it. . . . It was just a little less than seven miles."

John's early love of flowers continued during his sojourn at the university and he was able to collect specimens in a variety of plant habitats—on the hill, on the bank, and on the lakeshore. He described his room to his younger sisters:

"I like pretty flowers, but I haven't got the time to study much about them. I've got a fine posy at my nose here in an old ink bottle. And I've got a peppermint plant and a young bramble in an old glass bottle and on the shelf (the topmost one) stands my stew pan full of brambles 2 or 3 feet long and slips of gooseberry bushes and wild plums and I don't know all what, and further along you may see my tin cup in the same business. They keep a long time in water. I had a long yellow willow in my basin awhile but it died. I had always to take it out when I washed."[8]

That first spring Dan sent John a hook and eye box full of moss from home, the beginning of the family practice of enclosing flowers and bits of greenery in their letters. Wherever John's wanderlust would take him, he would tuck plant specimens into the envelope—a pressed flower from the shores of Fourth Lake or a tiny fern from a rock crevice atop the highest mountain of the Sierra Nevada. He shared the heart of his world with his family and they shared their world with him.

As the university year came to a close and John finished his studies, he became excited about going back to Hickory Hill. In all the months away he had sorely missed his home and family despite the negative aspects there.

"I already feel the thrill of true shakes and deep seeking looks," he wrote ecstatically, "and Hickory Hill breezes fan my face. I can see the dignified wave of those well known oaks. [During] these nine weeks vacation I shall not be in a hold-yarn mood . . . I am going home!"[9]

# V

# THE CORNERSTONE

*My eyes never closed on the*
*plant glory I had seen.*
*—John Muir*

John was ecstatic to be back at Hickory Hill after the long months away. Everyone in the family was happy to have him home if only for a few weeks. Anne Muir was especially so, for once again she could look after her eldest son, overhauling his clothes and taking pleasure in cooking meals for him. She baked the currant scones she so often mentioned in her letters over the years.

That summer of 1861 John worked with his brothers on the farm as he had always done, only this time he arranged with his father to be paid for his field work to help with expenses for the fall term. In one farm job, he and his brother David grubbed tree roots from the fields. While they labored together, David heard more about John's experiences and determined to go with him to Madison in August. He too worked for his father to earn money to attend the university. Daniel kept careful accounts of the boys' labors, figuring their accounts to the half cent.

The fall term started August 28, so in late August the two brothers said goodbye to the family and struck out on foot for Madison, sixty miles away. The first day they walked as far as Poynette where they stayed with their friends, the Watsons, completing the rest of the hike the next day.

"O how pleasantly and *contentedly* our feet lay on the prairie when they got the chance," John related to Sarah and David Galloway. "There was no more uneasy nervousness in them than in a fence post. I need not tell you how happy I was to see our lake and school for I was thoroughly rested in the harvest field. We could see the university and fourth lake quite distinctly when we were only half way to it."[1]

John and David viewed the buildings on College Hill from across the lake. When they finally arrived on campus, John was so happy to get back that he took the stairs of one building two at a time. After he showed David around his beloved campus, the two brothers settled into their room in the North Dormitory. Their living arrangements were better than John's the year before.

"We have been very busy for awhile getting our things put right and in running order," he told the Galloways. "We have got a nice alcohol cooking apparatus and a plate and a jug." He said that if David Galloway would pay another visit "we shall endeavor to entertain him in a manner more civilized and becoming than I did before."[2]

The family was pleased that the two boys were together. Joanna supposed that John wouldn't be so lonesome now that he had their brother David with him.

The previous university year had been divided into two terms totaling thirty-eight weeks. Nine students graduated. This year there were three terms of thirteen weeks each, the first from August 28 to November 27. In the catalogue under the heading "undergraduates," John Muir from Midland was listed with the thirty-seven first year students. In this catalogue there was no "s" designation by his name, but in the Student Account book he was listed as a freshman in the scientific course and was shown to have paid $10.50.

David Muir was listed with a group of sixty-one students in this same 1861-1862 catalogue under the heading of Preparatory Students. The "c" by his name indicated that he signed up for the classical course. He had a harder time with his studies than John had the year before. He did not have his older brother's study experience or all-consuming interest in learning. He had two years less schooling in Dunbar and during the early days on the farm he had not used scraps of time for reading as his brother had done. However, he did have the advantage of longer attendance at the district school. James Whitehead remembered going to the district school with the younger Muir children.

John reported to the Galloways that David was perplexed about his books, that he became tired and complained of having no leisure and ease. However, he said they were both well and happy.

A little later in the year, John wrote to Mrs. Pelton that "my brother never was accustomed to study and confinement so that though he promised himself much useful happy ease when he for the time being bade farm blessings goodbye, he found University toils far more severe than farm ones, his health suffered a little, so after a few complaints he suddenly threw his books aside and set out the other morning for the healing pill of a weeks ploughing on the prairie. He is going to teach a district school this winter and so am I."[3]

On October 5 Maggie wrote to her brothers in the North Dormitory about a troubling health problem. She said she wasn't well and had spent a week with Sarah at Fountain Lake and another week with the family at Hickory Hill, leaving her husband to boil his own potatoes and fry his own pork. She explained about her poor health:

"My nerves are miserable and I have had such hard nights I am good for nothing daytimes. You tell me the clouds will pass away sometime although 'tis long. I will live in hope and if [they do] not I hope I may have supporting grace while here and be fitted to meet you in that blessed home where sickness never enters. Boys pray for me. I think I have said too much about my troubles, but boys you know my failings."

Part of the basis for Maggie's nervousness and ill health was due to her reactions to her father. Recently Daniel Muir had talked with the Reids about getting help on the farm. "Now Pa talks of letting out his farm on shares," Maggie explained to her brothers, "and asked John if he would take a piece. Perhaps it would be as good a thing as we could do, but I'm afraid that would be getting too close [to Father]. I'm afraid my nerves wouldn't be the better for it."[4]

The following month she informed her brothers she had been feeling a little better the past few days. That was Maggie's health pattern—to sometimes be fairly well and then change for the worse. Maggie was destined to be a semi-invalid for most of her life. Over the years there were many references in the family correspondence to the poor state of her health and nervous state. Even now, at the age of twenty-seven, less than a year after her marriage, she was unable to handle her daily work for weeks at a time and needed a hired girl to help her.

As John and David went about their classes that fall, John was aware of the drastic change in Madison's atmosphere from the year before during the gala days of the 1860 State Agricultural Fair. When Fort Sumter was fired upon April 12, 1861, at the beginning of the Civil War, Wisconsin immediately switched to a war footing and Governor Alexander W. Randall took on the challenge of calling up the militia.

". . . the governor had little with which to work as he set out to mobilize troops. Although the entire male population of the state was considered part of the militia, there were only 2,000 men serving in a score of independent companies. Their arms consisted of a few rusty guns and some outmoded equipment, and their training was only in parade-ground rudiments."[5]

Governor Randall addressed the legislature:

"This legislature must determine for Wisconsin . . . the way of arming, equipping and uniforming its own citizens for military purposes,..by putting them in the shape of regiments, into camps to be drilled, inured to the hardships of soldier life and made skillful in the use of arms before being called upon to face experienced armies in battle. . . .The men sent to war should be *soldiers when they go*, or there will be few of them living soldiers when it is time for them to return."[6]

The State Agricultural Society offered the use of their fair grounds below College Hill—ten acres of gently sloping land—to the 2nd Regiment for drill practice. "A small army of carpenters removed the fences around the rings, and the animal sheds along the southern and eastern walls of the enclosure were cleaned, floors laid, and windows and bunk beds installed . . . 'the Temple of Art' was refitted for use as an indoor drill room, and a large shed was extended twenty feet on either side and equipped with long tables to serve as the mess hall."[7]

Thus, Camp Randall came into being on the grounds of the festive Tenth Annual State Agricultural Fair where the year before John had been tossed about by new everythings everywhere. The Temple of Art where he had so successfully displayed his whittled inventions was put to a far different use. The camp was the major training ground for most of Wisconsin's over 70,000 Civil War soldiers.

"These are stirring times in Madison,"[8] Anne Muir commented.

In the fall of 1861 John attended classes on College Hill while military companies drilled in the Temple of Art. He wrote home about the Seventh Regiment leaving Madison and he noted that the showy coverings of war hide its real hideousness.

John often walked down College Hill to Camp Randall to visit his friends there, and, following in his father's footsteps, he would minister to them as well. The differences between John and his father were profound, but during this period John was remarkably like Daniel Muir in the obligation he felt to provide moral guidance to the men in the regiments.

Two friends who marched at Camp Randall were Emily Pelton's cousins, Byron and Edward Dwight, from Prairie du Chien days. In a long letter to Emily, John told of his surprise at finding them at the camp.

"They appeared healthy and pleased with their exercises. Edward Dwight seemed to blow his pipe with great glee in the midst of the tireless army of chattering drums. Byron visited us in our room and went up town to church with us on Sunday. You would hardly know him in his great blue coat. I went down to the camp and spent an hour or two in their tent the night before they left for Missouri, and Oh dear such conversation. You have no idea how abominable it was. And yet when I expressed my abhorrence of such language Byron laughingly said, 'Why John this is not a beginning to what you would hear in other tents. This is one of the best in the regiment!' After lecturing them a few minutes upon the necessity of having the character formed and being possessed of tightly clenched principles before being put to such a trial as a three years soaking in so horrible a mixture, Byron growing grave dropped his *camp language* and declared with some emphasis that there was no danger of him. That his principles were 'firm as adamantine hills.'"

John went on to say, "... O it is so good [for them] to get letters from home and then to think that [there is]scarce one good influence reaches the poor boys, how much they need the holy influence of home. As they unfold the pages folded by a mother's or sister's hand they will forget where they are and as they anxiously read the pure thoughts and advices in the tent corner and those not half expressed sympathies which sisters and mothers only have, tears will fall and when he next joins his companions vice will not seem as before.

"I heard they had already seen the enemy," he continued. "The whole seemed anxious for fight. I was down the morning they left Madison and helped Byron to buckle on his knapsack. Dwight with his fife seemed uncommonly happy but O how terrible a work is assigned them. . . . how strange that such [men] can so completely compose themselves for such work and even march to the bloody fray in a half dance with a smile on their faces and perhaps a loud laugh."

Muir finished his letter to Emily with his own benediction: "May peace's blessings soon be ours again. May the time be near when the spirit of the Prince of Peace shall be in all hearts."[9]

The first term ended November 27, and neither John nor David Muir was listed in the Student Account Book as paying for the next term, December 11, 1861, to March 12, 1862. On November 27, Daniel Muir sent his sons $12, but needing more expense money, they signed up to teach at district schools in Dane County. John's school was located in McKeeley's District, a little log school on Lake Harriet, more than ten miles south of Madison. According to Charles E. Vroman, a later roommate, John kept up with his university studies at night.

Once again his mother was concerned about his comfort and hoped he would get a comfortable boarding place. John stayed at homes around the district, moving every five or six days.

His young sister Mary gave him some advice before he ever taught his first lesson. She urged him not be too hard on small scholars for she hated to see them abused. She had pitied them in her school the previous winter.

John, of course, felt the same way. He gave an account of his first day of teaching to Sarah and David:

"The usual blessings attending district school teaching do not seem to yield the injurious consequences which I had anticipated. The Monday morning that I commenced I did not know where to look or what to say or do, and I'm sure looked bashful as any maid. A mud turtle upside down on a velvet sofa was as much at home. I heard a scholar declare that the teacher didn't seem to know bran but all moves with regularity and ease now.

"I couldn't get my clocks with me at first and as I had not a watch I set to work and made a clock to keep time until I had opportunity of getting my other one from Madison. It cost about two hours' work and kept time by water passing in a fine jet through a three cent piece. I have a big wheel set on the wall which tells different classes when and how long to recite and a machine too for making me a fire in the morning at any hour I please so that when I go to the old log schoolhouse these cold biting mornings I find everything warmed and a good fire.

"I sometimes think of fixin' to box the boys' ears for at first the cry of 'He don't half whip' came loud and angrily from all parts of my parish, and indeed, I did think it awful then to skelp the little chaps even though so many did give proofs in rich abundance at times of mischief to the end of the toes. My voice would shake for hours after each hazel application. But now they cause precious little agitation or compunction of soul. My scholars, however, nearly all mean to behave themselves. They are neither good nor bad. Certainly not such children as Pollock speaks of so good and guileless as to seem as 'made entire of beams of angels eyes.'"

Not satisfied to teach only young people, Muir worked with adults as well. "I lecture every Saturday evening on chemistry or natural philosophy, sometimes to sixty or seventy," he continued, "You know it doesn't require much sapience to be a district school philosopher."

He then gave news about David. "Dave hasn't visited my school nor I his. But I saw him once and he said he was infinitely happy among his generous Dutch. He has singing schools and sabbath schools and writing schools."[10]

"You say you are still more thirsty for knowledge," Anne Muir noted in her December 1st letter to John. "I hope you will have opportunities for study until you are somewhat satisified."[11]

She had the same concerns for David leaving home the first time as she had for John the year before and felt anxious when she heard about the plan for both her boys to teach school. She didn't think David would like to board around in various district homes. Also, she was unhappy that she had received no word from him since he left.

"For all the time you have been from home you have never wrote one word to me," she scolded in a letter to David. "It seems strange. I want to know if you are well and I want to know if you like teaching. I hope you do. I hope you have made the best of your time at the university. I understand you are coming home after your school closes."[12]

That winter, as both John and David were having many new experiences, so too, were the rest of the family. Anne wrote to John about it from Hickory Hill:

"Affairs around here seem to have changed as much as the face of nature since you left home.

"About five weeks ago Daniel told his father that he had made up his mind not to be a farmer and he wished to go to Madison to study this winter. After his father had thought about it he decided to go to Madison and find a house suitable for us all to spend the winter in if he could get someone to take care of the farm.

"However, he afterwards thought Madison too far from the farm, so he went to Portage last week and hired a house there, so Daniel and the girls will attend school in Portage City this winter. I never thought I would like to live in Portage, but I hope I will."

She continued: "Mr. Everest has been here and has got John's farm back. John [Reid] never told Margaret anything about his affairs but Mr. Everest told her all about them. He told her John had paid very little more than the interest on the money. So he got the farm back and John has hauled off a good deal of wheat at low prices to give the money to Everest, and George claimed one horse, so John had little left. But Margaret said if she was poor she was out of debt and felt satisfied. So

John and Margaret are coming here to live as soon as she is able to ride this length."[13] Maggie had recently given birth to a baby boy, and was still weak.

When Daniel "hired a house" in Portage and brought Maggie and John Reid to the Hickory Hill farm, he found a solution to the family problems at hand. The Reids' financial plight was eased; John had work to do and his family had a place to live; young Dan Muir could go to high school in Portage; and the three younger girls could attend school there too. They would also have the excitement of living in town.

Anne Muir, however, was exceedingly unhappy with the change. She prayed to be shown her path of duty and given the strength to follow it. She told David that none of the family liked the idea of living in Portage City but expected to move there in a week.

This was only the first of many moves the Muirs would make around Portage and the area. With Daniel's restless nature, he was never satisfied to stay in one place for any length of time. He was always ready to move on.

The younger children eagerly described living in Portage to John and David. Dan told about the high school he and Mary and Annie attended. Like John, he was interested in science and had the same thirst for knowledge. Joanna went to intermediate school.

Mary told her brothers about their schools, the several churches, and the new people they met. She said she liked pretty well to live in the city and described the walk she and Annie took to the railway station to see the engines and trains.

Anne Muir missed her beloved Hickory Hill. "I cannot say I like to live in Portage," she said. "Your father doesn't like to live here either so he often goes away somewhere else. It is nearly a week since he was here."[14] Anne found the house they lived in a very cold one—a mere shell, and she found the neighborhood cold as well. No neighbor had yet called on them—only the nearest one sent her son to borrow.

After Daniel Muir settled his family in the Portage home, and bought them a needed cow, he turned his attention to other pursuits. Although he still spent a great deal of time at Hickory Hill, he had divested himself of the day-to-day farm responsibilities. He was now completely free to devote himself to fulfilling his burning religious needs.

He had long been engaged in religious activities. While the family still lived at Hickory Hill, Daniel Muir had turned more and more from farm work to evangelistic matters. As his children worked in the fields, he sat for hours in his bedroom study, translating his Bible and preparing for religious meetings.

When John first went to the university, letters from home were filled with references to the meetings his father attended and his preaching around the neighborhood. In the family letter from Hickory Hill, October 14, 1860, David noted that prayer meetings had commenced here again and that the first meeting was held the previous Sunday over at Midland [School]. Joanna wrote that her father attended a meeting on Thanksgiving Day, while Anne Muir explained that Daniel went to four prayer meetings a week.

In her February 19, 1861, letter to John, Mary said that "Father [is] going to a meeting at Mr. Arnot's house. Father goes to a meeting every other Sunday night at a school house beyond Belfountain. He goes through the week sometimes to a prayer meeting there too, and there is a prayer meeting every Sunday night at Gray's school house."[15]

When Daniel Muir died in October, 1885, John wrote of his father's evangelism in the obituary: "As an evangelist he went from place to place ... distributing books and tracts at his own cost, and preaching the gospel in season and out of season with a firm sustained zeal."[16]

The move to Portage was a major turning point for Daniel for it was the opening wedge in his expanding ministry and eventually led to his leaving home and Wisconsin without a qualm.

While Daniel Muir was roaming the countryside in his horse and buggy, John's district school came to a close. He went back to the university for the last thirteen week term of the year—from March 26, to June 25, 1862. He was listed in the Student Account Book as having paid $10.50 for the period. David did not return to the university with him. He was more interested in teaching school among his generous Dutch than pursuing a higher education.

Consequently, John was without a roommate. He was busily sawing boards in his North Dormitory room one day when the Preparatory Department tutor, John D. Parkinson, entered with fourteen-year-old Charles Vroman in tow. According to Vroman's later account of that first meeting: "We entered the northeast corner room on the first floor without rap or signal . . . After looking around awhile, Parkinson said, 'This is your room and there is your roommate.' Thus began my acquaintance with Mr. Muir, which quickly ripened into a close and delightful college companionship."[17]

Vroman said his first impression was that his tutor was showing him a branch of the college museum. "The room was a strange looking place for the room of a college student. The room was lined with shelves, one above the other, higher than a man could reach. These shelves were filled with retorts, glass tubes, glass jars, botanical and geological specimens and small mechanical contrivances. On the floor, around the sides of the room, were a number of machines of larger size, whose purposes were not apparent at a glance. . . . The floor was covered with boards, sawdust and shavings."

Vroman told of his campus life with John Muir:

"I never saw him read anything but his Bible, Burns, and his school books. . . . the study table was a . . . curious and amusing device which Muir made for his own use. It had little resemblance to a table; the legs were wooden compasses and imitation wooden books. The top was slanting and made of a series of cog wheels, the center wheel being solid and about fourteen inches in diameter. This wheel was cut through the middle into two equal halves and the parts so hung on pivot pegs that the two halves would flop up leaving an open space between them of about two inches. Underneath this wheel and on tracks was a car fitted with stalls. Muir would place his school books in the stalls in the order in which he wished to study them, lock the car and put the key where it was difficult to get, attach the clock to the machinery of the desk, climb on a high stool and await results. The clock would move the car to place and by a knocker arrangement underneath push a book up through the open space between the halves of the solid cog wheel, close down the halves and open out the book.

"Muir would study that book until time was up, when the halves of the wheel would flop up and drop the book in its stall. The car would then move to the next stall and repeat to the end of the list of books. Muir prearranged with the clock as to the time he should have to study each book, which arrangement was carried out to the letter. It was amusing to watch John sitting at that desk as if chained, working like a beaver against the clock and desk. The desk was built, he said, to make him more orderly and regular in his studies.[18]

"He had a thermometer made of parts of an old, broken washboard, which was so sensitive, that if one stood near it the index hand would quiver and move on the dial; also a miniature saw mill with a self-setting log carriage—ingenious but not practical; also a little device for measuring the growth of plants so delicate that when attached to a plant, one could see the hand move across the dial, measuring the growth from hour to hour; also other devices as ingenious and curious in construction and purpose as the ones described.

"Muir's manner of life at the University was very simple. He boarded himself, as many of the students did in those days. His diet consisted chiefly of bread and molasses, graham mush and a baked potato now and then. Being in the good graces of Pat [the janitor], he obtained a key to the basement where the old fashioned wood furnaces were. Here he baked his potatoes in the hot ashes and boiled his mush on the hot coals. . . .

"Muir's course of study, while irregular, corresponded closely to the then modern classical. He was a hard working student and very apt, and absorbed knowledge rapidly and accurately. The last two years of his course were devoted largely to chemistry and geology. He was acknowledged by common consent to be the most proficient chemical student in college. There were no laboratory facilities in the University at that time so Muir built a chemical laboratory in the room. With the multitude of things already there, the chemical laboratory capped the climax. It would require a vivid imagination to picture conditions in that room after the laboratory was constructed and in full operation.

"He was of a most gentle and loving disposition, a high-minded Christian gentleman, clean in thought and action. While he was not a very regular attendant at church, he read his Bible and said his prayers morning and evening of every day and he led the kind of life that all this imports. It must not be inferred, however, that he was austere and without any sense of humor, fun or frolic; far from it; he was as keen to a college prank as any of us, and always ready to 'put one over' on Pat, the janitor, who came to the University about that time with an exalted opinion of himself and his position."

After the snowy winter, spring came to Wisconsin and College Hill became green again. At Fountain Lake, David Galloway plowed his fields, planted crops, and planned ahead for harvest time. He pressed his brother-in-law about his summer vacation plans and wanted to know if John would be returning to Fountain Lake farm to help him with the harvest.

Sarah wrote from her own beautiful lake: "How beautiful it will look around your fine lake now with all the grasses and trees and flowers budding out so fresh and green. The closer you examine them the more perfect they seem . . ."[19]

Muir did not have far to look from North Dormitory for flowers and other plants. Just outside his window, tiny pink leaves appeared on the branches of the oaks on the wooded knoll, while flowers on the woodland floor and those down the bank and on the lakeshore bloomed again one by one.

Muir had an early love of plants. In The Story of My Boyhood and Youth he told the classic story of his first botany lesson from a fellow student, Milton Griswold.

"One memorable day in June, when I was standing on the steps of the north dormitory, Mr. Griswold joined me and at once began to teach. He reached up, plucked a flower from an overspreading branch of a locust tree, and, handing it to me, said, 'Mr. Muir, do you know what family this tree belongs to?'

"'No,' I said, 'I don't know anything about botany.'"

Thereupon, Milton Griswold, who liked to instruct others, launched into a textbook discussion of the makeup of the pea flower to which family the locust tree belonged.

"This fine lesson charmed me," Muir's story continued, "and sent me flying to the woods and meadows in wild enthusiasm. Now my eyes were opened to their inner beauty, all alike revealing glorious traces of the thoughts of God, and leading on and on into the infinite cosmos. I wandered away at every opportunity, making long excursions around the lakes, gathering specimens and keeping them fresh in a bucket in my room to study at night after my regular class tasks were learned; for my eyes never closed on the plant glory I had seen."[20]

Griswold later became Waukesha County (Wisconsin) Judge, a position he held for more than twenty years. He never forgot his classmate and kept up with John's career with great interest.

"I have often been prompted to write to you, and especially after reading some of your graphic descriptions of nature scenery as found in various articles which have come to my notice. I have always read such with pleasure, and when reading them there always comes up before me the vision our younger days, when we took our botanical trips around the lakes and woods of Dane County. What delight we used to experience in the haunts of the forests when we would meet with a new flower or some fossil among the rocks. I have yet the botanical specimens I there gathered, but the busy days of years past have prevented me from increasing them."[21]

Muir kept up his study of plants during the summers while he worked in the fields. "At the noon hour I collected a large handful, put them in water to keep them fresh, and after supper got to work on them and sat up till after midnight, analyzing and classifying, thus leaving only four hours for sleep; and by the end of the first year, after taking up botany, I knew the principal flowering plants of the region."[22]

John Muir continued his search for plants throughout his university days. Indeed, he studied and loved plants over his entire lifetime. He had such an affection for flowers he called them "flower people."

In years to come his nature studies took him into several scientific pathways, but botany was an enduring interest throughout his endeavors. It was the cornerstone.

# VI

# NATURE'S BASEMENT ROOMS

*. . . I walk with students in green fields and
forests, and show them in nature's basement rooms
how the foundations of the earth were laid . . .*
— *Professor Ezra Slocum Carr*

After David Muir's district school closed in the spring of 1862, he went home to Marquette County and began farming activities. He undoubtedly stayed with Maggie and John Reid at Hickory Hill where he worked for his father on shares. Although Daniel lived in Portage, he still kept an active hand in the farm operation.

David was now a property owner. His mother and father had recently given him eighty acres of the Fountain Lake land the Muirs acquired in 1850. This parcel adjoined the northerly eighty acres of the original farmstead and was adjacent to Davie Taylor's farm lying to the east. He acquired the land sometime before December 1, 1861.

On December 1, Anne Muir wrote to him about his farmland. She said that Davie Taylor had stopped in at Hickory Hill "inquiring if your father would join fences with him. Your father told him that land was yours so you will likely get help with your fencing when you come."[1]

As in previous Muir property transactions, the paperwork and recording of deeds was done some months after the fact. The deed to David was dated September 30, 1862. For the "amount paid," it read: ". . . in consideration of love and good will to them [Daniel and Anne] . . . paid by [David] the receipt whereof is hereby confessed and acknowledged."

At the same time David deeded this property to Charles Smith and his wife Delight for $400. Both deeds were registered at the Marquette

County courthouse November 5, 1862. At one time Charles Smith had done some work for Daniel Muir.

During the time David owned the Fountain Lake parcel he also acquired other land. In May of 1862 he dickered for the Everest property that John and Maggie had lost to debt early in their marriage.

Anne was aghast at the idea. "Perhaps you know," she informed John, who was attending spring classes at the university, "David is trying to buy [the] Everest farm that John Reid had. Would you believe he would be so very foolish as get into debt for such a place? John Reid says he has done all he could to prevent him from doing such a foolish thing but he seems determined to persevere in his own way. If he gets it he will be the first to repent of such a transaction when it is too late."[2] However, David eventually did secure the farm.

When his spring term was over, and John came home in June, he stayed with the Galloways at Fountain Lake, and, as usual, helped his brother-in-law with the farm work. All that summer both John and David Muir toiled and harvested on various family farms.

As the harvest season was winding down, John, still not drafted into the northern forces, returned to Madison for the fall term beginning August 27, 1862. This time David did not go with him.

Still interested in teaching, David decided to take a teacher's examination at Portage for a district school certificate. While he was in Portage an unexpected opportunity came his way.

"He was down at Portage at the examination," Maggie Reid related. "While there he got an offer from Forbes to be clerk. He thought he could do nothing else for awhile and so started down there yesterday. He got a nice certificate to teach but he didn't use it.

"Dave bought a yoke of cattle and plowed several acres up the hill [at Hickory Hill], but he willingly gave up the land and father paid him for what he had done. He has now let his [Everest] farm, part to Chauncy Hall and part to the boys."[3]

In a jovial mood, David also wrote to John.

"Johanes mine Brouder

"I have engaged in the haberdashery business till next July, making 9 months in all. I got a tip top 2d grade certificate, but I am not going to need it. I get $15 for the first month. I get $18 for the next 5 months and $20 for the last 3, making $150 for the last 8 months with board and washing, the former of which is tip top. You know I sold my oxen and am quite free again."[4]

David had joined a prestigious firm. *The History of Columbia County, 1880* carried a glowing paragraph about Forbes:

"'I noticed,' says a writer in 1860, 'some very extensive stores in which the quality of goods and amount of display were not a whit behind Milwaukee. In W. W. Forbes' magnificent establishment in Pettibone's Block, there are no less than a dozen clerks busily engaged in their various departments.'"[5]

On October 7, when David enthusiastically started his clerking job at Forbes, he launched a thirty-year haberdashery career on Cook St. in Portage. By making independent living arrangements, even though his parents lived nearby, he had truly set out on his own.

At Hickory Hill the Reids planted sixty acres of winter wheat and commenced fall plowing. John and Maggie were glad to get all their potatoes in the cellar, for it had been a rainy fall.

A few weeks later John Reid wrote his brother-in-law, "We had that droll chap David our clerk up here last Monday. He looks fine, quite smart." Reid said that David had seen Katie Cairns the night before and ended his letter with a hint: "So you see John, sparking must come in course."[6]

As the weeks passed David liked his Forbes job more and more.

"I am still trotting around the counter tearing rags etc. etc.," he explained to his brother John December 31, 1862. "[It is] a fine business for winter. It will do a fellow more good in the way of sharpening and trading than teaching. You should come if it were nothing else but to get your clothes here where they are cheap. . . .

"I had a most glorious visit last Saturday. Perhaps you don't know that C[atherine] C[airns] is teaching in the Town of Caledonia this winter about ten miles from here.

". . . I started on Saturday afternoon and got there early in the evening and staid [sic] all night . . . till three on Sunday afternoon. I declare it was the 'sweetest hours that e'er I spent.' I have got acquainted with lots of pretty girls in Portage, but I would not trade off my Katie for any ten of them. Now that's plain talking, but it is so. She is the best girl I ever saw or want to see. John, if you have not found a lass yet you are missing one of the greatest pleasures this earth affords. I wish I was out of debt so I could get married."[7]

John advised his brother not to rush into a marriage yet but to return to the university. David remained firm. "[I] have no idea of giving up the idea of marriage to go to school,"[8] he insisted.

While David was starting his new career and wrestling with romantic problems, John was once again settling into his North Dormitory room and the university routine. He wrote to the Galloways.

"After leaving the sheaves and thrashing machine, the merry sound of our old school bell made me all crazy with joy. I think I love my studies more and more, and instead of the time for dismissing them coming nearer, as one term after another passes, it seems to go farther and farther away.

"We live in changing times, and our plans may easily be broken, but if not I shall be seeking knowledge for some years, here or elsewhere.

"Our University has reached a crisis in its history, and if not passed successfully, the doors will be closed, when of course I should have to leave Madison for some institution which has not yet been wounded to death by our war-demon. . . .

"This war seems farther from a close than ever. How strange that a country with so many schools and churches should be desolated by so unsightly a monster. 'Leaves have their time to fall' . . . yet we hardly deplore their fate, because there is nothing unnatural in it. . . . But may the same be said of the slaughtered upon the battle field?"[9]

Upon entering the University during its early years, John had become well acquainted with the early luminaries who had done so much to keep the fledgling institution going through many a hard time. He came to know Professor John Sterling who guided him when he was first admitted. The grand scholar, Dr. James Davie Butler, professor of literature and Latin who came to the university just after its 1858 reorganization, was his friend. Dr. Ezra Slocum Carr was a great influence in Muir's life. Holding a medical degree from Castleton College in Vermont, Carr became the professor of chemistry and natural history in 1856 a little over a year after that post was established.

John was thrilled with classic literature, but his deepest interest was in the world of science and natural science. He found studying these subjects under Ezra Carr to be fulfilling.

Dr. Butler noted that "Dr. Carr came to Madison with high repute as a popular lecturer on Chemistry. His manipulations were adroit, his delivery impressive, and his experiments highly sensational."[10]

Under the heading, "Chemistry, Natural History and Their Applications," the 1861 university catalogue explained some of Dr. Carr's procedures: "The instruction in this department is given by lectures and demonstrations on the part of the professor and students, together with examinations.

"The recitation of the student consists in his giving a lecture, illustrated with experiments and demonstrations on the same subject and after the manner of the Professor, thus not only requiring an intimate knowledge of the subject discussed, but at the same time the faculty of communicating his knowledge."[11]

The Board of Regents' first record book described the examinations conducted at the end of the term. The university examiners reported that "the classes taught by Professor Carr evinced a thorough theoretical and a good degree of practical knowledge of the subjects discussed."[12]

They also noted that "The conveniences for the study of chemistry are somewhat limited. There is but one small room for the apparatus and chemicals." The examiners recommended that "some convenient room be set apart as a laboratory fitted with a few tables and open at all times to students . . . for practical experiments. The expense would be trifling and the advantages manifold."[13] Unfortunately, the laboratory was not set up at the time Muir studied chemistry, so he set one up in his own room.

Carr's teaching was not limited to the laboratory. "When I walk with students in green fields and forests," he once wrote, "and show them in nature's basement rooms how the foundations of the earth were laid, I see in them tokens of mental animation which are the strongest stimulants to my own exertion."[14]

". . . I shall not forget the Doctor who first laid before me the great book of Nature," Muir wrote to Mrs. Carr from Canada three years after he left Madison, "and though I have taken so little from his hand he has at least shown me where those mines of priceless knowledge lie and how to reach them."[15]

In this same letter Muir wrote, "I thank Dr. Carr for his kind remembrance of me, but still more for the good patience he had with so inept a scholar."[16]

John had been introduced to a number of Dr. Carr's theories. "I often think of the Doctor's lecture upon the condition of the different races of men as controlled by physical agencies."[17]

In an article the professor developed his theory of modern science based on the inductive method of reasoning. He felt that studying the effect to determine the cause was more important than the reverse as the deductive approach would have it. He said that "induction is the source of the great scientific truths," and that the treasures of knowledge were obtained by this process.[18]

Carr further felt that "education consists in the full harmonious development of the entire man" and that material interests should be united to education. "When men study for information which they need to use, they do not study languidly. The abilities used by the farmer, mechanic or manufacturer are not inferior to those of the professions."[19]

John formed a long-term friendshp with both Ezra Carr and his wife. He often walked over to the Carr residence on Gilman Street. After the austerity of his youthful years, he enjoyed the Carr home, especially the pleasant library with its "books and plants and butterflies." Jeanne Carr, a botanist in her own right, developed a special bond with the young Marquette County student.

He later wrote, "O how frequently, Mrs. Carr, when lonely and wearied, have I wished that like some hungry worm I could creep into that delightful kernel in your house, your library, with its portraits of scientific men, and so bountiful a store of their sheaves amid the blossom and verdure of your little kingdom of plants, luxuriant and happy as though holding their leaves to the open sky of the most flower-loving zone in the world."[20]

Professor Butler, a gentle, well-traveled, well-read man, also exerted great influence on John Muir. Butler took a personal interest in his students and shared with them his rich body of knowledge and experience. Educated in eastern schools with degrees from Middlebury College and Yale Theological Seminary, he had sailed abroad in the 1840s to study other civilizations first hand. He was a correspondent for several publications, a lecturer, Congregational minister, and teacher.

The *Wisconsin State Journal* of Madison reported on December 2, 1858: "Professor Butler is an eloquent and brilliant lecturer, possessing a sharp wit, and a graphic power of description."[21] In his memorial address for Dr. Butler, who died in Madison November 20, 1905, Reuben Gold Thwaites described him as a man "small and wiry of frame . . . gifted with unusual vitality. . . . His manner was genial and democratic; he had a quaint and often merry wit, tempered by shrewd wisdom. A man of such charming disposition, with an unending fund of material for cultivated conversation, could not fail to attract friends."[22] Thwaites said that Butler possessed a breadth of scholastic taste and winsome courtesy.

Butler felt that classic literature greatly enriched life in the present. Muir may have heard an early speech he gave many times titled "How a Dead Language Can Make a Live Man," or a "Defense of Classical Study."

Butler and his family lived in the South Dormitory, not far from Muir's North Dormitory. He delighted as John did in the beauty of the campus on the shore of Fourth Lake. In 1890 he described how the surroundings had looked in earlier years: "The outlooks around the buildings were then no whit inferior to those now so much admired. The trees close at hand were not high enough to obstruct the view, those in the distance were many of them patriarchs of the forest primeval. Gulls, ducks and loons were never absent from the lake. Three eagles were often swooping above me during my morning swims beneath the bluff."[23]

When the "central edifice," University Hall, was being built on College Hill one mile west of the state capitol, he said, "The chief aim in planning this third University structure was to make a fair show, a queenly crown . . . on the hilltop."

In later years Butler could recall many of his students by name and he remembered those who went on to a name for themselves. He remembered John Muir.

"No foresight, or Scotch second sight showed me to what acmes of dignity, legal, political and literary, these youths were destined to climb. So while entertaining angels unawares, I very composedly eked out their short-comings, and detected their blunders like those of ordinary mortals."[24]

When the Civil War broke, out many university students signed up for military duty. Some classrooms were emptied almost immediately and there was often difficulty maintaining enough students to continue classes. In speaking of his small Greek classes during the war Butler said that students whose last names were far apart in the alphabet sat close together on the bench.

In the fall of 1862, William H. Brown of the Town of Buffalo, who three years before had described the return of the birds in springtime, wrote to Muir about his recent visit to Madison in his effort to locate his brother Bradley, now in service. Unable to find him at Camp Randall, he had visited with John instead.

"I meditate frequently upon my visit to the capitol and although disappointed I did not see Bradley, I enjoyed myself first rate. I think Prof. Carr's lectures on chemistry were very instructive. Should I happen into your room tomorrow morning I presume I should find you digging away at your Latin grammar as usual."[25]

Bradley Brown, who had participated in log school escapades with John, was now ill in an army hospital at Camp Dennison, Ohio. Bradley gave an account of his illness to William, living on the home farm, who passed the news on to John.

Bradley thought he was gaining slowly and could rejoin his regiment in two or three weeks. Every day he and his friends would walk out to an old log where they sat and sunned themselves and talked together. The soldiers had plenty to eat and drink.

William said that the Town of Buffalo needed to raise seventeen men. "I suppose they will commence drafting tomorrow, the tenth [November]." He was angry at secessionists in the township and called them traitors.

A few days later Annie Muir gave her brother news of the town draft: "I suppose you have heard that they have drafted up in Marquette County and will be anxious to hear who are drafted. There are none of our folks taken. I will try and get the list of the names to send you and you may be glad you were not taken."[26]

The burden of war affected everyone—relatives, friends, and neighbors. James Whitehead, who grew up in the Fountain Lake area and was so devoted to Davie Taylor, was one of these.

Muir's correspondence with Whitehead about the harsh methods both Benjamin Whitehead and Daniel Muir used in rearing their children has been described in an earlier chapter. But Whitehead also held memories of an entirely different side of John's father. His most vivid remembrance of Daniel was after his service in the 17th Regiment. In a draft of a March 31, 1913, letter to Muir he wrote:

"I shall never forget when in Feb., 1863 I was discharged and sent home as only supposed to die, of your father visiting & for hours sitting beside my bed—reading—talking & praying for me with a sincerity that moved me greatly. How with tremulous voice he sought me to find hope and safety in God's forgiving love. For hours so it seemed in my weakened condition he read and commented on passages of scripture promises calculated to comfort & sustain the sick and afflicted.

"In a few days he returned bringing a couple of books (from a circulating library maintained at his own expense) which I promised to read. Do you wonder my dear friend that henceforth he became my ideal of a Christian. Animated by a faith that was imperishable he sought by his life & works to inspire others with the hope that was to him a fiery pillar. From these visits & the unselfish interest taken in myself we acquired a knowledge and understanding of each other."[27]

The Muir family could not escape the Civil War cloud and the worry over the new conscription law. On March 1, 1863, Anne Muir brought John up to date on the matter.

"Daniel left home yesterday for Canada. His father said he would not hinder him if he wished to go but he would not advise him. He wouldn't give him money, but said I might if I wished. It is a hard trial to me—all my boys have left me. I try to think it is for the best. You will have heard of this new conscription law exempting none. It seems hard."[28]

Despite the gloom, the family in Portage City continued their day-to-day affairs. "Father bought a house and lot," Anne related in her March 1 letter. "He is getting a small barn put up and getting a well dug. They call it three quarters of a mile from Miles corner—it is beyond the railroad station." She said they would not move for a month or so since the house was still occupied.

Anne also told her son about the elevator fire at the railroad station where thousands of bushels of wheat were stored. The Muirs lost about five hundred bushels in this disaster, including some winter wheat. As well as the grain elevator, the fire consumed a long row of houses.

After living in town for about two years, Anne Muir began to change her mind about Portage City. She told John she was glad now that Dan and the younger girls had such a good opportunity to attend school there and thought "it did the younger kids some good." She liked the location of the house Daniel had purchased at the bottom of Prospect Hill and gave John directions from the Ellsworth House so he could find it when he came for the summer.

"I like to live here very well. By going to the other side of the hill I have a very pleasant walk along . . . the Wisconsin river. I think you would enjoy a walk on Propsect Hill very much as there is such a fine view from it," she wrote John May 16, 1863.

"As yet there seems to be no end to this unhappy war. It is rumoured there will be drafting in this state in the month of June. I hope it will not take place. The dreadful miseries occasioned by this awful war can never be known. I hope it will speedily come to an end."²⁹

It did Anne good to get away from her daily tasks. When she walked along the river she could forget for a brief time her worry over the war.

A few months earlier the Galloways had been enjoying a wintery day in the comfort of their Fountain Lake farm house. That evening David described the scene for John.

"I am at home contented and happy. We have had quite a snow day, and if you could have peeped in this afternoon you would have seen us (all four) busy discussing a tin panful of popcorn. An hour or so later you might have heard us from the upper gate as if 'Bedlam' were loose and if you had not been scared to come near the house you might have seen me with one [child] on each knee shaking down the popcorn and singing and laughing like all possessed. . . . Sarah is learning to trip it on the light fantastic toe. It would make you laugh, John, to see me with a poker for a bow and left arm for a fiddle imitating all the motions. . . ."³⁰

In April Sarah and David looked forward to having John at Fountain Lake for the summer. She had much to tell her brother, much advice to give.

"I'm afraid you are studying too hard," she wrote on April 29. "Take time for fun. It will make you stronger and you will be all the better for it. You know we expect great things of you bye and bye if you keep your health, so you must take good care of yourself—mind that."³¹

John replied to Sarah's concern and expectation. "I had almost forgotten, Sarah, to tell you that I was elected judge in one of the debating clubs a short time ago, also President of the Young Men's Christian Assoc. You say that you expect something great bye and bye. Am I not great now?"³²

John had been elected to the Athenean Society in January and had been active the past several months both as a debater and judge. In April he debated in the affirmative with Milton Griswold and others on the subject "the American people are incapable of self government." The affirmative won this debate.

The following August, after the death of his dear friend, Frances Pelton from Prairie du Chien days, Muir wrote a letter of sympathy to her parents, Mr. and Mrs. Ambrose Newton. "I shall not again receive her letters of encouragement, or hear her words of earnest kindness, but the marks of her goodness shall never be ef[f]aced, and her advice shall influence me all my life.

"The cause of Christ has prospered of late in Madison, a great many especially from among the young have professed faith in the Saviour and joined themselves to his people. A few of the young men have formed a "Young Men's Christian Assoc[iation]" which it is hoped may do much good. Far more interest, too, is taken by Christians in the Sunday school cause. The Sunday schools of the city are in a more prosperous condition than ever before. All this is very cheering amid the din and desolation of war."[33]

At the university Muir had enlarged his circle of friends and widened his social experiences, taking some time for fun as Sarah suggested. His roommate, Charles Vroman, related one social event.

"Muir was absolutely without selfconsciousness. This was well illustrated on an occasion when we were invited to a reception at the apartment of Professor Sterling, the Vice-Chancellor. Quite a party of ladies and gentlemen were present. Muir became very much interested in a large square piano, which had been contributing to the entertainment. He managed to get the top up and then climbed onto the wires; when I first noticed him he was reaching into the back part of the instrument to discover what caused the music. After satisfying himself, he climbed down and mingled with the company. The host and guests smiled, but were not at all disturbed by the event, because it was John Muir and anything was allowable to him."[34]

As sunshine warmed the land, and flowers began to bloom at Fountain Lake, Sarah Galloway's thoughts again turned to her brother in the North Dormitory.

"How beautiful everything will be looking around the University. The banks around your lovely lake, the flowers, will be peeping out from under the withered leaves and grass, and all the trees just putting forth their buds and leaves. How pleasant it is to watch them and to think of that silent but mighty power that makes everything spring to fresh life and vigor. When he has placed so much beauty around and shown so much skill in the formation of the tiniest flower it is surely never meant that we should pass them by without a glance or thought."[35]

A strong bond existed between bother and sister, especially in their love of nature. No matter how busy she was with her daily tasks, Sarah took time to enjoy the natural landscape around her. Like John she had a fine imagination.

She described a recent ramble she had taken with Jane Mitchell, David's sister, around her own beautiful lake. The two women wandered as far as the oak knoll on the lake's south side. Sarah was intrigued with a vine that trailed along the ground, taking root as it went along. She sent John a leaf to identify since he was studying botany at the time, but he replied that he could not identify the plant without seeing its flower.

Sarah told her brother about their farm activities. David had begun sowing oats. Earlier in the spring he had planted more apple trees in the orchard. To fill out the rows he cut down two big oak trees in front of the house. She said there were a good many blossoms on all the trees, especially the two remaining that Daniel Muir had planted in the early years way out from the stables.

Sarah had planted a row of locust seeds the year before on the western side of the orchard to make a hedge border. "They grew finely,"[36] she said. This spring she planted a row on the other side of the orchard to complete the border.

By the first of June the trees on the Madison campus were in full leaf and many flowers were in full bloom. John, tired after a busy year, began to make plans with Sarah and David for his return to Fountain Lake for the summer. David needed him on the farm, and as always, Sarah looked forward to having her brother stay with them. John wrote Sarah that he expected to be at the Watson's home in Poynette by Thursday, June 18th. He said David could pick him up there.

"I mean to be happy for a few days around Fountain Lake collecting specimens for my herbarium. You would like the study of botany. It is the most exciting thing in the form of amusement, much more of study, than I ever knew. Very unlike the [study of] grave tangled Greek and Latin . . .

"I returned last Saturday evening from a long ramble of 25 miles through marshes, mud and brushwood with a heavy basketful of flowers, weeds, moss and bush twigs and have made five or six visits besides and pressed 30 specimens or more."[37]

John didn't go home to Marquette County immediately after his term was over. Feeling that a long ramble would do him good, he instead decided to take a long botanical and geological walking tour down the Wisconsin River to the Mississippi. Corn and wheat were just breaking ground, so he knew he wouldn't be needed just yet on any of the Muir family farms.

When he wrote to the Galloways about his short-term change of plans he touched on a possible change in his long range plans as well. His earlier idea that next year he "might be somewhere farther away" had begun to crystalize in his mind. "If I go to Michigan University Medical School," he informed them, "I shall be with you until October when I return from my tramp. . . . I wish you could go with me."[38]

Sarah imagined how it would be to go with her brother on his wilderness journey. "I wish, John, we could cast care to the wind and take a wander with you. It would do us all good if you did not go too fast . . . then Annie and George, if they had the strength, would skip all the way before us to see who would gather the most flowers."

After this flight of fancy, she voiced concern for her husband's health. "David is not able to be up this morning yet. Poor Davie is not strong for his work this spring."

With obvious difficulty, David added a note to Sarah's letter. "Don't forget about my winter wheat and rye. John, if it will put you about to come about four weeks from now, say so in your answer to this and I might get some help before spring wheat comes in. However, I should rather you were here at first, as I intend to make my hay before harvest. . . . Excuse me John, for a really don't feel like writing."[39]

So, at the end of the term, John embarked on his first wilderness tramp. Packs slung on their backs, he and two student companions, M. M. Rice and James A. Blake, made their way from Madison over glacially created hills, and up the long terminal moraine toward Sauk City on the Wisconsin River about twenty miles distant. After studying nature's basement rooms with Ezra Carr, John may have had some understanding of the geological processes that sculptured the landscape.

Sauk City was located near the edge of the terminal moraine where, ten or twelve thousand years before, the glacier had dropped its last load of unsorted rocks and gravels when it came to a stop and melted back. The meltwaters pouring forth from the receding glacier created a valley far wider than the Wisconsin River's normal flow could carve.

The young explorers hiked along this broad Wisconsin River valley on its southwesterly course toward the Mississippi through the unglaciated landscape of steeper hills and deeper valleys. Southwestern Wisconsin had escaped the glacier's bulldozing action that sculpted the rest of the state.

When the companions began their hike along the Wisconsin River at Sauk City, they picked up the route Father Marquette and Louis Jolliet had taken. The canoes of the French expedition had floated downriver here in June, 1673, as the the explorers searched for the legendary river to the west. The later hikers were also walking along the same route Muir had traveled by train with Wiard's Lady Franklin ice boat three years before.

With the sun on their backs and warm June breezes on their faces, they went where their feet took them. In complete freedom they explored the sand islands, the bottomlands, and the marshes. They scrambled up the river banks, the nearby hills, and rock outcrops as they made their way toward Prairie du Chien and the Mississippi River.

During this mild season, the river environment came alive in a hundred different ways. The June sun brought out every kind of life, from water beetles on the river surface to wetland vegetation—rushes and grasses, cattails, flowers, shrubs, and trees. The soft maple, elm, river birch, and the graceful willow trees were putting forth new leaves and new growth.

105

Filling the air with movement and song, the many birds in a variety of colors were building their nests in every conceivable location from a tuft of marsh grass to the end of an overhanging tree bough. Both migrating waterfowl and resident water birds were plentiful.

The friends had hiked over a hundred miles by the time they neared the mouth of the Wisconsin. On the south side of that river where it flowed into the Mississippi, a cliff rose abruptly five hundred feet, offering a spectacular view of the confluence. During Muir's 1860 sojourn at the Mondell House in Prairie du Chien, and on this 1863 hike, he certainly explored this magnificent bluff.

In 1673, Marquette wrote in his diary, ". . . we safely entered the Mississippi on the 17th of June with a joy I cannot express." Muir and his companions must have shared that same joy as they gazed at the legendary great river.

They probably gained access to the bluff by way of the wooden covered bridge, constructed in 1857, which spanned the Wisconsin at Bridgeport a few miles east of Prairie du Chien. They found a diversity of geological features on the bluff and the slopes leading to it, with each slope and valley having its own unique plant and wildlife. There was a maze of cracks, crevices, and small caves in the sandstone and limestone layers to explore.

From the limestone-capped blufftop, the boys could see for miles— the long expanse of both rivers; the wide Mississippi lined with bluffs covered by oak openings; and the breaks along the bluffs where streams had cut down from the prairie lands above to create short, steep valleys. Across the Mississippi on the Iowa side, about as high as the one they stood on, rose another steep bluff. They must cross the great river to explore it.

Muir was familiar with the busy Mississippi ferry landing at the Milwaukee and Mississippi Rail Road terminus in the Lower Town section of Prairie du Chien. He would not soon forget that adventurous 1860 train ride with Norman Wiard and his ice boat and how they had stored the craft at Holton's warehouse by the depot near the river. He and Blake undoubtedly boarded a Mississippi steam packet boat there and sailed around Horseshoe Island to McGregor's Landing on the Iowa side. Somewhere along the way Rice had left them and gone home.

Prairie du Chien and McGregor were both flourishing river towns. River traffic had greatly increased during the three years since Muir had lived in Prairie du Chien, and many more steamboats now plied the river. A large volume of grain from rich Iowa farmlands was ferried across from McGregor to Prairie du Chien for shipment east, while eastern goods and supplies were shipped across the river for transportation to the west.

After the railroad first steamed into Prairie du Chien in 1857 and connected with river packets at its terminus, McGregor, nestled in the Coulee de Sioux, grew by leaps and bounds. There was a military warehouse near the dock to service nearby Ft. Atkinson; there were foundries, hotels, grocers, mercantile establishments and banks; there were wholesale houses, feeding lots, and livery barns; grain elevators and other storage buildings lined the river.

Houses had been built in every nook and cranny of the coulee and perched against the steep hillsides. It was a homecoming of sorts for John. While staying with the Peltons at Mondell House, he had attended church services in McGregor.

As Muir and Blake crossed the busy river and landed at the bustling McGregor dock, they brushed up against the spirit of the country's western expansion. Ferry service to McGregor formed an important link for pioneers traveling westward, even during gold rush days. An early newspaper ad for MacGregor [sic] ferry service stated that there were good and easy roads directly into the interior "whither the vast tide of emigration is wending its way in quest of new homes."[40] McGregor was an important foothold in gaining access to the western lands for the military, traders, and emigrants alike.

A few months later, when John spent the winter with the Galloways, he recreated for Emily Pelton some of his adventures of those early July days of 1863.[41] The first in the series of backdated letters, dated July 7, 1863, was from a "recess in the bluffs near McGregor, Iowa."

That morning the boys followed the river downstream in search of a "romantic glen where a stream sought a path, turning the mosses to stone as it went, and watering many interesting flowers.

"'The road that leads to it,' said the man [giving the directions] 'lies close along the river brink—it is not very far and a loghouse marks the Glens [sic] narrow entrance.'"

In search of this ravine, John wrote, ". . . we could not withstand the temptation to climb the bluffs that butted so majestically overhead, and after many vain attempts we at last found a place where the ascent was practicable. We had to make many a halt for a rest, and made as much use of our hands as of our feet, but the splendid view well repaid the toil. After enjoying the delightful scenery and analyzing some specimens which we gathered on our way, we began to wish ourselves down again, as the afternoon was wearing away and we wished to visit the glen before night, but descending was still more difficult and we several times reached an unstoppable velocity.

"After traveling a good way down the river . . . when the sun's rays were nearly level and we had just emerged from a mass of low leafy trees we were suddenly struck with the most genuine astonishment at the unexpected sight so full before us. . . . judge, Emily, of our surprise when upon a piece of ground where the bluffs had curved backward a little from the river we saw the curious old house with four gaudily dressed females in an even row in front with two idle men seated a little to one side looking complacently upon them like a successful merchant upon a stock of newly arrived goods . . .

"It was long before I could judge the character of the establishment but I saw at once there was something very strange about it, and instinctively fell behind my companion. He was equally ignorant but boldly marched forward and asked for the glen where fossils were found. . . . They told us that the path was no farther—that the hills were unclimbable, etc. We then took the alarm—gained the summit of the bluffs after an hour's hard labor—built our camp fire, [and] congratulated each other on our escape."

The next day, July 8, "we found ourselves upon the brink of one of the highest points overhanging the river. It seemed as though we might almost leap across it. The sun was unclouded, and shone with fine effect upon the fleecy sea of fog contained by ample banks of bluffs—later it flowed smoothly away as we gazed and gave us the noble Mississippi in full view."

When the fog finally lifted, Muir and Blake found the distance was farther across the Mississippi to the mouth of the Wisconsin than it appeared.

That morning they returned to the upward reach of the glen they had found the night before. They could now enjoy at leisure the steep, secluded valley created by the little stream as its waters trickled toward river level. Here they "added some fine plants and fossils to our growing wealth."

We "soon found ourselves upon the shore of the great river. The genuine calm of a July morning was now master of all—the river flowed on, smooth as a woodland lake, reflecting the full beams of dreamy light, while not on all the dark foliage which feathered its mountain wall moved a single breeze."

As they walked along the river, they thought how nice it would be to make a boat and sail to the Wisconsin River entrance. They managed to fashion a little craft, but when they attempted to sail into the Wisconsin, the boiling current returned them to the Mississippi waters. That night, before camping on the river bank, they made two sets of oars, determined to try again the next day.

On the morning of July 9, the young adventurers climbed into their little craft and, rowing with all their might, once more entered the mouth of the Wisconsin. Again the river "came tumbling down rapid and restless as ever. At each pull of the oars our little fairy almost leaps from the water but we are now in the midst of the boiling water. We shook to this side, now to that, making very acute angles, and almost capsizing several times—again we pull harder than ever before—again are baffled. We are drenched thoroughly with steaming sweat, but we have strength remaining and have already conquered fifteen or twenty rods. The combat is prolonged amid splashing and boiling, now drifted back now gaining a few rods—now fast on a sandbar on this side, now aground on the other, till the victory was again wrenched from us and, drawing our boat upon a large sandbank we disembarked, [and] laid our packs at our feet. . . ."

Finally, Muir and Blake nailed a card to the boat addressed to John's friend from Mondell House days, Mrs. Goodrich, at Dubuque, Iowa. They pushed it into the Mississippi current and watched for a few minutes as it sailed away. "Then we again placed our old companion packs, and soberly marched away with unequal steps through the tall grass." They had begun their long hike home.

John continued the saga from "a farmhouse near Wright's Ferry," a tiny community consisting of the ferry, store, and post office, only a few miles upriver from Prairie du Chien. "After a wearisome walk over wet places and fallen trees we reached the farmhouse where I now write." The tired, hungry explorers asked the woman of the house for a meal, "only the fifth meal in two days, having had but one yesterday.

"We did not intend to stop here . . . but the old lady of the mansion gave us so good a welcome that we entered and she made us supper. She has invited us to stay all night." The grateful young Muir determined that "she shall know some time that I have not forgotten her."

Muir and Blake had just completed a memorable walking trip, but upon their return to Madison they were ready for more adventure. Within a week they boarded the train for Kilbourn City (now Wisconsin Dells) northwest of Madison, some thirty miles upriver from where they had begun their Wisconsin River walk to Prairie du Chien. Muir called it the best of all their rambles.

For miles above and below Kilbourn City the fast-moving Wisconsin had carved spectacular shapes in the sandstone as it flowed toward the Mississippi. The youths spent a day exploring the ravines and steep, rocky gorges along the river.

"On going up the river we were delightfully opposed and threatened by a great many semi-gorge ravines running at right angles to the river, too steep to cross at every point and much too long to be avoided if to wish to avoid them were possible. Those ravines are the most perfect, the most heavenly plant conservatories I ever saw. Thousands of happy flowers are there, but ferns and mosses are the favored ones. No human language will ever describe them. We traveled two miles in eight hours, and such scenery, such sweating, scrambling, climbing, and happy hunting and happy finding of dear plant beings we never before enjoyed.

"The last ravine we encountered was the most beautifully and deepest and longest and narrowest. The rocks overhang and bear a perfect selection of trees which hold themselves towards one another from side to side with inimitable grace, forming a flower-veil of indescribable beauty. The light is measured and mellowed. The walls are fringed and painted most divinely with the bright green polypodium and asplenium and mosses and liverworts with gray lichens, and here and there a clump of flowers and little bushes. The floor was barred and banded and sheltered by bossy, shining, moss-clad logs cast in as needed from above. Over all and above all and in all the glorious ferns, tall, perfect, godlike, and here and there amid their fronds a long cylindrical spike of the grand fringed purple orchis."[42]

After spending the night in Kilbourn City, the boys constructed a raft and sailed downriver through the swirling waters of the narrows and on to Portage. In contrast to their earlier effort to sail from the mouth of the Wisconsin in a homemade craft, their raft venture was a complete success.

John soon returned to Fountain Lake, glad to be home with the Galloways. Feeling much better after the weeks of hiking, botanizing, and collecting fossils and plant specimens, he was ready to help David Galloway for a summer of farm work.

# VII

# PLANTING THE SEED

The preservation of specimen sections of natural flora
—bits of pure wildness was a fond, favorite notion
of mine long before I heard of National parks.
—Muir before the Sierra Club,
November 23, 1895

While John Muir was finishing his final term at the university in the spring of 1863, and before he began his river tramp, his brother David was wrestling with romantic problems at home. He was eager to marry his beloved Catherine Cairns, but a difficulty arose with his mother.

"Kate had seen and met Mother several times," he confided to John in April, "and Mother would not speak to her nor look at her. At this [Kate] felt so grieved that she cried whole nights about it and concluded that we had better give it up. I don't know how it will end, but we won't give it up if I can help it.

"Write soon," he beseeched, "and tell me what I had better do about it. I hope you won't expose me nor make Mother angry, but I want you to help me."[1]

John's advice was to wait two or three years, but David's mind was made up. "We have taken a decided stand for the union," he declared. "You have not the slightest idea of how much we love each other. As for 'waiting two or three years' we would as lief be in purgatory. . . ."[2]

It was uncharacteristic of Anne Muir not to support her children in where they believed their happiness to lie. Perhaps one explanation for her opposition to David's marriage was that she did not want to lose the one son who remained nearby. John was in Madison and Dan had recently left for Canada.

By June that year David had risen to the position of cashier at Forbes store. He told John he liked the job first rate and that he was also making the twenty dollars a month he had been promised along with his board and washing.

He wanted John to follow him in the harvest fields as usual, but he wouldn't be able to spend much time away from the store this season. He asked his brother to stop in at Forbes as soon as he got into town.

Rejuvenated after his wilderness tramp to the Mississippi, John plunged right into farm work upon his return to Fountain Lake. David Galloway was relieved for the big lift his brother-in-law gave him in the fields. Occasionally, when Sarah could find the time, she and the children, George and Anna, roamed the woods and fields with him. Perhaps they found the trailing ivy Sarah had been so taken with in the spring, and he could now identify it.

When he wasn't working with David Galloway that summer, John worked on the other Muir farms. However, he probably didn't help much at Hickory Hill, for he could not get along with his father. "Father and I cannot agree at all," he later wrote Dan in Canada. "I could not live at Hickory Hill a single week hardly."[3] John increasingly looked on Sarah and David's home as his own.

Although Anne and Daniel Muir continued to live in Portage, Daniel spent many hours at the farm planting and harvesting. When he stayed with the Reids at the Hickory Hill farmhouse, he also prepared lengthy sermons for neighborhood religious services.

John continued his letter to Dan. "I have worked hard in harvest this summer and built John Reid's house over the hill from Father's. Also I plowed for John about two weeks."[4]

As the weeks went on, Anne evidently came around to David's way of thinking, for he and Catherine, daughter of John and Violet Cairns, proceeded with their wedding plans after all. On November 20, 1863, Almond S. Rounds performed the marriage ceremony, almost three years after he had married Maggie Muir and John Reid.

In a letter to Bradley Brown, John noted the long mile that Dave had marched on his long journey and said that he and Katy seemed to keep house very pleasantly together in Portage.

At Christmas time John wrote to Dan telling him all about the happy occasion.

"I was at David's wedding—he evidently thought that his lass was the most perfect piece of mortality this side of the new Jerusalem. We of course wished him happiness. I dined at his house in Portage a few days ago."[5]

John then showed the intensity of his feeling against marriage for both Dan and himself in this admonition: "You and I must not on any account permit ourselves to think of marriage for five or six years." He urged Dan to continue his schooling, saying he could afford to send him "Yankee greenbacks as I have but few expenses and can maul cordwood from gnarly trees at the tune of a pair of diems per diem."

He told Dan that he was splitting cordwood and rails for the stove this winter and that he was studying French, Latin, anatomy, and specimens for his herbarium. He added that if he weren't drafted, he planned to go to Scotland or Canada.

The preceding fall John had not gone to Ann Arbor to study medicine at Michigan University as he had planned. "A draft was being made just when I should have been starting for Ann Arbor, which kept me at home."[6] Instead, as the months stretched into autumn and winter, he stayed on at Fountain Lake.

As the snows piled up outside the house, he sat around the warm wood stove with the Galloway family. Perhaps, reminiscent of the festive evening David had earlier described to John when his brother-in-law was at the university, John bounced George and Anna on his knee as David had done, while Sarah popped corn for them all.

In January, 1864, he wrote to his old school chum, Bradley Brown who was still serving with the union forces. Painting a contrast between his life and Bradley's, he said, "I am living quietly at home and am too apt to forget you who are so much exposed to danger and disease."

He reminisced about their log school days: "When I pass the seat of the 'Academy,' I think of the funny times we had."[7]

Still not drafted into the union army by the Town of Buffalo, John could stay home no longer. The wilderness was calling and he was compelled to follow the call. On March 1, 1864, he boarded the train for Canada to join Dan.

Before Muir left Marquette County, an important incident took place, the significance of which would become clear thirty-one years later when he addressed a meeting of the Sierra Club November 23, 1895, in San Francisco.

"When my father came from Scotland," he said to the large gathering, "he settled in a fine, wild region in Wisconsin beside a small glacier lake bordered with white pond lilies. And on the north side of the lake, just below our house there was a carex meadow [wet sedge] full of charming flowers—and around the margin of the meadow were many nooks rich in ferns and heathworts.

"When I was about to wander away on my long rambles I was sorry to leave the precious meadow unprotected. Therefore, I said to my brother-in-law who then owned it, "Sell me the forty acres of lake meadow and keep it fenced; never allow cattle or hogs to break into it, and I will gladly pay you whatever you say. I want to keep it untrampled for the sake of its ferns and flowers; and even if I never see it again the beauty of its lilies and orchids are so pressed in my mind that I shall always look back to them in imagination, across seas and continents, and perhaps even after I am dead.'

"But he regarded my plan as sentimental dreams, wholly impracticable. The fence he said would surely be broken down and all the work would be done in vain.

"Eighteen years later, I found the deep-water pond lilies in fresh bloom, but the delicate garden sod of the meadow was broken up and trampled into black mire."[8]

Accordingly, as early as February, 1864, in the Town of Buffalo, Marquette County, Wisconsin, the seed of the idea of land preservation was planted in John Muir's heart and mind. The seed germinated, took root, and eventually grew into his major contribution to the formation of the national park system.

At the moment, however, John's precious time with his family was coming to an end, and he was concerned about his immediate future. As he explained to Emily Pelton, "I have enjoyed the company of my dear relatives very much during this long visit but I shall soon leave them all, and I scarcely think it probable that I shall be blest with so much of home again."[9]

Just before he boarded the train for Canada, he sent her a short note dated March 1, 1864.

"I am to take the cars in about half an hour. I really don't know where I shall 'halt.' I feel like Milton's Adam and Eve—'The world was all before them where to choose their rest.' Write to Midland soon. I have already bidden [sic] all my friends good bye. I feel lonely again. Goodbye Emily."[10]

The train route went via Chicago, around the southern tip of Lake Michigan, across Michigan to the international border at Windsor, Canada West. Then under British rule, that province would join three others in 1867 to create the Dominion of Canada and would become known as the Province of Ontario. Like the United States, Canada had been undergoing a process of European settlement. At this time many Scots, Irish, and English, were industriously clearing the heavily-forested land tree by tree in order to plant their first seeds for food or a small market crop.

At Windsor, Muir doubtless boarded the Grand Western Railway for the journey into the Province of Canada West. Alighting somewhere in present southern Ontario, he explored the area bounded by lakes Erie, Ontario, and Huron over the following several months.

"After earning a few dollars working on my brother-in-law's farm near Portage, I went off on the first of my long lonely excursions, botanizing in glorious freedom around the Great Lakes and wandering through innumerable tamarac and arbor-vitae swamps, and forests of maple, basswood, ash, elm, balsam, fir, pine spruce, hemlock, rejoicing in their boundless wealth and strength and beauty. . . ."[11]

Although he eventually got together with Dan, John was botanizing alone when he made the most exciting discovery of his trek through the Canadian wilderness.

"The rarest and most beautiful of the flowering plants I discovered on this first grand excursion was Calypso borealis . . . I had been fording streams more and more difficult to cross and wading bogs and swamps that seemed more and more extensive and more difficult to force one's way through.

"Entering one of these great tamarac and arbor-vitae swamps one morning . . . struggling through tangled drooping branches and over and under heaps of fallen trees, I began to fear that I would not be able to reach dry ground before dark, and therefore would have to pass the night in the swamp. . . .

"But when the sun was getting low . . . I found beautiful Calypso on the mossy bank of a stream, growing not in the ground but on a bed of yellow mosses in which its small white bulb had found a soft nest and from which its one leaf and one flower sprung. The flower was white and made the impression of the utmost simple purity like a snowflower . . . It seemed the most spiritual of all the flower people I had ever met. I sat down beside it and fairly cried for joy. . . .

"How long I sat beside Calypso I don't know. Hunger and weariness vanished, and only after the sun was low in the west I plashed on through the swamp, strong and exhilarated as if never more to feel any mortal care."[12]

When John wrote to Professor Butler about this thrilling experience, Butler sent the letter on to the *Boston Recorder*. It was the first time Muir's words ever appeared in print.

As well as learning the region's plants, Muir learned about the people. When his money gave out, he stopped again and again at farmhouses to do any kind of work for a few dollars. He chopped, cleared, graded, and harvested for farmers. When he tried to explain his mission to them, he found they did not understand the term botany.

Through Muir's dated herbarium slips, biographer William Badé traced Muir's route to Meaford, County Grey, Canada West. According to these identifications slips, Muir was wading the Canadian swamps in April, and by May he had hiked northward as far as Simcoe County. Begun on the eighteenth of May, his estimated three hundred mile ramble through Simcoe and Grey Counties took three weeks. In July he was botanizing north of Toronto in the Holland River swamps, and on the highlands near Hamilton and Burlington bays on Lake Ontario.

The herbarium slips showed that by August he was again wandering the Lake Ontario shores in the vicinity of Niagara Falls. By this time he had teamed up with his brother Dan and botanized with him for several weeks. Together, the brothers experienced the power and wonder of the falls as the Niagara River carried vast tonnages of water from the upper Great Lakes through Lake Erie to the edge of the Niagara dolomite escarpment. The water roared over the precipice crashing to the rocks below with monstrous white spray clouds rising up about as high as the precipice itself.

"The water in our lake would not last half a second," John later explained to his young sister Annie about the falls. "When Dan and I first saw them their enormous magnitude and grandeur so stunned and overwhelmed us that we could not realize anything, but when we had retired to the hills and returned several times we began more and more to see and feel that we indeed stood before the great Niagara, the grandest sight in all the world.

"Just in sight [above] is the calm blue Lake Erie; farther down the waters become troubled, and as they approach within a mile or two of the tremendous precipice they rush on in sublime fury, each feathery billow dashing on as if anxious to be first to take the fearful plunge. If the Falls were made into about ten thousand cataracts each would be grand and beautiful . . ."[13]

The brothers separated for a time, with arrangements to meet later, but unfortunately they missed their connection. Dan found his way to William Trout's sawmill and broom factory at Meaford on the beautiful Georgian Bay of Lake Huron. The mill was located a mile or two from the bay on a rocky stream in a secluded valley. Trout remembered the midsummer day that "a grown-up beardless boy showed up looking for work." Although he ran a large shop, the summer rush was over and he didn't need any help just then.

"His fine boyish face and frank open manners interested me," he chronicled in the *Trout Family History*.[14] Dan explained to Trout that he and his brother had been spending the summer botanizing. They found it best to separate for awhile, and planned to meet in a certain town, but somehow they failed making connections. His money was about gone and he needed to find work till he could get word from home or from his brother.

"A couple of my farmer customers were standing by, and that big new word 'Botanizing' caught their curiosity.

"'What's that?'

"'Why,' I said, 'the boys are examining and studying different plants.'

"'What for? For medicine?'

"'No! . . . for knowledge.'

"He left, and in the evening I was surprised to find him working for the man who was running the sawmill.

"I said to him, 'I'm glad you got a job.'

"'Oh, just working for my room and board.'

"'Is that all? Why, you come with us. You'll get better board and at least a dollar a week.'

"'Thank you. I shall be glad to do so.'

"'. . . he soon became a most companionable guest. He remained with us about six weeks; then through a few home communications, his brother was finally located, and he left us to join him."

Trout's account stated that the brothers did not return to Wisconsin "because of a positive order from their parents that Dan should remain in Canada while the military draft was enforced in the northern United States, and John, his elder brother, being of manhood age, was urgently requested to remain with him. While John's feelings did not coincide with their wish, . . . for his mother and Dan's sake, he complied."

John and Dan continued their botanical ramble in the Ontario wilderness "for a couple of months until winter was likely to set in, and snow would cover up nearly all of the plant life."

Then "like the squirrels and marmots and bears, the great question was 'Where shall we den up?.'"

Dan brought John to Trout's mill in the secluded valley and introduced him to Mr. Trout. The brothers arranged to work for him that winter.

"When I came to the Georgian Bay of Lake Huron," John later penned, "whose waters are so transparent and beautiful, and the forests about its shores with their ferny, mossy dells and deposits of boulder clay, it seemed to be a most favorable place for study, and as I was also at this time out of money again I was eager to stay for a considerable time. In a beautiful dell, only a mile or two from the magnificent bay, I fortunately found work in a factory where there was a sawmill and lathes for turning out rake, broom, and fork handles, etc."[15]

It was a good place to "den up." The Muir brothers' first job was to help build an addition to the shop for a rake factory.

When John and Dan settled into William Trout's log house for the winter, they joined a congenial group of young people—William's brother Peter, his sister Mary Trout who managed the household, and his business partner, Charles H. Jay.

Trout's three other sisters came to the hollow on Saturdays from their permanent farm home nearby or from the schools where they taught. Trout said they were all young, lively, intelligent people with common aims and purposes. Many a spirited discussion took place when everyone got together.

William Trout wrote in the family history that John was a systematic worker and a diligent student. In the Trout home he lived under his usual regimen. He rose early, worked hard, and read in spare moments at lunchtime. He spent his evening hours reading and studying. His usual bedtime was 10 o'clock, but if he were particularly interested in a subject, he would stay up till eleven or twelve o'clock. He always rose at five, awakened by his famous self-rising machine.

"Our house had only board partitions . . . so that when John's bed fell it was a wakeup signal for all in the house . . ."

Trout described the bed mechanisms:

"His bed was mounted on a cross axle, sustained by two high pedestals, one on each side, and nearer the head than the foot; so that if the foot was not held up it would fall and lie on the floor and the bed would be reclining at an angle of about forty-five degrees. A rod screwed to the ceiling, and hooked to the foot, sustained it in the level position. At night, however, a special trigger was affixed to the rod, and sustained the bed. A string connected the trigger to his specially constructed clock, which at the determined hour . . . would pull the trigger, and release the bed, which would instantly fall, leaving the occupant in a half upright position with his feet on the floor. . . .

"When the bed fell, an arm swung around into the fingers of which had been placed a match, which in swinging, rubbed over a piece of sandpaper, and being ignited, came to rest over the wick of an oil lamp perched on its regular place on a shelf. The lamp was thus lighted with the fall of the bed.

"A sponge bath in the tub was the next move, then dressing, which was followed by study till breakfast time."

John confided in a letter to Emily Pelton that his social advantages in the mill hollow were few, but he worked, studied, and dreamed in this "retirement."

The busy winter passed and spring finally reached the "retired and romantic" hollow. "Our tall, tall forest trees are now all alive. . . . Freshness and beauty are everywhere; flowers are born every hour; living sunlight is poured overall, and every thing and creature is glad. Our world is indeed a beautiful one. . . ."[16]

In May, Dan left his brother in Meaford and went to work in a Buffalo, New York, machine shop. John felt "farther from home and longer from home, . . . touched with melancholy or lonesomeness."[17] While John was soaking up the beauty of the Canadian spring, changes had taken place in Wisconsin. By January 1, 1865, the family had moved back to Hickory Hill. How glad Anne Muir was to be living on her beloved farm once again—to be there during spring planting, the growing season, and the harvesting. She was especially happy to tend her flower garden.

On Sept. 9, 1865, Annie described Hickory Hill for Dan, since her older brother had not been home for so long.

"There are fields of stubble, each containing a fresh straw stack. The willows have grown about twice as tall as before and also the trees in the orchard look much as [they] did last year. Also the mellon [sic] patch. But our flower garden—just step out the door and look around—moss roses north, moss roses east and moss roses south.

"But the farm itself has diminished as Dave Wallace has bought the log house 80, $1200 being the price."[18]

The following month Sarah and David Galloway sold the home eighty of Fountain Lake Farm to James Whitehead and moved to town where Maggie and John Reid were also living.

During 1865 David Muir became involved in a new venture. After clerking for Forbes for some time he joined with another clerk, William T. Parry, and a Mr. Bebb in establishing a new dry goods and clothing store—Parry, Bebb & Muir. When Mr. Bebb retired four years later the firm continued the business under the name of Parry & Muir. For over twenty years this prominent establishment was well known in Portage and the surrounding countryside.

Dan eventually did get home to spend some time with the family and then returned to Buffalo. In Oberlin, Ohio, he had checked into the possibility of going to college. In the fall he told John he had been doing little botanizing that season. Then he compared his abilities to John's: "I can't and I never did and never will pretend to be able to go on with any study the way you have."[19]

John stayed on at Trout's Hollow for a second winter. At Christmas time, 1865, there was a flurry of letters between him and the family. "I was glad to hear that Dan was visiting so long with you," he wrote his three younger sisters. "I suppose that he told you many a surprising and funny tale of Canada. I think that he can make and enjoy a joke very well indeed. I had a letter from him and he says that he has plenty of money, clothes and hope for the future."

Then he brought up a disturbing thought:

"My picture of home is in my room, and when I see it now I feel sorry at the thought of its being sold. Fountain Lake, Oak Grove, Little Valley, Hickory Hill, etc., with all of their long list of associations, pleasant and otherwise, will soon have passed away and been forgotten."[20] This was the first time anyone had mentioned the ominous possibility of selling Hickory Hill.

In her letter of January 7, 1866, Joanna tried to set John's fears to rest about any possible sale of the farm. "You say you do not like to have Hickory Hill sold but you need not bother yourself . . . for we have not much prospect of having it sold for Father did not agree with the man buying it."[21] She said the three younger girls were happy to be back on the farm going to school together once more.

During the New Year season Anne stayed with Sarah at Fountain Lake while Daniel went to Poynette to visit his friends, the Watsons. She took the opportunity to write her son Dan with the local news.

"David Galloway does not like to live in Portage at all. I would not be surprised to see him back to the farm again."[22] She could understand David's feeling very well, for she remembered how much she disliked living in Portage when she had first moved from the farm.

During his second year at Meaford, John contracted with the Trouts to make 12,000 dozen rakes and turn 30,000 broom handles. According to William Trout, the arrangement stipulated that Muir could improve the machinery as he might determine, and would receive half the economical results in a given period.

"He began with our self-feeding lathe, and by rendering it more completely automatic, he nearly doubled the output of broom handles."[23]

Trout praised the young inventor's work. "It was a delight to see those machines at work. He devised the construction of several automatic machines to make the different parts of the hand rakes.

"The broom handles were turned and stored in every available space about the factory for final seasoning, and a good start made on the rake contract, when one stormy night, near the first of March, 1866, the factory took fire; and sawmill and factory with broom handles and partly manufactured rakes were all completely destroyed, and no insurance." It was devastating.

When an accounting was made after the disaster, all that was left to the firm was a good span of horses and a wagon. The Trouts owed John about three hundred dollars. "After paying him what cash we could scratch up, enough to carry him a good journey into the United States, he cut down the account to 200 dollars, taking our individual promises to pay, each 100 dollars, without time limit and without interest."

Along with Trout's factory, John's first industrial career was wiped out overnight. Not for fourteen years did he call in his notes. And then it was because "he was contemplating marriage . . . he never began to feel poor till he faced the calculations regarding it."[24]

Although his stay in Canada ended all too abruptly, John had gained valuable experience and a firm foundation for his next career venture. In that country he and Dan had shared their mutual interest in botany and the experience of working together. There John received his first taste of factory work and had the opportunity to put his inventive genius to work.

Within a month after the Trout mill fire, John landed in Indianapolis, Indiana, and wrote home to tell his family of his whereabouts. Anne Muir was surprised to receive his March 20, 1866, letter postmarked Indianapolis. Upon learning of the factory disaster, she said she felt sorry for the mill owners.

John had made a careful decision when he relocated. "Looking over the map I saw that Indianapolis was an important railroad center, and probably had manufactories of different sorts in which I could find employment, with the advantage of being in the heart of one of the very richest forests of deciduous hard wood trees on the continent. Here I was successful in gaining employment in a carriage material factory, full of circular saws and chucks [sic] and eccentric and concentric lathes, etc.

"I first worked for ten dollars a week, without board, of course. The second week my wages were increased to eighteen a week, and later to about twenty-five a week. I greatly enjoyed this mechanical work, began to invent and introduce labor-saving improvements and was so successful that my botanical and geological studies were in danger of being seriously interrupted.

"One day a member of the firm asked me, 'How long are you going to stay with us?'

"'Not long,' I said. 'Just long enough to earn a few hundred dollars, then I am going on with my studies in the woods.'

"He said, 'You are doing very well, and if you will stop, we will give you the foremanship of the shop,' and held out hopes of a partnership interest in the money-making business.

"To this I replied that although I liked the inventive work and the earnest rush and roar and whirl of the factory, Nature's attractions were stronger and I must soon get away."[25]

Obviously, since the Trout fire had wiped out his earnings, John needed to earn enough money to pursue future wilderness travel. When he took the Osgood & Smith Company job, he was of two minds. He explained his feelings to Sarah:

"Circumstances over which I have had no control almost compel me to abandon the profession of my choice, and to take up the business of an inventor, and now that I am among machines I begin to feel that I have some talent that way, and so I almost think, unless things change soon, I shall turn my whole mind into that channel.

"I never before felt so utterly *hopeless* as now," he confided. "I do not feel sad, but I cannot find a good boarding place, to say nothing of a home, and so I have not yet unpacked my trunk, and am at any moment as ready to leave this house for a march as were the Israelites while eating the passover. Much as I love the peace and quiet of retirement, I feel something within, some restless fires that urge me in a way very different from my *real* wishes, and I suppose that I am doomed to live in some of these noisy commercial centers."[26]

While momentous changes were taking place in John's life, Sarah and David Galloway also experienced significant change. Anne Muir proved to be right, for David was not happy in town. After moving to

John Muir as a young man. (*State Historical Society of Wisconsin* WHi(X3)5766.)

Left: Tintype of Mary Muir at age 16. (Courtesy, National Park System.)

Bottom left: Daniel Muir, Jr., who became a successful doctor. (Courtesy, National Park System.)

Bottom right: Annie Muir, twin to Mary, as a young woman. (Courtesy, Sherry Hanna.)

David Muir at age 40. (Courtesy, National Park System.)

Joanna Muir in maturity. (Courtesy, Sherry Hanna.)

Memorial marker at John Muir Memorial Park, Marquette County, Wisconsin. (Photograph © Jill Metcoff.)

Portage City the previous fall, he had secured work at a grain elevator, but when the job fell through, he was anxious to return to farming. In mid-May he bought a 160-acre farm, with a small frame house, eight miles north of Portage City. The sellers had already put in thirty acres of wheat, ten of oats, and ten of corn. The Galloways called their new farm Mound Hill. Although Sarah liked the Portage schools, she was content to return to the country.

Feeling so homeless at the moment, John was keenly interested in Sarah's account of the new home. He imagined that Sarah "will have a fine flower garden. . . . Tell Anna and George to make a little garden to Uncle John." He advised David to "make this your fixed home and beautify, improve, and make it in all respects home as fast as possible. . . . I will venture to say that at your time of life under existing circumstances you cannot do better."

John realized how incongruous this advice was to his own situation.

". . . I am myself but a wandering star and move in as crooked an orbit as any star in the sky, but I believe you will admit the soundness of my advice nevertheless."[27]

Anne thought the Galloways' new farm was "a very pleasant place" and wrote of the "large fine orchard with . . . plenty of fruit of different kinds. They have a good school and a public road to it."[28]

During this lonesome time John thought a great deal about his friends and family in Wisconsin. He was concerned about his sister Maggie's "trouble." Chronically ill, Maggie was trying a water cure in Madison to see if it would help her.

Water cures had been in existence in Madison since 1854 when a sixty-room hospital-spa called the Water Cure had been built on the shores of Lake Monona, offering various forms of hydrotherapy. Other less auspicious establishments offered water therapy as well.

Not yet settled in Indianapolis, John found comfort and inspiration in nature. "The forest here is almost in full leaf. I have found wild flowers for more than a month now. I gathered a handful about a mile and a half from town this morning before breakfast. When I first entered the woods and stood among the beautiful flowers and trees of God's own garden, so pure and chaste and lovely, I could not help shedding tears of joy."[29]

On Christmas day, Joanna wrote to Dan from Hickory Hill that she had "been going to school for a few weeks," and was "contented to go to school here instead of Portage."[30]

She finished her letter with news of her father's religious ministry. "We have commenced going to the creek again every two weeks. . . . Father is going to get a grand stove pipe hat from New York. I suppose it will have the desired effect of making him look quite preacherly."

John always encouraged his three younger sisters in their interests and wished them good things in their lives. He recently advised the twins, Mary and Annie, "that now is the time for gathering stores of knowledge."[31]

Mary and Joanna loved beauty and poetry. Mary especially enjoyed sketching. Daniel did not approve.

"I believe we have all at some time been guilty of poetry, *so called*," John once wrote to Mary as he expanded on that subject. "Even merchant matter-of-fact David [Muir] when driving a brisk business in squirrel skins & hickory nuts, and in colt & calf exchange, wrote love songs to Katie Cairns on a stump which his father doubtless meant he should rather be grubbing out by the roots. Yes, we all have rhymed but I never saw a rhyme a Muir had made that was worth half a reading.

"You & I Mary began to sing at the same time of life, and our song was stimulated by the same causes & objects, viz, a shade or so of imagination and lakes, birds, thunderclouds and rabbits.

"Joanna began young. On seeing the hillside by the house covered with yellow solidagos [goldenrods] she broke forth, 'the flowers are very beautiful and *very yellow* too.'

"Marg, Sarah and David began at the pairing season like thrushes and canary birds and ceased at the usual time. Anna will likely whistle about the same time. As for easyminded Dan I believe if he were interrogated concerning the matter he would say with Robie Burns 'I rhyme for fun.'

"Mother made poetry when first acquainted with father and I think that father must have made some verses too. . . ."[32]

As well as writing to his brothers and sisters, John also corresponded with his nieces and nephews. Inspired by their uncle, their interest in nature increased as they grew older.

January, 1867, he wrote to Anna Galloway. "Dear flower loving niece, I have a great many pretty wild flowers to show you someday and I want you to keep some for me. . . . I wish you could come see me. I would learn you to draw pretty pictures and . . . how to find the names of all the trees and flowers and grapes and how to love them.[33]

As time passed, John began to feel more at home in Indianapolis. He was making great strides in his work in the factory, setting up new machinery to produce the carriage wheel parts. He drew a chart of detailed studies he made of three elements of factory operation: Chart of one days labor, Plan of sawyers end of shop, and Money profit chart of sawyers end of shop. His analysis of operations at Osgood & Smith was a forerunner of modern time-study.[34]

Under the heading, "Chart of one days labor," he drew a curve representing the results of work done throughout the day. His accompanying comments went straight to the point.

"The work-line B. C. begins in the morning far too low on account of disinclination [of the men] to take hold of work on a cold morning when no person capable of aiding in overcoming it is at hand. Also on account of the work not having been left in the easiest starting shape the preceding evening."

Muir drew a sharp upward projection of the chart's work line to represent a spurt of work on the part of the men when the masters passed through the shop. He felt this was inexcusable. He thought the workers should work well between times too. He noted: "Also at four o'clock there is an abrupt fall when lamps are lighted. Lamplighted labor is not worth more than two thirds daylight labor."

He concluded that "The grand central difficulty both with respect to the man and machine labor of this factory is lack of unity. Here is not one large and whole factory, but many small and incomplete ones."

He also concluded that presently all are work guardians of one another, that they stop to council with one another on how a job should be done. "It is self evident that one mind should direct—should do all the stopping-should weigh, deliberate, hesitate for all-any other condition of things is most preposterous in an establishment so complicated in its workings."

". . . in the departments of good factories no man or machine worketh to itself. The effects of but few delays and jars do not terminate where they begin, but are transmitted from operation to operation . . . which with most things produced here, are dependent on each other like the series of events connected with 'the house that Jack built.'"

In his plan for the "sawyers end of the shop", Muir drew an efficient layout designed to have everything in its proper place throughout the shop. He felt that one important key to a smooth-running factory was the efficient handling of the lumber. Muir suggested that instead of merely piling the planks in the yard when they were brought in, the men should unload them on plank tables within reach of the workers. This would eliminate "all fumbling, tumbling and hesitancy which last is the greatest of all factory time killers." Muir carried the plans for handling the wood all the way through the shop to using the refuse for firewood.

His third chart, labeled "Money profit chart of sawyers end of shop," showed that a well planned shop layout with its materials well organized throughout the operation would result in an "area of attainable profit" more than double the "area of actual profit." In dealing with the wood strips, Muir said profits would increase if the confusion and delays in the bending room could be eliminated with "half the forecast of a harvest mouse."

As at Trout's broom and rake factory in Canada the year before, Muir was once again fully immersed in methods and inventions to make a factory hum. Once again disaster brought him to a halt. It happened March 5, 1867.

Years later he wrote of the accident:

"I had put in a countershaft for a new circular saw and as the belt connecting with the main shaft was new it stretched considerably after running a few hours and had to be shortened. While I was unlacing it, making use of the nail like end of a file to draw out the stitches, it slipped and pierced my right eye on the edge of the cornea.

"After the first shock was over I closed my eye, and when I lifted the lid of the injured one the aqueous humor dripped on my hand— the sight gradually failed and in a few minutes came perfect darkness.

"'My right eye is gone,' I murmured, 'closed forever on all God's beauty.'

"At first I felt no particular weakness. I walked steadily enough to the house where I was boarding, but in a few hours the shock sent me trembling to bed, and very soon by sympathy the other eye became blind so that I was in total darkness and feared that I would become permanently blind."[35]

By way of a letter, Dr. Butler had earlier introduced John to his Indianapolis friends, the Merrills. Catherine Merrill brought an occulist to examine him. The doctor gave him the encouraging news that the aqueous humor would be restored, and that after the inflammation went down and the nerve shock overcome, he would be able to see about as well as ever after two or three months in a dark room.

"You have, of course, heard of my calamity," John wrote April 3, 1867, to his good friend Jeanne Carr. "The sunshine and the winds are working in all the gardens of God, but I—I am lost. I am shut in darkness. My hard, toil-tempered muscles have disappeared, and I am feeble and tremulous as an ever-sick woman.

"Please tell the Butlers that their precious sympathy has reached me. . . . My friends here are kind beyond what I can tell and do much to shorten my immense blank days."[36]

Jeanne Carr was concerned and supportive, and Muir was comforted by her encouraging and inspirational letters. "I cannot make sentences that will tell how much I feel indebted to you, . . ." he wrote April 6. "I believe with you that 'nothing is without meaning and purpose that comes from a Father's hand,' but during these dark weeks I could not feel this, and, as for courage and fortitude, scarce the shadows of these virtues where left me. The shock upon my nervous system made me weak in mind as a child."[37]

When the family received John's poignant letters about the accident they all rallied around him. He wrote them in almost total darkness, and his faltering script went uphill and downhill on the paper.

On April 12, he told Sarah and David about the first awful moments when darkness engulfed him.

"I could gladly have died where I stood, because I thought I never would have heart to look at the flowers and fields again."[38]

David Muir urged John to come to his home in Portage until he got well and promised to go to Indianapolis to get him.

Mary sent him one of her poems and some flowers. "Anna picked these windflowers [pasque flowers] two or three days ago, and we pressed them for you. They are the first we have seen this spring."[39] She told her brother she had taken teaching examinations in both Marquette County and Columbia County and signed a contract to teach at Graham's district school near Hickory Hill. All three of the younger Muir girls received teaching certificates.

Dan came to Indianapolis to visit his brother and urged him to leave the dirty, dusty city and come to Avery.

As the weeks passed, John's eyesight slowly improved and he regained some strength. Many visitors came to the William Sutherland home where he lived to cheer him, including Judson Osgood and Samuel Smith, owners of the carriage wheel factory. The Sutherland children came often. Miss Merrill and her sisters read to him as did her nephew, Merrill Moores. The children gathered early spring wildflowers for him and listened to his wonderful stories.

Finally, about a month after the disaster, Muir recovered enough strength to walk to the woods. "A little messenger met me with your letter of April 8th when I was on my way to the woods for the first time," he wrote Jeanne Carr May 2. "I read it upon a moss-clad fallen tree. . . . I will not try to tell you how much I enjoyed this walk after four weeks in bed."

He said he was happy to see his plant friends—violets, bloodroot, and meadowrue.

"The red maple was in full flower glory; the leaves below and the mosses were bright with its fallen scarlet blossoms . . ."[40]

As spring progressed, Muir began to feel better and his thoughts turned toward home. On June 7 he wrote to Sarah and David Galloway:

"I am coming home in a few weeks accompanied by a little friend of mine eleven years of age. . . . Merrill Moores and he belongs to that family that cared for me when I was in the dark.

"We may stay with you a week or two to gather flowers and strength for he is wearied with his school books and I with sickness. . . . I feel you will give him a cordial Scotch welcome for my sake."[41] The most welcome news was that his eye was improved.

On June 9 he wrote again to Jeanne Carr:

"I am not well enough to work and I cannot sit still; I have been reading and botanizing for some weeks, and I find that for such work I am very much disabled.

"I leave this city for home tomorrow accompanied by a little friend . . . We will go to Decatur, Ill., thence northward through the wide prairies, botanizing a few weeks by the way. We hope to spend a few days in Madison, and I promise myself a great deal of pleasure. . . .

"I am very happy with the thought of so soon seeing my Madison friends, and Madison, and the plants of Madison, and yours."[42]

Within a month he was home at last with Sarah and David at Mound Hill Farm. He could now see their "fixed home" for himself and roam about the farm while he recovered more fully from his accident.

In the course of his rambles with Merrill and the Galloways, Muir came upon a glacial pond over the hill from the house—Fern Lake. Sarah Galloway's daughter Cecelia later described the little gem as a cold pool, always filled with water, with no outlet or inlet, encircled with reeds, cattails, and blackberry vines. She said that royal ferns grew almost as high as her head on the steep slopes surrounding the pool like people in a theater looking down upon the water.

On July 12 Muir wrote to his Indianapolis friends, Janet and Chris Moores:

"... Last evening M.[errill] and I took a walk to the [Indian] mound on the hill. It was a fine evening—the clouds which attended the sunset were grandly colored, those to the east were like wool, but toward the west were laid in level layers at the bottom with high banks and broken rocky blocks piled on top. We could see beautiful waving, swelling green hills wherever we turned ... green, smooth hills that walled in the hollow and at those that were blue and far away and at the mound and the Fox River and the sky."[43]

He commented on the ripe raspberries and the wild strawberries and said that he was going up to his father's at Hickory Hill again in a few days.

With renewed joy, John drank deeply of the sights and sounds of the landscape he explored as a youth. He showed Merrill, who was the same age John was when he first arrived in Marquette County, many of his favorite places. All along the way he gathered fine plant specimens for his herbarium. They explored Wolf Hill where John had shot the wolf with John McReath and they climbed the Observatory. Once more he enjoyed the rhyolite promontory with its cedars and rock ferns at the top, and its slopes covered with white oaks and black oaks. They tramped through the ravines and especially admired the one that was "evidently scooped out for a fern garden. One hundred and twenty thousand of my favorite Osmundas live there, all regularly planted at regular distances.

"The highest point commands a landscape circle of about one thousand square miles, composed of about ten or twelve miles of the Fox River, Lake Puckawa and five or six nameless little lakes—marsh and woodland exquisitely arranged and joined—and about two hundred hills, and some prairie. Ah! these are the gardens for me! There is landscape gardening."[44]

"I am enjoying myself exceedingly," he wrote to Jeanne Carr. "The dear flowers of Wisconsin are incomparably more numerous than those of Canada or Indiana. With what fervid, unspeakable joy did I welcome those flowers that I have loved so long! Hundreds grow in the full light of our opening that I have not seen since leaving home. In company with my little friend I visited Muir's Lake. We approached it by a ravine in the principal hills that belong to it. We emerged from the leafy oaks, and it came in full view all unchanged, sparkling and clear, with its edging of rushes and lilies. And there, too, was the meadow, with its brook and willows, and all the well-known nooks of its winding border where many a moss and fern find home. I held these poor eyes to the dear scene and it reached me once more in its fullest glory."[45]

One August day John stayed at the Mound Hill farmhouse to sort his specimens. David Galloway was cutting wheat while his daughter Anna wrote a letter to her Uncle Dan.

"Uncle John is fixing his plants today. He has gathered a great many around here. He has some very pretty specimens."[46]

On August 8, 1867, Sarah informed Dan that the extremely pleasant visit with John would be finished all too soon. "He is in Portage just now visiting with Maggie and David. I expect him one more night before he leaves."[47]

So John's visit in Marquette County and Portage with his friends and family had come to an end. There was no more time to savor the landscape of his youth. Although Osgood & Smith had offered him a partnership and a share of the firm's profits, he could not return to the roar of the machines. The tragic accident had decided his life course. His future did not lie in the city factory, but in nature. Four years later he expressed thoughts in his notebook that were central to his being and foretold all his life to come:

"I will follow my instincts, be myself for good or ill, and see what will be the upshot. As long as I live, I'll hear waterfalls and birds and winds sing. I'll interpret the rocks, learn the language of flood, storm, and avalanche. I'll acquaint myself with the glaciers and wild gardens, and get as near the heart of the world as I can."[48]

# VIII

# THE HEART OF MUIR'S WORLD

*. . . it was by far the grandest of all the special*
*temples of Nature I was ever permitted to enter.*
*It must be the sanctum sanctorum of the Sierras.*
                                        —John Muir

A few miles south of Louisville, John Muir spread out his map under a tree and planned a foot journey through Kentucky, Tennessee, Georgia, Florida, and the Gulf of Mexico. He was thankful that his eye had healed, his health was restored, and he was free to tramp the wilderness. It was the second of September, 1867.

He had said goodbye to his friends and relatives in Marquette and Columbia counties; he had spent a week in Madison visiting with friends and botanizing with the Carrs; he had dropped off Merrill Moores in Indianapolis and made the rounds of his friends there. Then he boarded the train for Jeffersonville, Indiana, across the Ohio River from Louisville, Kentucky.

The accident and the roar of machines were behind him. Before him lay the woods and gardens of the south. As he sat beneath the trees contemplating his route through the southeastern states, he felt once again the loneliness of leaving family and friends. As he had written Dan the day before, he felt "touches of the old depressing melancholy which always comes when I leave friends for strangers," but he still anticipated "a great deal of pleasure from this walk."[1]

"Folding my map, I shouldered my little bag and plant press and strode away among the old Kentucky oaks, rejoicing in splendid visions of palms and tropic flowers in glorious array . . ."[2] Thus, John began his thousand-mile walk to the Gulf of Mexico.

He tramped through the "happy abounding beauty of Kentucky."[3] A few miles after he crossed the Tennessee border he "began the ascent of the Cumberland Mountains, the first real mountains that my foot ever touched or eyes beheld." He "reached the summit in six or seven hours a—strangely long period of up-grade work to one accustomed to the hillocky lands of Wisconsin . . ."[4] As he walked, he noted every landscape feature and marveled at the vistas.

On the eastern slope of the Cumberlands he "crossed a wide, cool stream, a branch of the Clinch River. There is nothing more eloquent in nature than a mountain stream, and this is the first I ever saw."[5]

All along the way, in contrast to the beauty surrounding him, Muir witnessed the "seal of war on all things."[6] His travel accounts described rickety villages and poor, filthy living conditions. He told of people whose grim faces showed the effect of the devastating war just past. He often met small bands of plunderers. Although he preferred to sleep outdoors, he had promised his mother to sleep indoors as much as possible. Consequently, he stayed in a number of shabby homes. It was an unsettled time, but Muir was not afraid at first.

He studied the hundreds of plants he met on the trail and noted in his journal that "These mountains are highways on which northern plants may extend their colonies southward."[7] He found that on the southern slopes of the Alleghenies, "the greatest number of hardy, enterprising representatives of the two climates are assembled."[8] In the mountains John was accompanied by familiar plant friends. As he walked farther south new plants constantly appeared, until, finally, all his old friends disappeared.

Muir pressed many specimens on his plant press. At Kingston, Tennessee he sent the first of his plant collections by express to his brother David in Portage.

On October 8, 1867, he reached Savannah, Georgia, almost penniless. The money he had asked David to send him there had not yet arrived at the express office and he needed to wait for it. He walked along a shell road three or four miles out of town and found his way to the Bonaventure graveyard located along a stream. In an isolated section, he made a hut in a dense thicket of sparkleberry bushes near an avenue of live oaks. Safe from maurauders, he lived for six days by the salt marshes and islands of the river where reeds and sedges and bird life abounded. "Bonaventure to me is one of the most impressive assemblages of animal and plant creatures I ever met."[9]

When the money from David finally arrived, John immediately booked passage on the Sylvan Shore sailing southward along the Atlantic coast. Debarking at Fernandina, Florida, he began his foot journey across the peninsula along the tracks of the Florida Railroad completed over the swamps just a few years before. By walking these tracks he managed to keep dry unless he waded into the water in search of plants. Discovering his first palmetto was a notable event.

Finally, he reached Cedar Keys on the Gulf of Mexico and on October 23 he noted in his journal:

"Today I reached the sea. While I was yet many miles back in the palmy woods, I caught a scent of the salt sea breeze which, although I had so many years lived far from sea breezes, suddenly conjured up Dunbar, its rocky coast, winds and waves; and my whole childhood, that seemed to have utterly vanished in the New World, was now restored amid the Florida woods by that one breath from the sea. Forgotten were the palms and magnolias and the thousand flowers that enclosed me. I could see only dulse and tangle, long-winged gulls, the Bass Rock in the Firth of Firth, and the old castle, schools, churches, and long country rambles in search of bird's nests."[10]

For about the next two months Muir lived on beautiful Cedar Key where he secured work at Hodgson's sawmill. His enjoyment of the island and the gulf was marred by a long illness, thought to be malaria, but he was well looked after by Mr. and Mrs. Hodgson in their home.

Upon his recovery he set sail on the "Island Belle" for Cuba where he spent about a month. The captain allowed him to stay aboard ship while they were in port. Not yet well enough to do much hardy exploring, he walked the beaches within range of the schooner. For some time his family did not receive his letters.

The Muirs occasionally lived through long, anxious periods when they did not know John's whereabouts. Since they had not heard from him for so long, they were particularly worried about him on this trip. Although he always wrote faithfully along the way to inform his family where he was and where to next send their letters, there were often long mail delays. Likewise, he occasionally waited for days at some post offices to receive word from home, or the money he requested.

Toward the end of February he sailed from Cuba on the trim little orange-laden steamer, "Santiago de Cuba," and docked in New York about the first of March.

"I arrived here from Cuba a few days ago. . . . I start for "California weeds and trees next Thursday,"[11] Muir wrote David from New York Harbor, March 3, 1868. He acknowledged receiving the $150 money packet his brother sent to Cuba.

Two weeks later Sarah wrote from Mound Hill that she was thankful to know his whereabouts and that Mother "was wearying very much for word from you."[12]

The preceding fall John had sent by express to David Muir, from Savannah, the balance of the plant specimens he had collected on his walk through the southeastern states. He gave explicit instructions as to their care.

"Please give them to Sarah to [take] care of until I return. Tell her to keep them dry and away from rats and if you or any of you open them to look at them please be extremely careful to avoid mixing or misplacing them."[13]

Interested in botany herself, Sarah, in her March letter, turned her attention to her brother's herbarium.

"I looked over your parcel of Florida plants and exceedingly admired your ferns. What a splendid variety you have got. Your Cuba ones have not arrived yet."

Sarah had painstakingly tended his increasing plant collection. She informed him that according to a new photography book she had heard of dried specimens could be used as negatives and a perfect picture produced. She thought this method could be an advantage to botanists—

that John could have a large book with the picture of one of his pets on every page along with its description.

Going on to family news, she told John about the new barn David was building at Mound Hill.

"David has been very busy this winter. He has got about all the lumber hauled for his little barn and has let the job. He had a stumping machine to work on the farm last fall. He has got all the stumps pulled on the broken land except a very few. He is busy today drawing them into a fence."

She recounted her younger sisters' school activities.

"Mary is still staying with Maggie [in Portage]. She has been out of school part of the time this winter but she keeps steadily at her music lessons. Her teacher told me that she was getting along very well and that she was way ahead of others of her scholars, she was so studious.

"Annie's school was out last Saturday, but I have not seen her since she got through." Earlier her mother had explained that Annie taught forty-three scholars and got along with them very well.

"Joanna feels pretty lonesome this winter," Sarah continued. "She went to school part of the time but could not go steadily because of the roads." The winter's deep snow made it difficult for Joanna to walk over the hill to the schoolhouse.

"Maggie is about her usual and John [Reid] is in the old place. David [Muir] has moved to another house [in Portage]."[14]

When he was in Cuba, John made the decision to move on to California, and in New York he booked passage on the steamship "Nebraska." He waited around the harbor for ten days waiting for the ship to sail, not daring to go very far away for fear of getting lost. He bought a pocket map of California to familiarize himself with the state and to plot his course from San Francisco. He was especially interested in the Yosemite Valley.

He had enjoyed the journey from Cuba on the "Santiago de Cuba," but traveling steerage on the "Nebraska" down the eastern seaboard was quite a different story. "There was a savage contrast between life in the steerage and my fine home on the little [fruit] ship . . . ," he recounted years later.[15]

John crossed the Isthmus of Pananma and booked passage on a ship heading up the Pacific coast. It tied up to the San Francisco dock March 28, 1868. On shipboard Muir met a young Englishmen by the name of Chilwell who was enthusiastic about exploring with him. Muir called him a most amusing and faithful companion. The two men stayed just one day in San Francisco before heading into open country.

They crossed San Francisco Bay on the Oakland ferry and struck out on foot in a southeasterly direction through the Santa Clara Valley along the Diablo foothills to Gilroy. They then walked through the Diablo mountain range by way of Pacheco Pass.

"At the top of the Pass I obtained my first view of the San Joachin plain and the glorious Sierra Nevada . . . extending north and south as far as I could see lay a vast level flower garden, smooth and level like a lake of gold—the floweriest part of the world I had yet seen. From the eastern margin of the golden plain arose the white Sierra."[16] Jubilantly, Muir and Chilwell descended into California's central valley.

Reveling in a botanical paradise, John described for Jeanne Carr the vast assemblies of flowers he saw. He said he examined hundreds and hundreds of blossoms, and listed them in their orders. Since he had no book to help him identify the flowers, he described their growth patterns and colors in minute detail.

"Crossing this greatest of flower gardens and the San Joaquin River at Hill's Ferry, we followed the Merced River, which I knew drained Yosemite Valley, and ascended the [Sierra] foothills from Snelling by way of Coulterville. . . . At the little mining town of Coulterville we bought flour and tea and made inquiries about roads and trails, and the forests we would have to pass through."[17] So began Muir's first adventure into the Sierra Nevada.

After roaming a month in the wonderful Yosemite region, the young men returned to the San Joaquin plain. In Hopeton they secured work in a harvest field.

"This Yosemite trip only made me hungry for another far longer and farther reaching, and I determined to set out again as soon as I had earned a little money to get near views of the mountains in all their snowy grandeur, and study the wonderful forests . . ."[18]

While John explored in the midst of all this glory, there was another long mail delay. Once again his family was alarmed for they did not know if he had actually arrived in San Francisco as he had planned. When the long-awaited letter finally arrived, Anne Muir sent a heartfelt reply from Hickory Hill.

"Words cannot express my feelings when I received your letter of June 10th. We were all thoroughly alarmed for your safey, as so many letters were sent to San Francisco and found no owner."[19]

Knowing that John was safe, the family went on more happily with their busy farm summer in Marquette County. On the Fourth of July they all went to the large church picnic held in the grove near Dates Mill a few miles west of Hickory Hill. Four or five area Sabbath schools attended the picnic by the millpond.

Anne said that Maggie, Sarah, David and their families, and Mary, Annie, and Joanna all got together and greatly enjoyed themselves. Joanna was teaching in the McKay district, but Anne and Daniel drove over to bring her home on Fridays so she could be at home a good part of the time.

All three girls taught in district schools that summer. Annie and Joanna's schools would be out soon, while Mary's school had let out the previous Thursday.

In a letter to Dan in Michigan, July 12, Sarah said how much Mary enjoyed her school. "She means to pick hops, be very saving and try to go to the Madison University the coming winter."

She described the new barn, now finished. David "has got a nice little barn built and painted. He has also got his clover and timothy hay into it and I tell you he feels pleased over it.

"We are having a long hot spell. The thermometer has been at 100 and 103 in the shade. The heat is hurrying things along so much that harvest will be earlier than usual. The Orchard and other crops look very well but we are troubled a good deal with potato bugs.

"Mother had a currant loaf made to celebrate your birthday," she continued. "A small thing, a currant loaf, but it is the loving remembrance. It happened to be two days before your birthday, but she thought if she waited till Monday there would be no one there to eat it but Father and herself. She seemed glad to think we were there to eat a piece of your loaf."

Sarah told of her mother's long-standing custom of baking currant loaves or scones to celebrate her children's birthdays, whether they could be home or not. On this occasion she baked currant loaves in honor of Dan's 25th birthday, but she baked them on John's birthdays as well.

"Father still thinks of selling [Hickory Hill]," she added, "but whether he will get a buyer or not is a problem."[20]

That summer, Mary carried out her plan to earn money by picking hops. Her twin sister Annie, and Joanna also worked in the hopyards, while Sarah's daughter Anna picked in a yard by the Galloway farm.

In October, 1868, Anne filled Dan in about the hop-raising in the neighborhood. "A great many of our neighbors have commenced to grow hops—so there are hop yards and hop houses in every direction—although they are rather discouraged this year. The prices are so low. A great many do not approve of the business at all.

"Our orchard has done well this year. We had about 70 bushels of apples. They were very large and looked beautiful.

"Your father has got the farm this year and he is busy ploughing and grubbing and pulling stumps and doing it all himself so far—he talks of hiring one or two choppers through the winter. He says he feels strong and healthy and appears to be.

"All the girls have left home and your father has hired a girl to do the work." She said the Muir girls were boarding with their brother David in Portage.

Anne ended her letter philosophically.

"These are great changes. I feel them to be so. We are apt to forget that we live in a world of changes, but time brings changes to us all."[21]

As for John, he was doing odd farm jobs on San Joachin valley ranches that summer. In late fall he hired on to herd sheep for a man called Smoky Jack. During the next five months he lived in a filthy cabin two miles from Snelling and learned how to manage the movements of about eighteen hundred sheep as they munched their way around the hillsides and valleys.

As John tended the sheep his eyes beheld the beauty around him—the cloud formations, the plants, animals and birds. He explored every inch of the hilly range and pressed many plant specimens. In the afternoon he would read or sketch the landscape.

To Jeanne Carr he wrote, "The Merced pours past me on the south from the Yosemite; smooth, domy hills and the tree fringe of the Tuolumne [River] bound me on the north; the lordly Sierras join sky and plain on the east; and the far coast mountains on the west. . . . I have abundant opportunities for reading and botanizing."[22]

By early April, the Wisconsin winter had not yet released its cold grip, but there were hints of spring around the countryside. Mary wrote her brother from Mound Hill where she was visiting Sarah and David Galloway.

"Warm spring breezes will soon awake to life and beauty the tender plants—even now I hear the [red-winged] blackbirds sing most merrily, although as yet the ground is covered with snow, having had quite a snow storm last week."[23]

Mary was deciding how to spend her summer. She thought she might stay with Sarah and David for a few weeks. She really didn't want to do farm work or pick hops but would rather spend time taking sketches and giving drawing lessons and teaching school.

From afar John carefully considered Mary's future. He said he didn't think she could make a living doing sketches and advised her to teach. He had faith in his sister's ability. ". . . I do not know of any business that would suit you better. I think that after you have practiced music & drawing sufficiently you will find the work of teaching these branches very pleasant & also very renumerative. You certainly have more than ordinary talent in both these branches of education & will I think eventually find a situation as teacher that will just suit you. . . . I think that you would do well to acquire a good knowledge of botany with a view to teaching it."

You will "escape martyrdom of such institutions [as district schools] when you are qualified for a higher place. . . . Madison is what you require." He told her she would gain knowledge at the University. Sometime earlier he had said that now is the golden time to gather stores of knowledge.

He stood ready to back up his advice. "If David has any of my money you and Anna can take it and go [to school] when you wish or let me know and I will send you some."[24]

The family was growing. David and Katie Muir recently welcomed a new baby. John referred to the event in a note to Dan from the Sierra foothills near La Grange:

"I am glad to hear that unto David a son is born. . . . I have always maintained that the Scotch are the salt of the earth. I rejoice in the birth of every Scot in general and every Muir in particular."

He said he was glad Dan had discovered both the medical profession and a girl. He went on to tell about his mountain explorations. "I might preach nature like an apostle,"[25] he said.

John was now sending Sarah beautiful specimens of California flowers and plants. He sent a fern to his niece Anna who was taking more and more interest in plants.

"The little fern arrived safely without being crushed or broken," Anna informed him. "I think it is very pretty. I will gather the flowers you spoke of and send [them] as soon as I can."[26]

In May, when the weather became oppressively hot in the central valley and the grasses were parched, John longed to go back into the mountains. In an unpublished manuscript he wrote, "When the heavy snows were melting in the spring sunshine, opening the way to the summits of the Range, and I was trying to plan a summer's excursion into their midst, wondering how I could possibly carry food to last a whole summer, Mr. Delaney, a neighbor of Smoky Jack's, noticing my love of plants and seeing some of the drawings I had made in my notebooks, urged me to go to the mountains with his flock . . . to see that the shepherd did his duties. He offered to carry my plant press and blankets, allow me to make his mountain camps my headquarters while I was studying the adjacent mountains, and perfect freedom to pursue my studies, and offering to pay me besides . . ."[27] John happily accepted the offer.

The plan was to move the sheep higher and higher up the mountains as the snows melted, till the party reached the headwaters of the Merced and Tuolumne Rivers. They would stop at the best grazing places for a few weeks at a time and Muir would then make explorations from the base camps.

On July 15, 1869, the group set up camp on Yosemite's north wall, two miles from the brink overlooking the valley. John was delighted with the site, for it was the very region he was anxious to explore. For nearly three weeks, with his notebook fastened to his belt, "I wandered among the valley domes & falls sketching & absorbing the inexhaustible treasuries of glory that are gathered here."[28]

One day, "Following the ridge, which made a gradual descent to the south, I came at length to the brow of that massive cliff that stands between Indian Cañon and Yosemite Falls, and here the far-famed valley came suddenly into view throughout almost its whole extent. The noble walls—sculptured into endless variety of domes and gables, spires and battlements and plain mural precipices—all a-tremble with the thunder tones of the falling water. The level bottom seemed to be dressed like a garden—sunny meadows here and there, groves of pine and oak; the river of Mercy sweeping in majesty through the midst of them and flashing back the sunbeams. The great Tissiack, or Half-Dome, rising at the upper end of the valley to a height of nearly a mile . . . the most impressive of all the rocks . . . marvelous cliffs, marvelous in sheer dizzy depth and sculpture, types of endurance. Thousands of years have they stood in the sky exposed to rain, snow, frost, earthquake and avalanche, yet they still wear the bloom of youth."[29]

At the previous camp, Don Delaney had brought John a letter from his beloved Wisconsin University professor, James Davie Butler. When his student was leaving the university in 1863, Butler had said, "Now John, I want to hold you in sight and watch your career. Promise to write me at last once a year."[30]

John did indeed keep in touch with the Butlers. He would always be grateful for their kindness during his Indianapolis accident, and before he left Wisconsin for good he enjoyed a memorable visit with them in Madison. In this recent letter Butler informed John that he was coming to California to visit a sister-in-law in San Jose. There was no mention of a visit to Yosemite, a plan that came about spontaneously later in the trip. Engaged in his sheep responsibilities and exploring, John had no expectation of seeing his good friend from university days.

On August 2, 1869, he settled himself for a day's sketching atop North Dome overlooking Yosemite Valley. He attempted to sketch every tree and every line and feature of the rocks of the spectacular valley vista. About four or five o'clock in the afternoon, he was suddenly seized with a strong feeling that Professor Butler was below him in the valley. He felt Butler's presence in a "strange, telepathic way,"[31] as if his friend touched him.

Muir sprang up and looked for a way down into the valley, but darkness was fast approaching. The next morning, dressed in clean clothes, he made his way down Indian Cañon and onto the valley floor. He went to the Hutchings Hotel, and checking the register, was thrilled to find the name of Jas. D. Butler, Madison, Wisconsin, written there.

"I could scarce believe my eyes & read the precious words over and over & at last got faith to believe that after two long cold years of isolation, a friend was really near in the flesh & that my eyes would be blessed that very day with light from a familiar face & I started from the house in pursuit."[32]

Upon learning that the professor and his company were traveling the valley to Vernal and Nevada Falls, Muir hastened after them. At Vernal Falls he caught up with Butler's companion, General Alvord. When he learned that Butler was climbing Mount Broderick beyond the falls he hastened upward to waylay him on the trail near the Nevada Rapids. He found that Butler and his climbing partner were lost and needed guidance to get back to their party. Butler and Muir had an exciting reunion.

With Butler on horseback, and John hurrying along beside him, the two men reminisced all the way back to the hotel. They talked of school days, of friends in Madison, of the students, and how each had prospered.

"He was weary with his day of hard climbing but was very cheerful nevertheless & on the way to the hotel gleaned delightful handfulls [sic] for me from the Poets & marked upon the surpassing glories of YoSemite [sic]."[33]

Muir passed a wonderfully stimulating evening at the hotel with Butler and the others gathered there. Everyone was intrigued with John's telepathic experience. When Muir compared notes with Butler it turned out that the professor was passing the sheer granite face of El Capitan just below John when he felt his presence.

Muir was disappointed that Butler must leave Yosemite the next morning in "scandalous haste urged by that man of war who is governed like a machine by military chronometers."[34] Hungry for the companionship of an old friend, he wanted Butler to stay two or three weeks. Muir was glad he himself wasn't "great enough to be missed in the busy world." But he was very happy that he acted on "the most unexplainable notion that ever struck me." He returned to the sheep camp rejoicing in his rare experience with Dr. James Davie Butler.

For a little longer, John continued his studies and sketching from the camp above Yosemite Valley. He knew now he must seek out the secrets of the valley and its environs. "I determined to return to it again and again if I was able."[35]

The last paragraph of *My First Summer in the Sierra* reads:

"Here ends my forever memorable first High Sierra excursion. I have crossed the Range of Light, surely the brightest and best of all the Lord has built; and rejoicing in its glory, I gladly, gratefully, hopefully pray I may see it again."[36]

Muir did indeed see the mountains and the Yosemite again. For the next ten years the valley would be his home base for a comprehensive exploration of the region and would be central to his life for all the years to come. In a real sense he had come home. He had found the heart of his world.

# IX

# A BIT OF WISCONSIN LANDSCAPE

*It is a splendid garden and I wish that I could*
*send a portion of myself to guard it*
—John Muir

"I was over at Hickory Hill a short time ago—the house seems so still, all of the girls being gone," Sarah wrote to Dan, October 3, 1869. "Still Mother seems to enjoy herself pretty well. She has a good girl and nothing in the way of work to distract her.

"[Father] is as busy as ever again. Up in the morning early, breakfast about six o'clock and works continuingly the day long. He has bought forty sheep from David and seems much pleased with the idea of having them to care for.

". . . David hired a boy for three months this fall and started off with John Reid to buy cattle for shipping to Chicago. The first carload proved rather an unsuccessful speculation and David has returned quietly to farming again."[1]

The Hickory Hill crops were all in and another farm season had come to a close. "David Muir and John Reid were here doing harvest and worked hard for a week," Anne Muir informed John in November. "Now we have only one man helping to build fences and I have a girl to do the work, so we get along very well."[2]

The family was scattered. Dan was studying medicine at Michigan University in Ann Arbor; Joanna signed a contract to teach in District School No. 3 near the Galloways and was boarding in Portage; Annieix was teaching in Whitman's school in Oconomowoc; and Mary was again enrolled in the university at Madison.

Anne noted the many changes that had taken place in the twenty years since the Muirs came to Marquette County.

"Nearly all the farmers around here have now all good frame houses and are very well off.The Presbyterians have got up a nice church near the graveyard . . ."[3] She was referring to the United Presbyterian Church standing near Sutfin's farm. A number of old settlers had died recently and there were many new graves in the cemetery behind the church. Anne added that the Methodists put up a church on the school section.

"The 9th of this month is the anniversary of my arrival at Fountain Lake twenty years ago," Anne reminisced a few days later. "How glad I was to meet you and the others after such a long journey. Many changes have passed over us since then and many blessings have been showered upon us since then and many blessings have been showered upon us as a family though distant from each other.

"It seems a very long time indeed since we had the pleasure of seeing you. Still I anticipate a happy reunion with each of you bye and bye."

After reading John's mountain accounts, Anne Muir was beginning to understand what her son was trying to accomplish.

"Your enjoyment of the beauties of Calif. are shared by me, as I take much pleasure in reading your accounts of the country around you. You have my best wishes and prayers that you may be protected and preserved in all your journeyings on earth and at last find a happy home in the mansions of glory forever.

Farewell dear John from your affectionate Mother"[4]

As he roamed the upper reaches of theYosemiteValley region with Delaney's sheep that first summer in the Sierra, John had indeed found Heaven on earth.

Upon his return to the San Joachin plain at La Grange, he worked for several weeks at the Delaney ranch. He yearned to return toYosemite. In November he and a young man, Harry Randall, arrived at the Hutchings Hotel near the Yosemite Falls where he had sought out Professor Butler the summer before. James M. Hutchings hired them to help around the place during the coming winter. Their job was to build a sawmill and cut lumber to erect cottages in the spring.The lumber would be obtained from pines brought down in a violent windstorm. Muir was ecstatic at the thought of spending a mountain winter in Yosemite.

He described the cabin he and Harry built for themselves near the Hutchings' winter home.

"This cabin, I think, was the handsomest building in the Valley, and the most useful and convenient for a mountaineer. From the Yosemite Creek where it first gathers its beaten waters at the foot of the fall, I dug a small ditch and brought a stream into the cabin, entering at one end and flowing out the other with just current enough to allow it to sing and warble in low, sweet tones, delightful at night while I lay in bed. The floor was made of rough slabs, nicely joined and embedded in the ground. In the spring the common pteris ferns pushed up between the joints of the slabs . . ."[5]

No matter how grand his California setting, John still maintained a keen interest in the welfare of his Wisconsin family.

On March 20, 1870, he wrote to his brother David who was still working hard to make a success of the Parry & Muir store in Portage.

"Your last of January 6th reached me here in the rocks two weeks ago . . . I am sitting here in a little shanty made of sugar pine shingles this sabbath evening. I have not been at church a single time since leaving home. Yet this glorious valley might well be called a church.

"Your description of the sad, quiet and deserted loneliness of home made me sorry, and I felt like returning to the old farm to take care of father and mother myself in their old days, but a little reflection served to show that of all the family, my views and habits and disposition made me the most incapable for the task."[6]

Going on to practical matters, he told David that his money receipts were all right. John and David had begun the practice of helping family members financially when the need arose. John sent money to David, who, acting as his brother's banker, would disburse funds as John directed.

John took special interest in Dan's and his younger sisters' education. On February 15, 1870, he sent David $350 toward their expenses.

He said he planned to send more the following fall to help Dan through medical school at Michigan University.

John felt a sense of kinship with his sister Mary as she eagerly sought knowledge at Wisconsin University. He was reminded of his own experiences in Madison nine years before.

"What do you think of Lake Mendota in these quiet, sunny evenings," he asked her from Yosemite Valley in March, 1870. "I used to walk around Lake Monona every Saturday for plants.

"David will send you some of my money any time you write for it and next fall I will send you as much as you will require for a year at least."[7]

"I will have about a thousand dollars in the fall," John informed David a few weeks later. "I may need one or two hundred doll[ars] myself and I promised to let Mary have enough to keep her at Madison a year or so if she wishes it, and you may have the rest. Dan or the girls may want some of it, and if in the course of human events I be overtaken with calamities such as sickness or marriage I shall *need* it myself. I fear that so small a sum with so many indeterminate conditions dangling about it will be of little use to you."

At the same time he expressed his thoughts concerning his brother's quandary. David was discouraged with his dry goods business and thinking of leaving Parry & Muir. When John attempted to bolster David's spirits, he showed a good grasp of economics as he addressed the problem at length.

"You say that you have some thoughts of retiring from the dry goods business. I think you had better not be discouraged by these hard times. So great a number of depressing influences do not often occur at the same time. After learning your business 'stay with it,' as Californians say, until you make a competence.

"If, however, you have come to dislike your business . . . apart from the accidental losses and depressions of hard times then by all means leave it [as] soon as possible. You are still a young man and it is well worth your while to battle with the vexations and inconveniences which attend the labor of making a new home if by so doing you can make yourself and family permanently more happy.

"If business is overdone in Portage, seek another market for your goods, and if you decide to move at all, give a serious thought to Calif. and to the Pacific coast in general. Money is much more abundant here than in the Atlantic states. Still there is a good deal of competition in the dry goods business, but you may find a place where you can establish yourselves.

"I'm not qualified to give advice about the matter in anything like particular terms, but I am sure that in a new country, rapidly developing which abounds in the essential elements of material wealth, success is sooner or later sure to the talented and enterprising.

"If you resolve to spend your life in agricultural pursuits do not choose California for a home. But I will likely see you ere you are found following the plow to your old song of 'success to the jolly old farmer.'"

In this letter John made an important statement that revealed the depth of the Muir family ties:

"As a family we are pretty firmly united and you know that no one tree of a close clump can very well fall. In my walks through the forests of humanity I find no family clump more interwoven in root and branch than our own."[8]

In early May, Anna Galloway wrote to her Uncle John with Mound Hill news.

"Mr. Van Brunt is building our new house just now so that when you come back we will have a nice big room for you to spread out all your curiosities (when you show them to us) and a nice big bedroom for your special benefit.

"Mother has been sowing her flower seed and we have nice times helping her. We have a great many flower shrubs among which are snowdrop, snowball, flowering almond, climb rose, variegated rose, damask rose, white rose, Scotch rose, blush rose, Persian lilac, white lilac, honeysuckle."[9]

The following week Sarah added her comments to Anna's about the upright addition to the west end of the house. Then she mentioned a secret. "Enclosed [is] a picture of Mother. Acknowledge this to me as Father likes to see your letters and you know it would not do for him to know of this." Father disapproved of family likenesses. He would never sit for a portrait of himself.

"Father is very busy. You know he never does anything by halves and he is farming."[10]

At the end of June, when the Hickory Hill barley field was ready for harvest, the Muirs' loyal buggy horse died. Anne reported the sad loss to Dan.

"Our faithful favorite Nan that has been with us in all our journeys for so many years is dead and buried. I don't know whether her place can ever be filled."

On a more optimistic note she added, "John is quite well and still resides in the beautiful valley. How pleased I am to think that the sun of happiness shines upon him for the present."[11]

With the coming of fall, 1870, another harvest season was done. Dan was still studying medicine in Ann Arbor, and, once again, Joanna and the twins, Mary and Annie, left home for their various pursuits. Sarah observed that her mother was so lonesome when all the girls were gone.

In early September, Sarah was busy with sewing projects—making a bedspread, shirts, and drapes; and baking pies, cakes, and bread. She somehow found time to bring her brother Dan up to date on the family news.

"[Mary] has found a very pleasant boarding place [in Madison] and intends going to the University for another year at least. She had a very pleasant visit at Father's and he even gave her a little of the needful so that you may be sure she went schoolward rejoicing more on account of the good will than the money. She has been taking another drawing of the old home."[12]

Mary had always felt badly that her father disapproved of her crayoning pictures as much as he did the taking of photographic likenesses. Consequently, she was especially pleased when he gave her a little money towards her university expenses.

"David, Celia and I rode over to Father's yesterday," Sarah wrote two weeks later. "The house seems very quiet but all seem comfortable and happy. Father ploughs two acres a day and does his chores so you may be sure there is not much spare time with him. [He] looks well.

"Mother looks well and takes great pleasure in caring for her flowers and keeping the chips well raked up in her door yard. It is a pretty place and she seems to enjoy the country around her in her own quiet way."

Sarah was happy about Maggie and John Reid's new baby, not quite a month old. She knew that little Harry was a comfort to her sister and helped "fill the vacant place occasioned by the death of her other little pet."[13]

Five years earlier, on July 7, 1865, the Reids lost their first son, Andrew, at the age of one month. They buried him in the pioneer cemetery near Hickory Hill. With Harry's birth, they felt their family circle to be more complete. They had two little girls, Annie, nine, and Jessie, seven.

In the meantime, John wandered the Yosemite region, and thought often of his family. He shared with them the magnificence of his surroundings. Sprinkled throughout his letters were passages written in the same beautiful, poetic prose for which he later became famous.

To his brother David he once said: "Yosemite rocks and all the peaks and spires and broad shouldered mountains beyond are jeweled, clothed with winter's first born snow flowers."[14]

And to his niece Anna he wrote: ". . . the hills [were] strewed with quartz crystals—they made the ground look starry as the sky. Here is a precious little fern that I found far up in the Yosemite rock. After a walk to Ribbon Falls when I was sitting at the camp fire that night I looked up past the top of the rock and happened to see two stars that belong to the Great-bear and they made me think of home.

"Whenever I feel bad I always find something good to make up for it so, sure enough the next day I found this delicate little creature of a fern. Its little cave home is on the north side of the valley a thousand feet up the rocks. Some of the spray of the great Yosemite falls come to it.

"I hope when spring comes you will gather some flowers for me and send them in a letter. Some of the big *anenomes* I want. You call them gopher blows."[15] Once again an exchange of flowers symbolized close family ties.

John not only remembered his immediate family in this way, but others as well. He remembered David's mother, Jean Galloway, who had been his dear friend and strong supporter for many years.

"How shall I begin to express my thanks for those dear little tokens of remembrance you sent us from a far off land," Sarah wrote her brother January 15, 1871.

"We each prize them highly, but none of us more than Grandma Galloway. She tells us to tell you that she is very grateful to think you thought of her when you were so far away.

"She keeps her little flower tied up in her mother's Bible with its history as she calls the description you sent along with it, and thinks of it as one of her treasures.

"The little buds and flowers seem to tell us of rocks and mountains and of a warm enthusiastic heart very nearly allied to us wandering among and admiring their beauties."

Sarah reminisced about the old days at Fountain Lake. "Annie helps at home . . . she is as old as I was when I left Scotland. When I think of it it seems as though it could hardly have been real and these thoughts lead us back twenty-two years, and then our shanty experience comes rushing back. . . .

"Many of these events in our history seem like a dream or a tale that has been told. George and Celia take me back to where you and I as children kept the house in perfect commotion, so much so that they tell me if there was any extra noise, going on they would say, 'O that's John and Sarah fechtin.'"

"I believe C[elia] and G[eorge] romp and play with as much noise and zest as we ever did. When George is at home from school they are almost inseparable. To be with him Celia is perfectly willing to help him tend to the cattle and clean the stables."[16]

Although John Muir had found his wilderness home in the Yosemite Valley, he carried fine memories of the rolling Wisconsin landscape of his youth. In 1864 he had failed in his effort to set aside Fountain Lake farm acreage. Once again he tried to preserve a treasured area for its beauty alone. Now he wanted to purchase from the "Ennis boys" a forty acre wetland parcel adjacent to the old Muir farm. He also wanted to preserve Fern Lake at Mound Hill Farm from the trampling hooves of the cattle. He had enlisted Sarah and David's help.

Sarah wrote to her brother about it May 30, 1871.

"Well John, I have done my best to get David to write you a few lines about that land affair but I find I may just as well speak to the wind. He says he is too busy to think, the weeds among the corn are growing big and he must away with Nell to cultivate, but he says to tell you that the ferns [at Mound Hill's Fern Lake] shall not be disturbed and it shall be called yours until you come home and then you will both see about it.

"Also he says he will see the Ennis boys about the Fountain Lake forty but he says he doubts about its being bought as it connects with the old Muir farm. You know they own that too but he will see about it."[17]

In September of that year, John wrote David Galloway, "I am truly much obliged to you for the pains you have taken concerning that strip of Fountain Lake land."

He stipulated: "If you think that the cattle & hogs can be kept off by any ordinary care & fencing considering the character of the neighborhood I wish that you would offer Ennis from 2 1/2 to 10 dollars per acre as you can agree, but if you think that the stock cannot be fenced out I do not care to have the land at all. It is a splendid natural garden and I wish that I could send a portion of myself to guard it." Even then the pioneer ecologist understood the damage done by cattle impacting the soil and the destruction caused by erosion.

"I am glad to hear that you are making so comfortable a home for yourself and precious little ones. Few portions of the world can be so beautiful and healthful than Wisconsin.

"Tomorrow I start upwards again in the summits to study. I will be very busily engaged for the next two yrs. upon the works and ways of the ancient glaciers wh[ich] did most of the work of forming and fashioning of this grand Yosemite."[18]

Sarah, always with John in her imagination, wrote in November, "Once more I have gathered my writing materials together to write a few lines to my wandering brother far away among the rocks and mountains in and around Yosemite. How often I imagine I can see you seated among the wonderful scenery, admiring and writing. . . . How I long for a ramble with you whose words and thoughts were always as fresh as the woods themselves."

She finished her letter by giving information on the land affair. "David spoke to the Ennis boys about the Fountain Lake forty and without their knowing what you were able to give. They do not think of selling it for less than $10 per acre. David gives his opinion that cattle and hogs could hardly be kept out, and so thought of doing nothing till he heard from you."[19] This second effort to preserve a treasured bit of Wisconsin landscape ultimately failed.

As for Fern Lake, although David Galloway had written his brother-in-law that the mudhole was safe and the frogs were singing merrily, Muir was disappointed to find that twenty-five years later the little glacier bog had been virtually trampled away.

Anne was following her son's career with great interest. On November 9, 1871, she wrote from hickory Hill:

"Your very welcome letters are always a source of much pleasure to me. With my mind I often follow you in your wanderings in the valley and on the mountains ever praying that the Lord will comfort and protect you at all times.

"This summer and fall I have enjoyed a ramble in the woods very much. The trees and flowers and plants looked more beautiful to me than ever before, and I took care of the garden sowing the seeds and gathering the vegetables for the first time.

"Perhaps you do remember that it is 22 years today since I first met you and David and Sarah at our first Wisconsin home. How very thankful I was to be at home with you again. Many changes have taken place since then, and many blessings have been showered upon us mixed with some trials and though the family is widely scattered, yet we are still all spared by His great mercy.

"Around home everything moves on about the same as usual. Your father is very busy husking corn. Anna intends staying at home this winter but Joanna intends to teach. We were glad to have Mary home during the vacation. She looked very well and is very thankful to be able to study at Madison so long. I am very thankful to you for your kindness to her. . . ."[20]

The Wisconsin season was changing as was that of the Sierras where high mountain snows brought John down into the valley. He told his mother that he planned to remain at Black's Hotel for the winter taking care of the premises and "working up the data which I have garnered during these last months and years concerning the ancient glacial system of this wonderful region.

"For the last two or three months I have worked incessantly among the most remote and undiscoverable of the deep cañons of this pierced basin, finding many a mountain page glorious with the writing of God and in characters that any earnest eye could read."

Muir explained to her that Yosemite Valley was not the exceptional creation that the few scientific men who had looked into it believed it to be. Having made painstaking studies, he said he knew that "Yosemite is one of many, one chapter of a great mountain book written by the same pen of ice which the Lord long ago passed over every page of our great Sierra Nevadas. . . . someday I hope to show you my sheaves, my big bound pages of mountain gospel."

And then, as a kind of benediction, he ended his letter:

"Wisconsin winter will soon be upon you. May you enjoy its brightness and universal beauty in warm and happy homes."[21]

# X

# DANIEL MUIR'S ABDICATION

*Father is a comet whose course only heaven knows.*
—John Muir

At Hickory Hill Daniel Muir was becoming restless and bored with farm life. Preaching only in the local area, he burned with desire to enlarge the scope of his religious ministry. On January 7, 1872, he wrote to John, who was exploring Yosemite, and Dan, practicing medicine in Racine, Wisconsin. He told both sons that he loved them though he didn't write often.

In his letters he enclosed tracts from two organizations he had been distributing to local churches and friends. One was from Dr. Charles Cullis describing his work as steward of a consumptives' house in England where poor consumptives and their families lived free of charge. Cullis took care of the children of the forty or fifty people who died there annually. Daniel Muir was concerned about those who died unconverted to Christianity. The other tract described George Muller's orphan's home in Bristol, England, where eighteen or nineteen hundred orphans lived in five houses.

John became uneasy as he read the tracts, fearing that his father was again about to uproot his mother and the girls still at home. As early as 1868 Daniel had spoken of selling Hickory Hill. There was no telling what he would do now. When John received his mother's letter of February 26, 1872, he knew his fears were well founded.

Anne's nearly-identical letter to Dan read:

"We were surprised to hear your father say he had decided to sell everything he owned or possessed in Marquette Co. by auction. He is now busy distributing bills of sale—the sale to take place on Tuesday the 5th of March. He wishes to keep some of our best furniture but nothing more.

"Only think the farm to be sold by auction. He says he cannot decide on where he will go or what he will do until after sale day is over. . . ."[1]

Anne and Daniel had owned her beloved Hickory Hill farm for seventeen years, but she had no part in her husband's decision to sell it. He would prevail as usual.

Although Anne was upset about the coming sale, she showed her concern for John's happiness when she commented: "I feel much interested in all that interests you although in many of your studies you leave me far behind. Yet I rejoice in all your joy and hopes of further advancement."[2]

John's earlier letter to his brother David detailed the studies his mother mentioned: "I will be busy as soon as the snow leaves our surrounding mountains measuring heights and depths, sketching, describing, etc. for my 'Glaciers.'"[3]

The Hickory Hill sale took place according to the terms of the hand bill.

"I wrote to you in Feby.," Anne sadly informed Dan in April, "that the sale your father intended to have on the 5th day of March—well all the farm implements and stock were sold—and two days afterwards the quarter section with the houses and orchard were sold to John C. Mahaffy and John Madden bought the north eighty and John Turner bought the west eighty.

"So on the 19th day of March we bid farewell to our dear old home and came to Portage. We rented a house on Cook Street as our own houses were all taken up. We expect to move again very soon to one of our own houses—and when we get settled we will be glad to have you and your wife make us a visit."[4]

The family was happy to hear of Dan's recent marriage. John extended his congratulations. "Tell your love I stretch my hand to welcome her to the family of Muir."

He added with justifiable pride, "You know how people used to say that I was a genius in mechanics. Well they say the same things about my readings of nature."[5]

The family's traumatic move weighted heavily on John's mind. On April 25 he wrote to Sarah and David from the New Sentinel Hotel in Yosemite Valley. He was in the process of building a cabin for himself up the valley in a clump of cornus bushes on the Merced River bank.

"I am sorry about the selling of Hickory Hill. In my opinion it was a diseased act, but father is a comet whose course only heaven knows."

He then brought up the subject of the Galloways' effort to preserve Fern Lake at Mound Hill.

"Hearty thanks, David for your care of the mud pond dear to nature and to me."[6]

At the end of April, John received a long, newsy letter from his brother David.

"Business is improving and becoming more profitable. Father and Mother are now living in P[ortage], working hard improving the place where John Reid used to live and own—painting, papering, making an addition, gardening, etc. etc. Father looks as tired as though he were farming."

David described their brother Dan's success and how he bragged about Emma, his new wife. "Dan is doing pretty well in medicine in Racine. He keeps her in the office with him making pills. Won't let her keep house, so they board and have nothing to do but love each other."

As for the younger sisters, he reported Joanna had a beau; Annie was teaching in Caledonia where she was considered a good teacher; and Mary still studied at the university.

John and Maggie were doing well. "John Reid is doing a large business in cattle, hogs, beef, pork, wool, pelts, furs, etc. etc. and making money. He will be well off some day."

David was proud of his children. "Carrie, 7 years old, reads in the fourth reader, studies arithmetic, geography, etc. Annie is four years old, reads in second reader, and Willie, 3 years is a bright boy and will be one of the big guns someday.

"Portage is going to be a big place sometime. We are going to have seven rr's and a ship canal. No doubt it will be a great R R center with shops, etc."[7]

"After much moving," Anne wrote to Dan May 30, 1872, "we now begin to feel that we are settled in Portage. We moved to the smallest house we owned but we had an additional room put up—quite comfortable."

She still felt badly about leaving Hickory Hill.

"I do not allow myself to think often of our dear old home. It seemed hard to leave the place that we had built planned and planted." But her ever-present philosophy helped her to become resigned. "Time brings changes."[8]

With the dreaded move complete, Anne Muir would live in Portage the rest of her life.

That summer the Galloway family participated in the Columbia County fair. Each year farm families entered animals, produce and handiwork into competition. The Galloways did well. Sarah received a first premium for her white bedspread and colored mat that were so admired by the other women; Annie won a premium on ten different kinds of apples; and her brother George won one for his corn.

In September Mary returned to the university at Madison, while Annie and Joanna attended a six-weeks teaching institute at Oshkosh.

"After they were all gone," Anne wrote to Dan and Emma, "your father decided to move to the brick house by the high school. So we have been here over a week. The house seems very large for us two, but it reminds me very much of our old home across the ocean, although it is not so large."[9]

Daniel's fetish for moving underscored his chronic restlessness.

While the Muir family was readjusting to town life, John was still exploring the Sierras. He shared a bit of mountaineering with Sarah:

"While waiting for [Asa] Gray this afternoon on the mountain side I climbed the Sentinel Rock 3000 feet high. Here is an oak sprig from the top." Asa Gray was the foremost botanist of the time and one of a number of people beginning to seek out the young naturalist, John Muir.

John ended his note with a special thought for David's mother. ". . . and always remember me to Mrs. Galloway who though blind sees better than most people."[10]

The Muirs had been having their share of illness. Sarah related how David Muir suffered from a dyspepsia condition and was unable to work in the store for a long time. When he was somewhat better, Parry & Muir purchased a nice horse and buggy. It helped David to ride out into the countryside as often as he as able.

Annie reported to John that her father was very ill with a pain in his stomach and that he had nearly fainted from overexertion.

"Mother says she does not think he was ever so sick in his life," Sarah explained. "Dan came to see him and he willingly took his medicine."[11] At the same time Sarah noticed how worn and weary Dan looked.

The situation was brighter for the Galloways. While Sarah penned this letter, David was lying in the grass by the door cracking hickory nuts. The children were growing up. Annie helped Sarah in the house and George helped his father in the fields.

Christmas that year was a happy occasion as all the families gathered at Anne and Daniel's Portage home to celebrate. Annie Reid was happy that that her grandpa went downtown on Christmas and got everyone a present.

Daniel had softened somewhat during the passing years, but he continued to be exceedingly restless. He was still obsessed with the idea of enlarging the scope of his service to God and now spoke openly of the possibility of going to England to work in Muller's home for orphans.

When John heard of this latest plan from his brother David, he realized that his father was ready to abdicate family responsibilities for the larger ministry he sought. Over the years Daniel Muir had provided little financial help in his children's efforts to get an education, nor did he aid them when they were in financial trouble. It had fallen to John, as eldest son, to step in with advice and financial assistance for his three younger sisters and his brother Dan. He now faced the possibility that his father would pull up stakes without even providing for his mother.

John understood his father only too well. Though he and Daniel Muir were opposite in many ways, they were surprisingly alike in others. Both men were driven by strong inner compulsions, yet each responded to a different call—Daniel to preach religious gospel; John to preach the gospel of the wilderness.

While he was growing up under his father's iron-handed regime, John had taken issue with him many times as he struggled for his personal freedom. Daniel was stern and unyielding, but John early learned flexibility. Daniel endured a lifetime of underlying dissatisfaction and restlessness, but John early found fulfillment. He once said, "I am always happy in the centre."[12]

Now at age sixty-nine, Daniel was driven to go out into the world on an evangelistic mission and was in the throes of deciding where to go. The uncertainty dragged on throughout the winter of 1872-1873.

John tried to help from a distance. On the first of March, 1873, he wrote urgently to his brother David from Yosemite Valley.

"I answer your letter at once because I want to urge you to do what you can in breaking up that wild caprice of father's of going to Bristol and Lord Muller. You and David Galloway are the only reliable common sense heads of our tribe, and it is important when [the] radical welfare of our parents and sisters is at stake that we should do all that [which] is in our power.

"I expected a morbid and semi fanatical outbreak of this kind as soon as I heard of his breaking free from the wholesome cares of the farm. Yet I hoped that he would find ballast in your town of some sabbath-school missionary kind that would save him from any violent crisis like the present. That thick matted sod of Bristol orphans which is a sort of necessary evil induced by other evils is all right for Muller in England but all wrong for Muir in America.

"The lives of Anna and Joanna, accustomed to the free wild nature of our woods, if transplanted to artificial fields and dingy towns of England would wilt and shrivel to mere husks even if they were not to make their life work amid those pinched and blinking orphans.

"Father, in his sick and feeble-minded condition, is sick and requires the most considerate treatment from all who have access to his thoughts and his moral disease is by no means contemptible, for it is only those that are endowed with poetic and enthusiastic brains that are subject to it.

"Most people who are born into the world remain babies all their lives, their development being arrested like sun-dried seeds. Father is a magnificent baby, who instead of dozing continually like most of his neighbors, suffers growing pains that are ready to usher in the dawn of a higher life.

"But to come to our work, can you not induce father to engage in some tract or mission or Sabbath School enterprise that will satisfy his demands for bodily and spiritual excercize? Can you not find him some thicket of destitution worthy of his benevolence. Can you not convince him that the whole world is full of work for the kind and loving heart?

"Or if you cannot urge him to undertake any independent charity can you not place him in correspondence with some Milwaukee or Chicago society where he would find elbow room for all his importance. An *earnest* man like father who also has a little money, is a valuable acquisition to many societies of a philanthropic kind, and I feel sure that if once fairly afloat from his shoal of indolence upon which he now chafes, that he would sail calmly the years now remaining to him.

"At all events, tell Mother and the girls that whether on this side of the sea or that, they need take no uneasiness concerning bread."[13]

"Your father had not yet decided where he will go," Anne declared to Dan in April, "but lately has talked and read a great deal about California. He thinks that is the Goshen of the United States. But where he will go I do not know—he is much dissatisfied with our present home. So what will come of this I do not know."[14]

Anne said that Joanna and Annie might go to California, but not England. Joanna planned to return to the Portage second ward school during the summer while Annie would stay home.

In the meantime, John, still happily mountaineering in the Sierras, wrote to Sarah September 3, 1873, that he had just completed a long hard trip in the mountains. "The mountains are calling me and I must go,"[15] he said.

Once again he closed his letter by remembering his old friend from long ago. ". . . Mrs. Galloway who though shut out from sunshine yet dwells in light."

That fall Daniel finally came to a decision. He would not go to England after all, but to Canada. Anne Muir faced a dilemma. On October 27, 1873, she explained the situation to Dan.

"Your father got very tired living at Portage so he left home on the 15th and went to Hamilton in Canada. He wrote to us that he likes the place very much and says that he has bought a house there. He wishes us to sell all our furniture and all the houses and says I must come there at once, but I objected to this arrangement and wrote to him that I could not think of moving at this season of the year.

Then, touching upon a key element of her nature, she continued," . . . I have no wish whatever to leave my present home especially as I do not think he will settle anywhere. I would like to know what you think of all this. I trust my path of duty will be made plain to me and that grace will be given me to walk in it. I hope he will come home again."

Anne told of more trouble, this time financial.

"Our bank is shut. They are bankrupt. Your father had over two thousand dollars in the bank. John Reid put in two thousand dollars only about three days before it was closed. He felt dreadfully about it. David did not have any money in it but very many had. Business is not so good as before. Our bank was not chartered. It was only a loan bank. The president has given up all his property so people will get part of their money if not all."[16]

Daniel's move to Canada threw his family into turmoil. Joanna, attending normal school in Oshkosh, Wisconsin was especially upset.

"Isn't it too bad?" she asked Mary in her letter of November 16th. "Certainly Ma does not want to go away out to Canada and yet now that he has bought a house there, I suppose he will be very determined."[17]

Two weeks later Joanna wrote, "As for the Hamilton abomination it's too much for me. . . . I don't think Ma will ever commit to such foolishness as to leave a place of safety and expose herself to the power of the whirlwind."[18]

Daniel Muir stayed in Canada for three months and then temporarily returned to Portage City.

"I expect, my God willing to leave Portage City for Hamilton, Ontario on the last day of this month," he informed John March 19, 1874. "I bought a house last October there and without my family at present I mean to go in the way of God's providence to spend all my time in His service and wholly by his grace to glorify Him. I shall be glad to hear from you there any time. I will get your letters at the post office there.

"We are all well. Your dear Mother sends her love to you.

"Your affectionate father in Christ."[19]

An interesting sidelight to the selling of Hickory Hill was later told by Thomas Kearns who bought the farm in 1873 from interim owner John Mahaffey. When Kearns stopped by the Muirs' home to pay off Daniel's mortgage on the farm, there was a trunk full of religious tracts in the room. Daniel told him he was taking them with him to Canada.[20]

The Muirs' troubles were not yet over. In April Joanna was struck with a severe illness. She could neither study nor teach. Her eyes were affected and she wore dark glasses to protect them. Devastated, she was forced to leave her normal school classes to go home to Portage to recuperate. On the way she stopped at her brother Dan's home in Racine. As a practicing physician, he gave her medical advice. It would be six years before she was completely well again.

In May Joanna was living with her mother in Portage. Managing to write to Dan and Emma, she said she helped plant the garden, "a beautiful row of peas, a good bed of lettuce, and several rows of corn. My geranium is doing finely.

"We had a letter from Father last night who is delighted with his new home and as usual is busily employed in improving both house and grounds after which he will doubtless become tired of it. He, however, enjoys it at present."[21]

In Hamilton Daniel improved this property as he had done so many times before with other properties. He painted his house and set out trees. He still expected his family to join him. He wants "to know if mother has not yet repented," Joanna related to Mary, June 3. "He says he is very happy and distributes tracts every day."[22]

"It seems a strange thing that he should live in Hamilton while we are living at Portage,"[23] Anne commented sadly to Dan.

But Daniel did not tire of his life in the busy Canadian port city on Lake Ontario as his family predicted. With renewed zeal he pursued his missionary career, preaching at Hamilton's large agricultural market and passing out religious leaflets. He was embarked on a new phase of his career and did not seem to need his family.

As the summer progressed, the Portage family continued their life as usual. Mary was teaching oil painting between university terms. Joanna's health and eyes were improving.

As fall approached, Sarah and John exchanged letters. On August 30th Sarah commented from Mound Hill that "the season has been so very dry the leaves are falling around the dooryard [in] all the different hues that precedes their decay."[24]

John was spending some time in Oakland, California. On September 7 he wrote to Sarah about the maidenhair fern he had discovered in high mountain country, "perhaps the most graceful and delicate of all the ferns of North America." He noted that in the Sierras, the fern, even more delicate than in Wisconsin, grows at 9000 feet.

"Instead of growing in soil as in Wis.," he explained, "it is found only as a rock fringe where it is sheltered from storms.

"How delightful it will be when I come to visit a year with you all and see the plants and streams and ponds of Wisconsin."

As he so often did, he finished his letter with a thought for Mrs. Galloway. "How seldom one meets human benevolence of so magnificent a kind."[25]

About the same time, Joanna penned a letter to Mary who had returned to the university. Father said "he would not live in Portage ten minutes if he could help it and desired Mother to come to Hamilton, but Mother says, nay verily."[26]

Anne wrote to Dan in the same vein.

"Your father is still in Hamilton and says he has no wish to come back to Portage but thinks that the girls and I might come to Hamilton.

"I rode out to Sarah's pleasant home yesterday. Everything there looks well and thrifty. They were all as busy as bees. They reminded me of long ago."[27]

Anne further thought of long-ago times when she received word of her sister Margaret's death in Dunbar at the age of 78. She told John that her mother had also died when she was 78 and her father at age 88. Anne said she was "the last remnant of a numerous family."[28]

As for the present, she said that Daniel was rather impatient about her staying behind in Portage. He had gone his way, fully expecting his wife and the younger girls to follow him to Hamilton. He little thought that Anne would not obey him as she had done for so many years. But Anne Muir had had enough of moving, and Daniel could not uproot her again. Thus, their pattern of separate lives was established.

The winter of 1874-1875 passed and summer came. On June 29, 1875, Anne wrote to Dan:

"Your father writes that he is well and has got his new brick house finished and thinks of letting the frame one—he still likes Hamilton much better than Portage." She mentioned he had been distributing so many religious tracts at the market that he ordered a second box of books from England.

As for the home news, she related that "David Galloway has sold about 50 dollars worth of strawberries and has still a great many. They are very plentiful here this summer."

She said that her health was better than it was last summer but "I feel the effects of old age more." Then, despite the strangeness of her situation, she concluded, "My comforts and blessings are great. . . . there is in a bright beyond a happy home for the faithful."[29]

As busy as she was that fall, Sarah took a short boat trip on the Wisconsin River at Kilbourne City, not too far from Mound Hill. She was intrigued by the sandstone bluffs—the dells lining the river that had eroded into such fascinating shapes. She enjoyed walking through the cool, rocky ravines that were cut away from the river and filled with ferns and greenery.

Early in November, John commented on her trip.

"Here is your letter with the Dalles in it. I'm glad you have escaped so long from the cows and sewing and baking to God's green wild Dalles and dells for I know you are young again and that the natural love of the beauty you possess had fair play. . . .

"I will never forget the big happy day I spent there on the rocky gorgery in Wisconsin above Kilbourne City. What lanes full of purpil [sic] orchids and ferns: aspidium fragrans I found there for the first time and what hillsides of huckleberries and rare asters and goldenrods.

"Don't you wish you were wild like me and as free to satisfy your love for whatever is pure and beautiful?"[30]

Satisfying her love of nature in her own way, Sarah drank in the beauty around her as she went about her chores. She often walked over the hill behind the farmhouse and down to tiny Fern Lake that John had so wanted to preserve for its beauty. She described it for him in a letter. ". . . the ferns were waving and making beautiful arches in the shade of the oaks, the young timber is growing so thick and fast it is quite a trial to get there unless we go around by the marsh and come to it on the further side."

Then she spoke of Grandma Galloway.

"David has gone up to his father's today. We heard that Grandma was feeling very low-spirited and not very well at all. I was up in the spring and was much pleased to find her looking so well. Still she was quite feeble, feeling very tired by the time she got up and dressed herself.

"But I daresay you would not see much difference in her except that she looks more pale and languid than she used to be, but it always seems to wake her up to talk about you. You remember in your last letter to the children when you sent your picture to Mother. You said you would have sent one to Grandma Galloway too if she could have seen it. I mentioned it to her and she told me to tell you that your picture would be welcomed by everyone in the family, but that it was already hung up in the halls of her memory—and that she could see you now as plainly as the day you sat near her with some little flowers in your hand, telling her about a little bird that always sang 'the day's done—the day's done.' She said the picture was so plain she could tell which side of you was next to her.

"'And tell him,' she said, 'he will yet see *all* the glorious works of our Father for he is one of those whose day will never be done.'

"She also showed me the little sprig of pine or cedar you sent her some time ago. It was carefully laid away—corked up tight in some fanciful little bottle where she said it would look *always* just the same."

Sarah had received a letter from her father the week before. It had been almost two years since he moved to Canada.

"He was quite well. He seems to think it was good for him that he had broken away from among us for he had found a number who were of like mind with himself. They were holding open air meetings, every night where thousands were hearing the gospels preached.

"There is also a meeting at his house every Sunday. He seems to be enjoying himself very much.

"I hear by Mother's last letter he is very anxious for her to go there and bring as many of the girls as care to come."[31]

Jean Millar Galloway died December 22, 1876, and was buried in the pioneer cemetery behind the United Presbyterian Church. John deeply felt her death. On January 12, 1877, from his friend John Swett's home in San Francisco, he eulogized her:

"The sad news of dear old Mrs. Galloway though not unexpected makes me feel that I have lost a friend. Few lives are so beautiful and complete as hers and few could have had the glorious satisfaction in dying to know that so few words spoken were other than kind and so few deeds that did anything more than augment the happiness of others. How many really good people waste, and worse than waste their short lives in mean bickerings when they might lovingly, in broad Christian charity enjoy the glorious privilege of doing plain, simple, every-day good. Mrs. Galloway's character was one of the most beautiful and perfect I ever knew."

Wistful about his Wisconsin family and the Christmas season just past, John went on, "How delightful it is to gather on the holiday, and what a grand multitude you must make when you are all mustered. Little did I think when I used to be, and am now, fonder of home and . . . domestic life than any of the boys that I only should be a bachelor and doomed to roam always far outside the family circle.

"But we are governed more than we know and are driven as with whips we know not where. Your pleasures and the happiness of your lives in general are far greater than you know, being clustered together, yet independent, and living in one of the most beautiful regions under the sun. Long may you all live to enjoy your blessings and to love one another and make sacrifices for one another's good. From your wandering brother John."[32]

During the winter Daniel fell ill in Hamilton. About the first of February, unable to care for himself, he took the train to Portage. Joanna was still at home continuing to improve after her illness three years before. She didn't need to wear her dark glasses now unless the sun shone too brightly. Anna was teaching the winter term and Mary would soon be home as well, "engaged in crayoning."

On February 22, 1877, Anne wrote to John about his father's situation:

"About three weeks ago your father arrived here. He had been sick for some time and thought he should be home. He is quite yellow as he has the jaundice. He is much better since he came home and rides out every day being too weak to walk much."[33]

Anne Muir merely stated the facts about her husband's stay in Portage, but she must have been pleased to have him at home, if only temporarily. She made him as comfortable as she could, and hoped for his recovery. But when he began to feel better, he was anxious to return to Hamilton. Although he meant to return to Canada sooner, Daniel stayed in Portage for six months.

"Your father did not get away as soon as he intended on account of the railroad strikes," Anne informed Dan on August 8, 1877, "but he left here on Monday the 30th of July and he had the pleasure of seeing our nice new sidewalk, it being finished by that time. He also made me a present of four large books."[34]

Daniel Muir was truly a dedicated missionary with his work cut out for him and like-minded people to work with. Hamilton was a large city, so he could preach to large audiences. There were endless souls to save and tracts to hand out. He was accomplishing his religious goals and his inner restlessness was subsiding. As Joanna put it to John on March 6, 1878, "Father reports himself very well, very useful and very happy."[35]

# XI

# THE STREAM OF TIME

*It all seemed to be like enchantment and I*
*thought of the . . . time to come when we will*
*all be gone, and other generations will be here*
*and enjoy this scene.*
— Mrs. Louisiana Strentzel

"Hard times, hard money, hard work, hard hearts."[1] Joanna thus summed up her mood in February, 1878, and that of the times. It had been four years that month since she returned home so very ill from the Oshkosh normal school.

David's April 2nd letter to John, written on his Parry & Muir letterhead, echoed Joanna's pessimistic thoughts. The partners, at their 20 W. Cook St. store in Portage, were "Dealers in Clothing, Hats, Caps, Boots & Shoes, notions &c Singer's Sewing Machine."

He too commented on the ". . . hard times, unprosperous times and the terribly hard scratching to make business go at all. Last harvest everything looked more than usually promising, good crops, fair prices, etc. It rained all fall. We had no winter—mud all through the winter months. So we had no fall trade and no winter trade and as we had a large stock we had to pay for our goods before they were sold. Consequently [we] had to borrow a great deal and then goods sold so slowly that the profits did not half pay expenses.

"So I've been blue and worried and fretted and it seemed to me that I would be glad to move away without a cent just for freedom's sake. I wish you could find a rich gold mine so that I could get enough to pay our debts.

"Our hope is that the tide will turn and if it does I'll get out of this as soon as I can do so with a whole hide. We have an expensive establishment. In good times it pays and in bad times we lose money and lately we have had worse times than usual for the last fall and winter.

"I have envied your freedom from care and trouble and still I wouldn't take your single blessedness."

David said their brother Dan was having problems with his large medical practice in Racine, Wisconsin. "Men from Racine all report him successful, and in high standing in that city as a physician." Although Dan was doing a large business and could book $4,000 a year, he couldn't collect because of hard times.

David's letter included a comment on his sister's health. "Joanna has been pretty well all winter. She deserves lots of sympathy and love. Her sickness seems to make her more lovely and sweet in her disposition every day."[2]

About the same time, Anne also wrote about her daughter's health. "Gardening has commenced here. Joanna is quite interested in planting flowers and seeds. Her health slowly but surely improves. She has suffered a good deal, but we have much to be thankful for—blessings and mercies have followed us all the days of our lives. I often think how I am surrounded with blessings and comforts that many are denied."[3]

April 21 marked a special event in John's life: his fortieth birthday.

"We all partook of currant scones," Anne wrote May 16. "Your fortieth birthday was remembered with many heartfelt loving wishes for your prosperity and for your preservation in the many dangers to which you are exposed.

"I have had the pleasure of reading about your favorite bird and also your late trip to the mountains about Lake Tahoe. You know I am extremely interested in all your travels and writings and enjoy reading about them very much."[4]

Another time she wrote, "[It is] a great blessing that you so much enjoy the glorious and wonderful scenery that continually surrounds you. I think very few can appreciate and understand the wonders of that part of the world as you do. . . ."[5]

Mary too had read her brother's article, "The Humming-Bird of the California Water-Falls," published in *Scribner's Monthly*, February, 1878.

"Everyone likes it,"[6] she said of Muir's charming and detailed account of the sprightly, melodious water ouzel of mountain waterfalls and streams. Muir well described the cheery robin-sized bird as it flew directly into the falls' white torrent or dived many feet below the stream surface in search of insects and larvae. He drew a fine word picture of its interrelated habitat of mosses, mountains, falls, seasons, and geologic processes.

The family continued to follow John's nature articles. Through "A Wind Storm in the Forests of the Yuba," in the November, 1878, issue of *Scribner's Monthly*, Sarah experienced vicariously his exciting ride atop the Douglas spruce.

"The windstorm must have been *terribly grand*," she wrote in February, 1879. "You must have clung to that tree like a vice or you would have gone the way of the leaves."[7]

In this article Muir discussed the universal influences of wind in a forest and told about his scramble through one forest at the height of a storm.

"There is always something deeply exciting, not only in the sounds of winds in the woods, . . . but in their varied waterlike flow manifested by the movements of the trees, especially those of conifers."[8]

He wrote that after drifting through "the midst of this passionate music and motion," he was inspired to climb to the top of a one hundred foot Douglas spruce, lithe as it rocked and swirled in the wind. "Never before did I enjoy so noble an exhilaration of motion." He kept his "lofty perch" for hours watching the forest "as over fields of waving grain."[9]

"We all travel the milky way together, trees and men,"[10] Muir penned toward the end of the article. This classic gem written so early in his career, demonstrated his literary power that persuaded his readers to the appreciation and preservation of nature.

Through articles like these, Muir was educating the public on the wonders of the native landscape. It had been eleven years since he left Wisconsin for his thousand-mile walk to the Gulf of Mexico. For the past ten years he had been studying every corner of the Sierra Nevada and had accumulated a vast amount of knowledge on its natural history.

As he led scientists and others through the region, he shared his knowledge with some of the finest minds of the time. His fame was spreading and people began to heed his preservation message.

In Portage, on May 27, 1878, Mary Muir wrote a long letter to her brother revealing her innermost thoughts about her dreams and accomplishments. Like John she had a thirst for knowledge, and, with his encouragement and financial aid, had attended the university in Madison for at least four years. She had been home for two weeks working on her music and painting, her favorite pastimes.

"I could show you some of the pictures that I have made, but I often wonder what you would think of my work. I wonder if you would be disappointed in it, and I wonder if you would be pleased with it, and all my wondering is vain and amounts to no good for you never see any of it.

"But if there is anyone in the world I should like to please it would be and is you—for no one has done more to help me to what I am and can do than your own dear self and I owe it to you to do so. I enjoy my work and do not tire of it any more than a natural tire when I do too much, which is not very often.

"Oh! if I had such or even a little mental wealth [as yours], not for the sake of being wondered at by fellow beings, but because I want the wealth of mind. Perhaps you say, go to work, which is good advice, but it is not easy to churn butter from skim milk. Still, I am glad to recognize a little butter after my long University churning.

"I still enjoy study. Work takes nearly all my time. For some time I have been very busy, but it is hard to dispose of pictures these times that I have to work for [so] little and so [I] am not getting rich at all except in practice and training. I have been crayoning portraits more than anything else in the past 2 years."[11]

Then she shared the happy news that she was to be married in about three months to Willis Hand of Phillips, Wisconsin. She and Willis had become friends when they both attended the university in Madison. He was graduated from the law school there. After their marriage they planned to live in Phillips, a new town far to the north on the Northern Central Railroad.

In the meantime, Daniel Muir was greatly involved in his evangelistic activities in Hamilton. According to an April, 1878, letter from his home at the corner of Queen and Robinson streets, he visited sixty patients in the Hamilton hospital twice a week; visited eighty-six boys at the Boys Home once each week; and preached at the great agricultural market in Hamilton three times weekly.

Sometime during his Canadian sojourn Daniel broke his hip. At the time of Daniel's death in 1885, John mentioned in the obituary that his father suffered a "fall eight years ago from which he never recovered."[12] Accordingly, Daniel's accident would have occurred sometime in 1877. However, Anne's letter to her son Dan March 8, 1879, undoubtedly referred to this same accident.

"Latest news from your Father is that his limb is much stronger, and he is now able to go downtown as usual but still uses his crutches." Daniel was determined to let nothing stop him from preaching.

Anne reported that Sarah and David's son, George Galloway, "has been staying with us for the last three months and attending the High School. He has now returned home to work on the farm." In a disappointed tone she concluded, "He was not at all ancious [sic] about his studies."[13]

Anne had gotten to know her eighteen-year-old grandson well during the months he lived with her and she wanted him to be successful in his school work. At the end of the term, George was no doubt relieved to leave school to return to his family at Mound Hill to help his father with the spring planting.

Three months later tragedy struck. On June 19, 1879, George drowned in the Fox River that flowed within sight of the Galloway farmhouse on the hill. By June the weather was warm enough to swim, a favorite pastime for the neighborhood young people.

Sadly, Anne recounted the event for John. "Sarah has met with a very sad trial indeed in the loss of her only son. In June George was nineteen years of age and on his birthday he went with others to bathe in the Fox River and was drowned—how very sad. How we shall all miss him."[14] It was a crushing blow for them all.

When the accident occurred, Joanna was in Phillips visiting Mary and her husband Willis. Her eyes had not completely recovered, but she was improving.

At the end of May, 1879, she described for John her love of the Wisconsin northwoods. Her brother, who had just sent her a bit of Sierra moss, had always inspired her botanical interest.

"How precious these wild wood rambles are, so prolific of darling little flowers which I have never seen before, of luxurious mosses and beautiful ferns, are to me. The noble old pines, the hemlocks and the graceful balsams and spruces too, are all new to me—they are so near us that I can enjoy their company even when I do not feel like walking far.

"I am moreover recovering some of my forgotten knowledge of botany. If ever I have the full use of my eyes again I am determined to pursue this study, for I love it more than ever."[15]

Joanna realized that the native plants of the northern woods were quite different from those she knew in south-central Wisconsin.

Meanwhile, Muir's travels were taking him farther afield. On a July day in 1879, dressed in a Scotch cap and a gray tweed ulster, he alighted from the mail steamboat at Fort Wrangell, Alaska. He had come to do some exploring in southeastern Alaska. It was the first of seven Alaskan journeys.

For the next four months he and the young missionary, S. Hall Young, accompanied by a crew of three Indians, voyaged by canoe among the coastal islands and into bays from Fort Wrangell to Glacier Bay. They climbed mountains, investigated the terrain, and studied icebergs and living glaciers. All along the way they visited Indian villages.

The high point of the journey was the discovery of Glacier Bay and its magnificent wall of ice, with fast-breaking icebergs, later to be named Muir Glacier. During the week they spent there, Muir took a one-day foot journey on the glacier, and ecstatically described to Young how "I've been wandering through a thousand rooms of God's crystal temple. I've been a thousand feet down in the crevasses, with matchless domes and sculptured figures and carved ice-work all around me. . . . Such purity, such delicate beauty!"

During their explorations and discoveries, Hall came to understand his companion's new glacial theories:

"He pointed out to me the mechanical laws that governed those slow-moving resistless streams; how the lower valley and glacier were often the resultant in size and velocity of the two or three glaciers that now formed the branches of the main glaciers; how the harder strata of rock resisted and turned the masses of ice; how the steely ploughshares were often inserted into softer leads and a whole mountain split apart as by a wedge."[16]

John's Wisconsin family anxiously awaited news of his Alaskan journeys and of his safe return to California. In early February, 1880, after his second journey to Alaska, they rejoiced when they heard of his arrival in San Francisco.

Maggie and John Reid learned of it first.

"A week ago Friday evening," Maggie wrote to her brother John, "John (Reid) was sitting with his boots off reading the notice of [Muir's] arrival in the *Chicago Interocean*.

"I felt so glad I said to John, 'This is too good news to keep till morning.' He got to Mother's before she had retired. Joanna had gone upstairs and I guess was partly ready for bed, but coming to listen at the head of the stairs, called out, 'What is that about John?' It had a very restful effect on us all, as it was over a week before the letters came.

"Monday John and I went out to Sarah's carrying your letter to her. Poor dear Sarah and all of them have had hard stroke. Little Gracie didn't seem to realize much about it [George's death], but David, Annie, and especially Sarah have suffered keenly. She has seemed a little more cheerful lately. . ."[17]

Maggie, who often suffered much illness, commented that her health was better and that she had lots of help at home.

That winter Annie went to Phillips to visit her twin sister Mary and Willis Hand, while in Portage the time passed pleasantly for Joanna and her mother. Anne often read aloud to her daughter and they took many walks together.

The spring of 1880 marked six years since Joanna had taken ill in Oshkosh. Her recovery had proceeded slowly, but her health and eyesight were at last greatly improved.

During this period many Portage people were moving west. Anne had brought it up two years earlier when she wrote, "Now very many of the citizens of Portage are turning their faces towards Nebraska. Some have already gone and others are getting ready to go."[18]

Dan, too, decided to leave Racine and join the westward movement. On March 12, 1880, he came to Portage for a week's visit with his mother, and then it was on to Lincoln, Nebraska, to the farm he had procured there. Taking a man along to help him, he transported a carload of animals and materials with which to begin his farm work. He planned to bring his wife Emma and their three little girls out in the fall. One daughter was named Sarah after her Aunt Sarah Galloway.

So the Muirs' westward trek began. The family was spreading out. John and Maggie Reid would soon follow Dan to Nebraska. Daniel still lived happily in Canada, although he was still lame from his accident. Mary and Willis Hand lived in Phillips in northern Wisconsin where Willis practiced law and ran for a county judgeship.

In Portage, David was working as hard as ever at the Parry & Muir store, while Anne remained in the same home she had lived in for several years. Annie and Joanna still lived at home. Not far away the Galloways farmed Mound Hill.

Sarah told John they were all older and grayer and wore spectacles sometimes, adding that David's hair was nearly white and that he was reading with spectacles, too.

"April will bring around another birthday for you dear John," Anne wrote in March. "What need we have to improve the precious moments as they carry us down the stream of time."[19]

On April 14, 1880, just one week before his forty-second birthday, John passed an important milestone when he married Louisiana Strentzel of Martinez, California. She was the daughter of Dr. John

Strentzel, a prominent Alhambra Valley rancher, and his wife, also named Louisiana. John had known the Strentzels for about three years, and he and Louie had been engaged for a year.

The *Contra Costa Gazette*, Martinez, California, carried this item:

"While we feel, as will all her friends, that he has found a worthy mate in one of the most accomplished and highly respected daughters of our county, we may all join in congratulating Miss Louise Strentzel on her marriage with John Muir, whose studies and graphic descriptions of the grand features of the Sierra Nevada and other Pacific coast formations have won him recognized rank among the foremost of the world's living geologists and naturalists."[20]

The Muirs were overjoyed that their wanderer had finally married. Happy letters flew back and forth between California and Wisconsin. John and Louie even sent wedding blossoms and wedding cake.

"I do heartily congratulate you on your new found happiness and trust it will increase as years pass on," Anne wrote May 2. "I send my earnest loving greetings to you and your wife and would be most happy to meet you both. It gives me much pleasure to think of your increased happiness. Lovingly, Mother."[21] She thought it would add so much to her eldest son's comfort to have a permanent home.

John had married into an adventurous and enterprising family. Louie's father, a physician, had come to America from Poland in 1840 after the Polish revolution. In Texas, he married Louisiana Erwin. That remarkable couple then made their way by wagon train from Texas to California in an adventure-filled journey.

The doctor, as Mrs. Strentzel fondly called her husband, bought many acres of land in the beautiful Alhambra valley hills at Martinez and beyond on the Coquinez Straits of Suisun Bay. There he turned his scientific mind to agriculture and eventually became known as the father of California horticulture. With the aid of a large Chinese crew, he planted many kinds of fruit into at least two thousand acres. He was active in the Horticultural Society, the Winegrowers Association, the local Grange, and other agricultural groups.

The Strentzels had provided Louie with an atmosphere of affection and rich culture. They often read aloud in the evenings from one of the many books in their library. Louie became an accomplished pianist, and Dr. and Mrs. Strentzel spent many hours listening to their daughter play.

Louie, who loved plants, grew beautiful flowers and learned from her father about cultivating peaches, grapes and other fruits. She delighted in the wild plants too and roamed the hills in search of native ferns.

Muir first became acquainted with the Strentzels through Jeanne Carr, his mentor from university days, who now lived in Oakland. Dr. Carr was then a chemistry professor in the medical department of the University of California, though he would shortly be named superintendent of public instruction. Jeanne Carr had continued her avid interest in botany and her abiding interest in John Muir and his career. One day in 1874 she introduced him to the Strentzel family when they all met briefly at her home. She felt that John and Louie would make a splendid pair.

The Strentzels and the Carrs shared mutual pursuits. Both Dr. Carr and Dr. Strentzel held medical interests in common and they all shared a love of plants. Both families were active in the Grange organization. Each had a wide circle of friends and often entertained scientific and culturally-minded people.

For many years Mrs. Strentzel kept a delightful daily journal written in her unique, concise style and grammar, chronicling the Strentzels' daily adventures and expressing her feelings.[22] For some time the Strentzels had been following John's adventures and reading his articles. Upon reading his account of a trip to Mt. Shasta, Mrs. Strentzel wrote in her diary August 20, 1877, "O why is it that no other can write like him."

A friendship developed between Muir and the Strentzels, and during several treks he carried on a correspondence with them. He and the doctor exchanged plant specimens along with their comments and analyses. Eventually, Muir gravitated to the Strentzel home in the

Alhambra Valley. By the spring of 1878, he visited them frequently from San Francisco where he was working on his manuscripts. As time went on, he took more and more interest in the gracious and popular Louie.

Mrs. Strentzel's April 20, 1878, diary entry related one Eastertime visit from John Muir. The Strentzels were attending a Grange meeting in Martinez that day. "I had to fill the lecturer's place, read Mr. Colby's address. At the close of the meeting, Charley told us that Mr. Muir had come and was already at our house. We were very sorry to be from home, and hurried on as fast as we could, arrived home, found he had gone on the hills and did not come in till near night, said he lay down and slept on top of the hill. We had dinner soon after he came in and spent the evening in pleasant conversation.

"Easter Sunday, partially cloudy, but a very pleasant day. At breakfast Louie made 4 tiny bouquets of pale fleur de lis and orange buds, one for each place, set in small glasses. We intended going to church, but gave it up on account of the visit of our friend. At 11, Dr., Mr. M., and Louie went walking in the orchard and on the hills. At 3 they returned laden with flowers and very tired and hungry. In the evening Mr. M. read some Scottish poetry for us. The evening was so cold we had to sit by the fire in the dining room, having taken out the stove some time ago. . . .

"This afternoon Mr. M. left for the City. He and Louie prepared a great bouquet of ferns and flowers for him to take with him, it must have weighed two or three pounds. Many of the roses were from little Johnnie's grave. Louie and the Dr. went with him to town." John and Louie Strentzel had lost their nine-year old son John Erwin in 1857, while their infant daughter Lottie had died in 1851 at the age of four months. Both children were buried in the nearby family cemetery.

In a few weeks Muir returned to Martinez. According to Mrs. Strentzel's diary, he arrived on the boat from San Francisco at the end of May looking pale and tired. "He carried a quantity of writing to do while resting here."

As usual, there was plenty of activity in the Strentzel home, but Muir probably did work on his manuscript during his six-day visit. One evening he and the other guests all sang Grange songs to Louie's piano accompaniment.

With the letters, the boxes of fruit the Strentzels sent to John, and his frequent visits to the Alhambra Valley ranch, the bond between him and the Strentzel family grew stronger. One day John, Louie, and the doctor drove around the area to look at a possible location for a new house for the Strentzels. John liked the site atop the hill where the doctor spoke of building. He and Louie did not realize then that they were looking at the future location of the home where they would live for many years.

According to Mrs. Strentzel's diary for December 27, 1878, John arrived in the Alhambra Valley on the overland train to spend a few days. On the 29th she commented: "this evening was so pleasant it seemed like a foretaste of Heaven. Louie and I dressed nicely and at 6 we all sat down to dinner. . . . after dinner we all sat by the fire in the dining room. Louie read from Scribner Mr. M's article 'The Birth of a Lake.' Mr. M. read many selections from Tennyson and Jean Ingelo. also read 'the wee, wee Bairnie.'"

May, 1879, found John once again at the Strentzels. This time he stayed about a week. He and Louie were spending more and more time together and often walked on the hills.

Two weeks later John returned for an overnight stay, an especially important occasion in his life. On June 17, 1879, Mrs. Strentzel's entry read:

"Yesterday evening Louie and Mr. Muir became engaged for life. Papa and I had retired, when about 7 o'clock Louie came to me, overcome with emotion, threw her arms around me, and said, 'O, Mother all is well, all is well.' we both thanked God for his mercies. She then went away, and I awakened papa and told him all. he seemed very much pleased but quiet. this morning we all arose with thankful hearts. I wonder if there ever were 4 happier people than we were. Mr. Muir seemed more beautiful and pure than ever before, and Louie seemed perfectly glorified and Angelic, and when we all sat down to breakfast, I felt that my own Son, my *Johnnie* had been given back to me. Mr. Muir

190

is the only man that the Dr. and I have ever felt that we could take into our family as one of us, and he is the only one that Louie has ever loved, altho' she has had many offers of marriage. O, can we ever feel thankful enough to God for sending us this man. after breakfast Louie and Mr. Muir remained in the parlor awhile, then walked in the orchard. at 3 o'clock he bade us good by and left for the City. O, it did seem so hard for him to leave so soon. Louie went with him to the cars, promising to go down to see him off on the steamer."

Seven years earlier Mrs. Strentzel had written in her diary with a sense of prophecy:

"Went with Dr. in vineyard, how delicious the fresh morning air, and how lovely everything looks, the peaches plums, cherries and quinces are now in bloom making the air fragrant with their rich odor. . . . I stopped about midway opposite the cañon, and stood gazing at the surrounding loveliness. The sun came shining down aslant the hills, throwing a flood of light over the pale green slopes, and the dark rich green of the buckeyes, laurels and live oaks while the sycamore and willows glittered in the sun like diamonds. It all seemed to be like enchantment and I thought of the future time to come when we will all be gone, and other generations will live here and enjoy this scene."

When John and Louie married that rainy day in April, 1880, they were well on the way to making her mother's vision come true. Future generations of the family did indeed enjoy this scene.

John's wedding was not the only one that took place that season. In Portage Joanna planned to marry Walter Brown in September. However, before they could be married, a problem arose with her father.

David wrote to John about it, June 26, 1880:

"Father reported himself very sick a month ago and urged Joanna to come to him. She went taking her intended with her to whom she is engaged to be married Sep. 7th. Mr. Walter Brown of Phillips, Wis. They found him feeble, unable to walk without crutches, but he has since regained his usual health. They have done all in their power to get him to come home, but as yet he says the Lord has not ordered him to return to Portage yet, but we expect Joanna will make out to bring him with her in August."

Then he turned to other family news.

"Jno Reid and family will go to Crete, Neb. in Sep. if all is well. He owns half an interest in 200 cows near there and intends to take a half interest in a meat market also.

"Dan, overworked, health threatened, couldn't collect his money now. [He is] located at 18th and K sts., Lincoln, Neb. [and] takes office business only. [He] has a large farm.

"Portage is certainly becoming worse for business. . . . For the past ten days we have been surrounded by water so that not a single customer could come in from the country."

David said his wife, Katie, was pretty well, and he brought John up to date on the ages of his children: Carrie was 16, Annie, 13, Will, 11, and John, 8.

"Mother is alone," he continued. "One of our or Jno Reid's girls generally stay with her nights.

"Sarah is getting over her trouble [the death of George] but still there is a sadness about her.

"Maggie is a feeble creature.

"P. S. I have a 20th interest in 14 claims, lodes and mines in Silver Cliff, Colorado, out of which I expect to make up for my lost time partly."[23]

July found Joanna and Walter still in Hamilton with Daniel Muir. Joanna explained to John that their father was sick and had sent for her. Walter had just come from Phillips to visit Joanna in Portage. He felt the long train trip and the care of her father would be too much for his fiancee and insisted on going with her.

"Accordingly I packed up at once and arrived in Hamilton four weeks ago today." She said that her father was nearly recovered now, but needed both a crutch and a cane to get around with.

"I cannot become accustomed to see Father thus crippled and I think he at last begins to realize he is growing old. He seems very happy to have me here, and is suited with everything I do thus far but he is just the same man he has ever been, and by this you know just what I mean."

Joanna was concerned about the welfare of both her parents.

"Mother had consented to stay with us which she with pleasure had consented to do, and so break up housekeeping entirely, and then when we came here, we used all our power to induce father to come too, that we might have the great pleasure of taking care of both in their old age, but unhappily, we could not persuade him. Now if it were not that Our Father always provides a way, I would be very much troubled, for certain it is, father can never be left again in his present condition. But I am praying that his mind may be changed and that he may feel differently towards us all, but in all probability he may be very many years in this world yet, and I could not stay always."[24]

On September 20, 1880, Anne completed the story for John:

"About the first of Aug. Joanna returned from Hamilton, her father and Mr. Brown accompanying her. Her marriage took place on the first of Sept. about thirty being present, mostly our own folks. The Baptist minister performed the service assisted by the Presbyterian minister. We could not think our company complete while you and your wife were absent."[25]

After their marriage, Joanna and Walter Brown set up housekeeping in Phillips in the midst of the northern Wisconsin pine forests where Mary and Willis Hand lived. Mary was happy that her sister and her new brother-in-law lived nearby.

"Your father remained here about six weeks," Anne wrote later to John, "but is now at Phillips with Joanna. His health is good but [he is] very lame indeed, being quite unable to walk across the room without his crutches. They were quite anxious to have me move to Phillips too, but for the last nine years I have lived in a brick house near the High School and it seems so like home to me that I decided to remain in Portage during the winter.

"You know how I always feel inclined to be stationary wherever my lot be cast—so Annie will remain with me for the present as she is the only one left to me now."[26]

Anne had never really said no when her husband urged her to come to Canada or Joanna urged her to come to Phillips. She just didn't do anything about it. The result was that she did indeed remain stationary.

"My dear Brother and Sister," Joanna wrote October 25, 1880.

"The [story of the] glacier was refreshing and interested my husband exceedingly. He has traveled a great deal in wild woods and loves the beauties of nature as much as I do.

"We have a cozy home in the bosom of the pine forest, and I can step out the back door and gather darling little ferns and mosses just at the farther end of our lot. We have mosses like those you sent in the letter, and many others.

"We are located at the end of the village from Mary, but can see each other often. M. is very well and has a nice little boy.

"You will be sorry to hear that father after coming here with us and staying about a month again became restless and determined to return to Hamilton. He said he had not been able to withstand our entreaties and had come almost against his sense of right and that though he enjoyed his stay with us very much he must now return to a place where he might labor for the Lord as he could find nothing to do in so small a place [as Phillips].

"It seemed we could not let him go away into the cold world again but words were in vain and he left us with tears in his . . . eyes.

"We have this satisfaction, however, that his health aside from his lameness is now excellent and his mind more composed than I have . . . ever known it, and I think he has a kindlier feeling toward the whole world.

"Moreover the end is not yet and I believe he will yet spend his last days with us. I told him that the room we had arranged for him would be his still, and would always be kept for him till he should come back to it.

"Mother intends coming up in the spring if she can dispose of her property satisfactorily."[27]

Daniel Muir was glad to return to Hamilton. Annie explained to her brother Dan on December 22, 1880, that "Your father is happier than ever since he got back to Hamilton but writes that he is ashamed to think that he allowed himself to come to Wisconsin."[28]

By November of 1880 Maggie and John Reid joined in the westward trek. They left Portage to settle in Crete, Nebraska on the Big Blue River about twenty miles from Dan and Emma Muir in Lincoln. Sarah was especially sorry to see them leave. She had once referred to herself and Maggie as "the other twins."

"So Maggie has left us for the far west," Sarah wrote to her brother John December 3, 1880, "and how we miss them all. Our family took so much pleasure in each other's company and were so much together."[29]

Crete, with a population of two thousand, was the hub of a thriving agricultural community surrounded by nearly-filled homestead lands. It was a stopover point for settlers headed farther west.

A letter to the editor of the *Wisconsin State Register* January 2, 1880, from a Crete resident described the area.

". . . now the land is under cultivation for hundreds of miles, and every ten or twelve miles you can find a lively little town.

"Business in the town of Crete is all the time on the gain; the town is filled with teams from the country with all kinds of produce; also you will find any amount of cattle and hogs on the market. One can hardly get across the street for teams.

"The emigration still continues to pour in. There is scarcely a day that we cannot see teams on the street, bound for the far west. . . . There will be quite a rush from this part of the state in the spring, as they are starting new towns and building railroads in all directions."

The writer noted the warm weather they were having compared to the cold weather in December.

"I think that to be about the time John Reid, of Portage, was out here with two car-loads of young cattle. I was down to the corall [sic] one day this week, to see them. I think the warm weather has made a decided improvement in them—they are looking fine."[30]

John was well underway with his cattle business, and the family was well settled in their new location.

The past two years had brought momentous changes to the Muir family as they were carried "down the stream of time." They were now spread out across Wisconsin, Nebraska, and California. Three of Anne Muir's children remained nearby—David and Annie in Portage, and Sarah at Mound Hill farm.

Sarah said to John, "How truly you say 'we are like winged seeds flying off in all directions and taking root so far apart.'"[31]

# XII

# MY DEAR WANDERER

*In all our devious ways and wanderings*
*we have loved one another.*
—John Muir

"We have all been busy as bees all day,"[1] Annie informed Dan on December 22. She was helping her brother David at Parry & Muir during the 1880 Christmas season.

"It leaves Mother alone a good deal," Sarah commented, "but she does not seem to mind it. She says she is not lonely and always seems cheerful. She goes out quite frequently and seems to enjoy herself."[2]

After the Christmas rush was over, Annie went to Phillips for the balance of the winter where she enjoyed a good visit with Joanna and her twin sister Mary. The three younger sisters had always been close, and welcomed the chance to get together as they used to do when they were growing up.

It was a snowy winter, with drifts piling up ten and twelve feet high in Portage and the surrounding countryside. Anne went out to Mound Hill to stay with the Galloways. The eight miles to their farm was about as far away from her own home as she was willing to go for any length of time. Her visit may have helped the Galloways with the loss of their son. It had been a year and a half since George's death, and they missed him still.

Later she wrote to John that "Sarah and I went up to the garret and saw a good many of your things that were put into her care when we left the farm."[3] Among them were the precious plant specimens from his walk to the Gulf of Mexico he had entrusted to Sarah fourteen years before.

Anne stayed with Sarah and David during January, February, and March. When the weather warmed up somewhat and the snow melted, they brought her back to Portage.

She was happy to hear the good news from Martinez of the birth of Annie Wanda to John and Louie on March 25, 1881.

"It pleases me much to think that you have now a home and family," she wrote her son on April 8. It gave her joy that her eldest son who had roamed outside the family circle for so long had found such a happy home.

Then Anne shared some of her underlying philosophy that daily provided her with serenity in the face of problems and disappointments.

"God has dealt very tenderly and kindly with me in many ways but he has especially blessed me in sparing all my children to grow up to be useful members of society—and a great comfort to me. True they have nearly all left the old farm but still I do rejoice in all their joys and happiness."[4]

That summer Anne Muir sold to the city the brick house by the high school where she had lived for nine years, the agreement providing that by paying rent she could continue living there as long as she wished. By September she and Annie were settled in another home in Portage, the sixth house they had lived in since the first time the family moved to Portage from Hickory Hill twenty years earlier.

Sarah called upon her mother and informed John how delighted she was to see how neat and cozy everything was arranged. News of her husband was not good. "David does not feel able to work as he used to do when you were here—keeps doing all he can."

She wrote fondly of her girls.

"Anna is just the same good, willing trusty girl she has ever been to us. She taught school this past summer. She will be 24 next Dec. Celia is a lively laughing body, a help in the household, quite a musician, 16 tomorrow. Gracie, our little girl, is fond of going with her father and helping him do chores. Quite a reader. 8 years old next month."[5]

In great contrast to his family's daily domestic affairs, John was in the midst of exciting adventures and icy danger. Eager to study the ice and glacier patterns of northern lands and seas, he was aboard the revenue steamer "Corwin" sailing the Arctic region off the northern coasts of Siberia and Alaska. The "Corwin," under the command of Captain Calvin L. Hooper, had sailed from San Francisco on May 5, 1881. One of its missions was to look for signs of the lost vessel "Jeanette" carrying Lt. George W. De Long's Arctic exploration expedition which had not been heard from for two years.

There followed an odyssey of travel through the treacherous ice floes that had crushed many a whaling vessel; of coastal mountain explorations; of visits to death-ravaged native villages; of glorious sights amid the Arctic twilight; and, important to Muir, landing at unexplored Wrangel Land, an Arctic Ocean island. At the time it was not known whether the area was an island or a land mass.[6]

Later, Portage area people shared a part of Muir's adventurous journey when they read his account from Plover Bay, Siberia, reprinted in the *Wisconsin State Journal* from the *San Francisco Bulletin*.[7] He emphasized the need to explore the bleak and mysterious Wrangel Land to see whether or not it was a land formation. He did not mention he was present when Captain De Long raised the flag there and claimed the land for the United States.

Muir did not know then that the "Jeanette" had endured until June 12, 1881, when she was crushed by ice and sank in the Arctic Ocean. Only thirteen of the original thirty-four crewmen survived. De Long perished with the others. Ironically, the "Corwin" was then sailing Arctic Ocean waters.

Once again the California and Wisconsin families anxiously awaited word from John. At the end of September Louie wrote joyously to her mother-in-law. Anne and Louie had never met, but they maintained a friendly correspondence.

"Glorious news today from the far, far north! Our beloved wanderer is coming home. . . . Surely in all the wide world there will be no woman more blessed than I when I have my husband and our baby once more safe and well by our own fireside."

Louie had both an open heart and an open home. In the home where she grew up and during her marriage to John she was accustomed to providing warm hospitality to the many people who made their way to the ranch, no matter how long their stay. She was happy in her beautiful Alhambra Valley and wanted now to share it with her husband's mother.

"Dear, dear Mother, if only you could be here to welcome your beloved son! [Think of] John's intense joy. California is only five days' journey from Wisconsin.

"Do you not sometimes think of coming in our blossom time— to behold the wonderful Yosemite and the beautiful Sierra forests that John loves so well? How glad I should be to give you a true home, welcome and to thank you in more than words for the precious gift of your son who has brought joy and steadfast blessedness to my heart and life.

"However, it be, I trust that before many months we shall all meet in the delight of a grand reunion, parents and children and grandchildren.

"I long to see that lovely Fountain Lake where John first knew the charms of a fresh wilderness and the exquisite water-lilies. How the blue eyes of baby Annie Wanda will shine over the snow chalices."[8]

Anne was pleased with the love for John Louie expressed and for her gracious invitation, but, as usual, she was inclined to remain stationary.

In November Anne had news of a less happy nature to report to John.

"Your father has been home for a short time and has now gone to Phillips. I don't think he will go back again to Hamilton as he has sold his property there. Mr. Brown intends going to Arkansas to make a home there and your father is determined to go with him, he using your father's money. Your father is well, but very feeble and lame, walking and leaning on two crutches, but as strong minded as he ever was."[9]

She wrote again in February. "Your father came home about Christmas and stayed until Joanna and Walter came to make us a visit on the way south, and when they left he accompanied them. His health is quite good, although [he is] still quite lame."[10]

It is not known how deep Anne's feelings were about the events she chronicled so matter of factly. After they bid each other goodbye, and the door closed behind him, Anne and Daniel Muir never saw each other again.

Their situation in recent years was an enigma. When Anne did not follow her husband to Canada, their pattern of separate lives became permanent. She never visited him in Hamilton. Although Daniel came back to Portage from to time, he always felt compelled to return to his evangelistic activities. He was achieving an inner satisfaction he had never before known.

When her father first became disabled, Joanna had been able to coax him to leave Canada and stay with her and Walter in Phillips, but Daniel soon returned to Hamilton to preach at the agricultural market. In the end, when he was no longer able to keep up his property or continue his evangelistic work, he returned to the Browns' home in Phillips. He had always doted on his youngest daughter, and when his health became precarious, depended on her more and more to provide him comfort. At this time in his life Daniel was completely self-indulgent.

It is not clear why Joanna would again seek to take her father away from Portage and her mother, where he would have received good care from the family. Anne was in good health and her daughter Annie was usually home. David Muir lived nearby, while Sarah was just eight miles away at Mound Hill.

After Daniel's departure for Arkansas, Anne continued her usual way of living. "I have near neighbors and a very comfortable house,"[11] she said.

The Browns settled near Jefferson, in Jefferson County, Arkansas where Walter engaged in an extensive logging and milling operation. Joanna said they were located twenty-four miles southeast of Little Rock and sixteen miles north of Pine Bluff near a railroad where excursionists come. She commented on the magnificent weather.

Anne explained to John that Walter was one of a company of wealthy men who had invested in pine lands and had erected a sawmill, a store, and boarding house and employed over twenty men. There was no settlement near them.

By the next month Joanna was having problems with her father.

"Father, although entirely satisfied with this climate, has become restless once more and expresses his wish to return to Canada," she confided to John on April 22, 1882.

"He can't take care of himself. He wants to rent rooms and board himself. He can do more good there, can go into the market, see many people without moving about. You can't reason with him.

"All that remains of his possessions, Walter owes $1100 business loan, $200, promissory note, 2 small houses in Portage.

"Can't detain him against his will or we won't have a moment's peace. Won't board with a family. He must have his own way about everything or he is unhappy." [12]

Joanna's last statement held an important clue to Daniel's life and behavior. He had always insisted on his own way, and he was not about to change now. A few days later Joanna touched on an equally important part of her father's character—his restlessness—in one of her frequent letters to Mary.

". . . his restless spirit never forsakes him. He says that he can do more good in Hamilton market than in any place he ever was and that he must go back for he is only happy when employed." [13]

On June 7 she wrote to Mary again.

"John is very much excercized about it but of course realizes the helplessness of us all to do anything in the case." [14]

Anne wrote to John in August. "I am not surprised at you fretting about the news you had about Father as you are entirely ignorant of his proceeding for many years. But our fretting is of no avail whatever. He was still with Joanna two weeks ago." [15]

Although John was upset with his father, Anne Muir had resigned herself to whatever took place. It was the secret to her serenity.

Earlier, she had commented on the times:

"Portage is now a very busy place, and her boundaries are much enlarged. Every season many fine large buildings are going up.

Farmers produce of every kind has so much more value than for many years."[16]

If Anne did not like to travel, Sarah and Maggie did. That September Sarah and her sister Annie boarded the train for Crete, Nebraska. Annie stayed on at the Reids while Sarah and Maggie went on to California to the Martinez ranch where John and Louie gave them a warm welcome. The sisters had a fine time amid the pleasant surroundings.

From the tone of their letters, Mary concluded that Maggie and Sarah thought that in California they were in the enchanted land.

David Muir envied his brother and sisters staying in such a fine climate. In Portage the thermometer registered between 18 and 24 degrees below zero and he had to get up in the night to stir the fire in both wood stoves to keep the house warm. He told the California family he weighed 150 pounds and felt better than he had in years. It was Christmas time and he was again busy in the store.

"Thought of you climbing mountains and getting flowers, mentioning oranges and trees, also blossoms made us think less of home and sigh for the ability to fly south with the birds."[17]

On New Year's day, 1883, John wrote to Mary and Willis Hand at Phillips. "Maggie & Sarah still here—though husbands grumbling. They need rest and change of climate and scene more than any two other women I have seen out of bed."

He contemplated on how far apart the family was.

"One strikes root more or less deeply whenever we chance to stop any length of time and in the case of a family like ours growing in different kinds of soil and with varying pursuits etc. Death is about the only harvester than can bring us together."[18]

Anne Muir was delighted with the arrival of the boxes of greenery on New Year's day that John sent from California. She appreciated what an undertaking it was for him to pack up the beautiful specimens of trees and flowers. She and the others admired the plants, and as they spread them on the table and read the labels, they felt closer to the California family.

Maggie and Sarah felt a special holiday joy this year. They loved the fine weather, the beauty of the hills and vineyards, and the busy town of Martinez on the Coquinez Strait. They came to know and love Louie and Wanda, their little niece, and they relished spending time with John. It had been such a long time since they had seen him.

The two sisters spent the winter in the Alhambra Valley, returning to Crete at the end of March greatly refreshed. David Galloway met Sarah at the Reids. He had missed his wife during her long absence and was glad to take her home.

Several months later Sarah reminisced about the wonderful time she and Maggie had at the ranch in the Alhambra Valley.

"Oh, John, it is so pleasant to think of you all now—I can almost see you. The pleasant home among the trees and flowers, and surrounded by those grand old hills. I can remember the form of every one of them, and something of the wonderful beauty of their light and shade. When I look around your dooryard I can see the door open, and Louie comes out with little Wanda, the darling."[19]

Once again spring arrived in Wisconsin, and summer with the strawberry season was close at hand on the Galloway farm. The warm weather returned and the landscape was at its finest. Sarah described the countryside in her June 2, 1883, letter to John and Louie.

"I had a beautiful walk in our woods a short time ago away down at the little pond where there are so many ferns. They are just as plentiful and beautiful as ever. The wood is cleared off on the further side, which spoils the effect, but still I wished that you Louie, could have been with me, for I know you would have enjoyed a little wandering about in woods that John was telling you about last winter.

"I wish you could see the country now. Everything is so fresh and green.—Anna [Galloway] was calling me to come out and see the beauty of the sunset near the hills all about us."[20]

In the meantime, Walter Brown had sold his Arkansas logging operation and moved his family to Kansas City, Missouri, to pursue a career selling real estate. They took Daniel with them. Joanna reported to John June 1, 1883, that Daniel was comfortable, but stayed in bed.

The year since Sarah began her California trip had passed quickly. On October 19, 1883, she wrote to John and Louie.

"It will soon be a year since Maggie and I started on our journey to California. Truly time flies swiftly. The woods here are already brown and wintery looking. . . . the days . . . will soon be upon us, when there is no place so comforting as the fireside. We are still at the Mound Hill farm, but . . . it may not be for more than the coming winter."[21] Sarah explained that David was anxious to sell because he was not able to work the farm alone and didn't think it paid to hire help.

The sisters and brothers were concerned about Annie. Sometime in November, 1882, their sister had taken a cold and been ill off and on ever since. Joanna said Annie's lungs were consolidated. During the summer of 1883 Annie stayed with Mary in Phillips hoping the air of the northern pine forest might help her, but when she returned to Portage in September her cough was worse than ever.

Sarah informed John in her October letter that several doctors advised Annie to go to Nebraska. John Reid was visiting in Portage at the time. He was telling everyone about life in Crete and about his farming operation and the four thousand sheep he would be feeding that winter. When he returned home he took Annie with him.

At the Reids that winter she was under the care of her brother Dan who came down from Lincoln to examine her and give her medical advice. She was able to sit up during the day, doing fancy work to pass the time. She also took short walks and looked after her room. John urged Annie to come to California, but she couldn't muster the strength to make such a long journey. She was even too weak to go as far as Kansas City to see Joanna and her father.

In November Joanna reported from Kansas City: "Father well, but weak. He spends most of his time lying down and thinking. As fleshy and healthy as ten years ago, and seems happy and contented all of the time now." Joanna said that her father took pleasure in Ethel, his little granddaughter.

"Mother is well but deaf. I think Mother holds her grounds wonderfully with old age. So well and strong at seventy."[22]

"For the first time in my life I am quite alone," Anne Muir informed John that fall. "Celia G. [Galloway] goes to school in Portage and is with me overnight. I try to keep myself very busy at home and I go out a good deal. I enjoy a long walk on green hills or in woods when the weather is fine. David Muir is very kind. Always gets my wood for me and assists me in more ways than I can tell of."

Her usual serenity shown through as she added, "I hope you will not think of me as lonesome as I daily feel that I am loaded with benefits and blessings far beyond what I deserve."[23]

At the end of January, 1884, Joanna wrote to John from Kansas City about their father's condition.

"Father is indeed contented and happy at last. He seems to be enjoying an abiding peace with God. He has no other thought or theme and seems gentler and more considerate than I ever knew him. He spends almost all of his time in bed now and complains of great weakness in his back. Otherwise he is perfectly well."[24]

As the winter wore on, David was working hard to make a go of Parry & Muir. In February he explained to John, "We do our share of business here and keep a good assortment of goods and stand well in the community, but we have to sell on small margin and have to pay interest on so much of our capital that we make little headway."[25]

In February Sarah described her mother's way of life for John. Mother looking well. Her manner of living is simple and easy. She must have her poritch [sic] and milk in the morning, goes out to dinner at an eating house kept by an Edinburgh Scotchman near her home, and for supper she takes just a morsel of something, or often nothing at all, thinking she can sleep better without it. So as not to disarrange her plans, we send Celia to dinner at the same place with her, and I prepare and send provisions for her other meals. She has a washwoman come to the house when required. So you see, Mother keeps house in the easiest manner possible."[26]

John was concerned about his mother and he and Louie made another effort to persuade her to come live with them on the ranch.

"I thank you for your very kind offer of a home with you in Calif.," Anne answered March 6. "I think it would be pleasant but you well know that I am such a homebody that I never could even think of it, but I shall not forget your kindness in this matter."

She added philosophically, "Father reaches his 80th year this month and I am just nine years behind him, so we have reached the span of life allotted to us."[27]

When John's 46th birthday rolled around, Anne reminisced sadly, "The currant scones are not forgotten, but where are those that used to gather together at such times—all scattered everyone."

She continued her April 21st note to her eldest son with news of David Galloway's poor health which had long been of concern to the family. She said that someone else had to drive him to Portage and that he came to town twice a week.

Anne said that David was offered $3,000 for his farm. "Some are advising him to keep it as there is a good home on it and a good orchard, and let the land to some of his neighbors."[28]

While her brother-in-law's health declined, Annie Muir began to feel somewhat better. On April 5, 1884, she left the Reids to spend a few days in Lincoln with Dan and his family.

"Four bright little black-eyed girls as happy and rosy-cheeked as you could wish to see, fill the house with the clatter and glee of joyous childhood."[29]

Annie was able to continue on to Joanna's home in Kansas City. "Her little girl is a great comfort to us all, so sunny and happy is she in disposition. Father has changed but little since I saw him two years ago. He stays in his room most of the time and seems quite content."[30]

That summer there was more worrisome news from Portage. David Muir's beloved wife Katie was very ill with cancer. At the end of June his mother wrote to Dan, "Katie is much worse. Now she fully understands her situation. David is much tried about all this."[31]

In early September, 1884, according to Anne, there was "nothing encouraging about Katie Muir or David Galloway. Tires him to walk across the floor."[32]

David died September 28, 1884. It fell to David Muir to tell his brother John.

"David Galloway died today at 12m at the house of John Foster. I suppose you know he had been very sick for a long time. For the last five or six days his death has been hourly expected. His remains will be buried at the Louden Graham Cemetery in Buffalo on Tuesday, 30th inst. They rented a nice house here and moved in but took David to John Fosters while they were settling the house and there he died. D. G. Muir for Sarah."[33]

So Sarah, who had always made such a pleasant home for her family, was left alone at the age of forty-six. She and David had been married twenty-eight years. Within five years' time she was devastated by the loss of both her son and her husband. She and her three girls must now make it on their own.

A few weeks after David's death Sarah wrote a sad, lonely letter to John and Louie. She said Annie was at home as was Gracie who attended school in Portage. Celia was teaching school about eight miles out in the country. Her mother was well and came to visit frequently. Katie Muir was still very ill.

John was having his own problems in Martinez. He confided to David that he wanted someone to learn the fruit business and take the personal supervision of the ranch off his shoulders. Without the day-to-day burden of running a large fruit ranch he would be better able to travel and to continue his writing and other conservation efforts.

On March 28, 1885, David Muir wrote a second sad letter to John and Louie. It was not unexpected.

"Katie died last eve at 6. She had been feeling [as] well as usual up to 26th at noon, when she took a chill, then a fever and when that passed off, died. Buried here on Monday."[34]

Ironically, David's marriage to Catherine Cairns may never have taken place if John had had his way twenty-five years before. He had tried so hard to talk his brother out of marriage in favor of continuing his university studies. He now sent him a long letter of consolation on the death of his beloved wife.

"Not many I think have enjoyed more in marriage union and walk through life than yourself and Katie Cairns."[35]

Anne was glad that Katie's suffering was ended and thought David could take comfort in his children. In her letter to John on his forty-seventh birthday she said that Carrie, 20, was a bright girl and a good housekeeper, and Annie, 17, expected to graduate in the summer.

"Sarah has moved to a larger house and I am going to have rooms with her. Her 2 daughters are both teaching so there is only one at home."

Their new home was located some blocks farther from the center of town. "I go rather reluctantly so far up on 'Prospect Hill' as I am not quite capable of taking the long walks I used to enjoy so much, but now I am doubting if I will be able to get to church or Post office."[36]

However, Anne adjusted to the move very well. She had three rooms and the use of the kitchen in the large pleasant home on the hill overlooking the Wisconsin River.

"We find our home on Prospect Hill to be very comfortable," she wrote John, on June 15, 1885, "but the long walk to church or to the business part of the city seems quite an undertaking. However I did get to church yesterday and enjoyed the services very much."[37]

On the 29th of June Anne was happy to tell Dan the good news that Annie arrived home from Kansas City in time to enjoy his birthday currant scones. Her daughter was feeling better.

There was more sadness in store for the family. On July 15, 1885, while the Browns were staying in WaKenney, Kansas, during the summer, their six-month-old daughter Winnie died of cholera infantum. Joanna and Walter took her back to Kansas City immediately and buried her the next day in Elmwood Cemetery near their home. It was the second time they suffered the loss of a baby.

There was more to come. Years later John Muir told about the premonition he felt that August day in 1885 while working in his Martinez study. He had received no word that his father was ill, but knew that he must go to Kansas City if he were to see him before he died. He first took the train to Portage.

"I am with my mother at last, and Sarah and David, all that is left of them," he wrote to Louie August 30.

"Arrived here yesterday morning at 12:30 o'clock and went to bed at a hotel.

"Found David's store in the morning. He recognized me instantly, strange to say, and took me to Mother and Sarah. They saw me afar off, guessing by Dave and the Satchel who I was. Anna, too, is here living with Mother and Sarah, who have rented a house in common. All are well as usual.

"Mother does not seem so much older as I expected, is yet erect and quick in conversation, though her voice has failed somewhat. Sarah is easily agitated and is far from strong.

"Anna is much better since her return to Portage but whether she is out of danger yet I am not all sure. She sits up most of the time, but any slight walk or exertion in the kitchen exhausts and sends her to bed for an hour or two. I don't know what to do as to advising her to stay here or undertake the journey with me to California. David is much bent and worn and bears the marks of all these years with their burden of care and grief."[38]

John described his nieces, Carrie, the eldest, and Anna as fine, sensible, well-behaved young women. Carrie was to leave home the next day to travel two hundred miles northward to teach music. She would stay with an old friend of the family. Anna was keeping house for her father and young brothers, Wilberforce, 16, and John, 12. Muir described Wilberforce as quite a carpenter who was building a boat and said that his nephew John was an amiable little fellow. In another letter he wrote that young John was a "queer, cute, quiet, narrow faced clipper built boy, noticing everything, saying nothing, knows every dog, cow, horse, man, woman and child in Portage."[39]

"Sarah's girls are fat and strong," John continued his August 30 letter to Louie, "well able to take care of themselves excepting Gracie, the baby who is bright and interesting.

"Of course they are like to eat me up and I have a busy talking time rambling over all the occurrences of the 18 years since last we met and as I lost some sleep arriving in the middle of the night I have not been feeling very well.

"We are sitting today at Sarah's and Mother's house by a fire. The sky is all dark and rainy, all the grass rank and green.

"I mean to stop with Mother about ten or twelve days, then go to Fountain Lake one day to see the lilies that used to charm me when a boy and the calopogons and cypripediums and Osmundas and a few of the old settlers who used to care for me and lend me books, especially Mr. Duncan, a Scotch mason who still remembers me, then on to K[ansas] C[ity] & Crete. I should like to spend a few weeks about the Lake region [the great lakes] to learn the inscriptions recorded there. . . . How cool the weather is and how green the grass and how small the trees look and how low the hills, nothing high enough for a landmark—and how lavish the flow of waters in the streams."[40]

For the next three weeks John roamed his boyhood haunts. Reveling in the landscape of his youth, he wrote to his five-year-old daughter Wanda September ninth from her "Grandma Muir's house."

"There is a pretty lake here where Papa used to live when he was a little boy and pretty ducks and fishes swim about in the lake and beautiful lilies like roses grow around the edges of the lake, and violets and lilies and ferns in a meadow and blue flowers and some white ones and pink ones.

"Papa hardly knew the places where he used to live because somebody else lives there now and new houses have been built and fences and the trees have been cut down and many little trees have grown up and the apple trees that papa planted most all died last winter because it was so frosty although they were so big and old but the crab apple trees and the kind they call Duchess of Oldenburg.

"Papa had to buy an overcoat to keep warm it is so cold and people make big fires in stoves to keep warm."[41]

The next day he wrote a long letter to Louie about the family.

"I have just returned from a visit to the old people and old places about our first home in America ten or twelve miles to the north of this place.

"Mother is still strong and well and alive to everything, and takes long walks to church and to visit her many old friends in town, and evidently enjoys life here. She will never leave Portage while any of the family remain here."

John told Louie that Annie would go at least as far as Kansas City with him for she dreaded the cold Wisconsin winter. Then, if she could stand the fatigue of a journey, she would go on to California with her brother.

"Sarah is looking very sick and miserable and I am troubled about her. She cannot bear any excitement or exertion without suffering from nervous prostration. The death of both son and husband, the breaking up of home, sale of the farm etc. have been too heavy and she is badly crushed.

"I suppose she will remain here with Mother. The girls can take care of themselves, except Gracie, who is rapidly growing and will soon be a woman, and there is property enough to support her in comfort, as far as property can.

"John Reid has been investing some of her money in Nebraska land, and I think if she leaves Portage she will settle in Nebraska." However, in a letter to John on July 4, Maggie said that her husband invested money for Sarah in cheap land in Kansas, not Nebraska.

"David is tied up securely in his store," John continued. "He is looking very old and gray and shows too plainly the scars of life's battles. The death of his dear wife to whom he was unreservedly devoted, was a terrible blow and her long illness (cancer of the breast) with its night and day waiting and watching, with the suffering of sympathy, has made sad havoc with the David Muir I used to know. Still my visit with him to the old home and meeting all the old neighbors has brightened him up considerably, and all the rest say that it was worth my journey here just to cheer and revive Dave. He looks older than I do.

"I saw nearly all of the old neighbors, the young folk, of course grown out of memory and unrecognizable, but most of the old I found but little changed by the 18 years since I last saw them and the warmth of my welcome was in most instances excruciating.

"William Duncan, the old Scotch stone-mason, who loaned me books when I was little and always declared that 'Johnie Moor will make a name for himsel' some day' I found hale and hearty, 81 years of age, and not a gray hair in his curly bushy locks, firm of step, voice firm with a clear calm ring to it, memory as good as ever apparently, and his interest in all the current news of the world as fresh and as far-reaching. I stopped overnight with [him] and talked till midnight.

"We were four days in making the rounds and had to make desperate efforts to get away.

"We climbed the Observatory that used to be the great cloud-capped mountain of our child's imagination but it dwindled now to a mere hill 250 feet high, half the height of that vineyard hill opposite the house. The porphory outcrop on the summit is very hard and I was greatly interested in finding it grooved and polished by the ice sheet. . . ."[42]

John had a wonderful time visiting the family and friends he hadn't seen for eighteen years and roaming the landscape he knew so well as a boy. Finally, it was time to make plans to proceed to Kansas City. On September 19th he informed Louie in another long letter that he had persuaded David to accompany him to Kansas City and, perhaps, Nebraska.

"He is so set in his business here that he fancies he cannot spend a cent or minute. The small trip around the neighborhood waked him to some semblance of his old, joking, laughing, witty self, and everybody remarks the change I compelled in him. . . .I convinced him that he would never again see father alive unless he made this visit this year.

"I found that the firm of Parry and Muir still owed [me] $800, and interest for ten years making altogether about $1600, as he showed me a note bearing interest at 10 per cent. I had not the conscience of a Jewish banker and therefore reduced the interest to 7 per cent, then drew the $560 interest and gave back half of it to David as I did not wish to charge him anything for the use of the money, but Parry only. Therefore, I have received $280 which will be enough to bring Anna and I home, and I have not been compelled to draw on Upham at all. The $800 is still left with the firm and is safe enough I guess.

"And I have directed David to give little John $100 out of the interest money as soon as it accrues and invest it for him until he is of age, leaving us, of course, a clear 3 1/2% on the $800.

"As I had forgotten all about the debt and expected nothing I felt that I have been quite generous and at a very moderate expense while actually getting rich in the middle of generosity.

"David has been 20 years in the business and is well known and doing fairly well. Do not think he will ever leave Portage or change his business materially though yet young.

"I have been regarded as a great curiosity here and have been called on to recognize about a thousand people that I never heard of, but who declared they knew me passing well, etc. Willis Hand is expected here tonight.

John continued that he had been "writing and drawing nice album pages for heaven knows how many of these sentimental nieces and nephews and all this introduction to every man woman and child in Portage, 7000 or so."

But he was concerned about his current manuscript. He hadn't worked on it since he had been in Portage, but he maintained that "I shall lock the door tomorrow" and work on it then.

"The weather here has been very like California winter—wet and dry with occasional frosts, cool and pleasant with slight hints of rheumatism."

At Sarah's John looked over his treasured possessions he had originally left at Hickory Hill Farm. When the Muirs moved from Hickory Hill she stored them in her attic at Mound Hill, and later brought everything with her to Portage.

"I found the plants from Florida and the South in good condition and have had a grand overhauling of them and repacking for Cal. Also the wooden clock and some other old traps of queer construction, some of which I will bring with me, with old drawings, letters, etc."[43]

In another week's time John's Wisconsin homecoming finally came to a close. Then, he, David, and Annie boarded the train for Kansas City. When they arrived at Joanna's home they found Daniel Muir very ill.

"Father is very feeble and helpless," John explained to Louie, September 26, "and within the last month or two has failed very much. He is often for a few moments in a kind of bewildered stupor, out of which he awakens with a start and is conscious in a bright, keen way for a few moments or so, and again loses the power of attention. He is very emaciated also, and he eats but little. I feel the end is near.

"He does not know me and I am very sorry. He looks at me and takes my hand and says 'is this my dear John' and then sinks away on the pillow exhausted without being able to understand the answer.

"This morning when I went to see him and was talking broad Scotch to him, hoping to stir some of the old memories of Scotland before we came here, he said 'I don't know very much aboot it noo' and then added, 'You're a Scotchman aren't you?'

"When I would repeat that I was his son John that went to California a long time ago and came back to see him he would start and raise his head and say 'O yes, my dear wanderer' and then lose all memory again—the next minute when he awakes he has to be told again who I am, but David and Anna and all the rest of the family he knows readily.

"He is conscious that his last days are drawing nigh and seems resigned, though eager for love and encouragement. It was only a few months ago that he said, while yet in full possession of his faculties, that he had made terrible mistakes in dealing with his children and in particular mentioned some of the cruel things he had said and done to his poor wandering son John, and advised Joanna to be careful to rule her children only by love.

"I sent for a physician last evening to consult with him about his condition and how best to smooth his way to the grave. He said there is no disease—that he might live for months or die at any hour, and that he should not be left alone.

"I had already consulted with Joanna and Walter about hiring a nurse at once. When the doctor came father asked whether he was going to die now, and seemed glad to be told that there was no probability of his dying yet.

"Though I expect to be here only a week I fear that David and I will see him laid at rest. I'm sorry I couldn't have been here two or three months earlier though I suppose all may be well as it is."[44]

At this last reunion John made peace with himself concerning his father. The stern facts of his childhood had not changed, but he came to terms with them. As for Anne Muir, it would be difficult to tell just how she felt about her husband's final illness. Daniel had gone his own way long ago and she had continued her life quite well without him.

On September 30, when she answered a letter from Louie, she did not refer directly to her husband's situation. She only expressed her feelings about John coming home. "His presence here has been to me an unspeakable pleasure, for which I have longed and do now feel thankful that circumstances enabled him to come amongst us even for a short time. I think his health improved a little while he was with us."[45]

In Kansas City, John wrote daily to Louie. On October 4 he said he was glad he persuaded Dan to come "to make as sure as I could that everything possible was being done to smooth these last sad childish days of old age as well as to gather once more about him." On this day, six of the Muir brothers and sisters were there—John, David, Dan, Joanna, Mary, and Annie. Sarah was not able to come, and Maggie remained in Crete.

"I want Mother to come as soon as possible," John continued, "and will call her by telegram today. She ought to have been here weeks ago, but I am afraid she will not be able to endure the fatigue of the journey, as she is not used to travel."[46]

On October fifth he wrote, "I have been thinking of calling in a photographer, as no portrait of any sort of him has ever been made, but Mary has just completed a crayon sketch, partly from memory that is better than a photograph now that he is so emaciated and his features all over-shadowed by death. . . . The command 'Thou shalt not make unto thee any graven image or likeness of anything,' was his ground of dislike of pictures in general."[47]

Daniel Muir died in the early morning hours of October 6, 1885. The Kansas City, Missouri death record states that the cause of his death was old age and that his medical attendant was C. P. Catheart. He was buried in Elmwood Cemetery a little over three miles from Joanna's home at 803 Wabash in the same plot where Joanna and Water had placed their baby Winnie just three months before. Maggie came from Crete, but Dan did not attend the funeral.

John's obituary information given in his letter to Louie October 6, summed up his father's life and personality.

"Few lives that I know of were more restless and eventful than his— few more toilsome and full of enthusiastic endeavor onwards toward light and truth and eternal love through the midst of the devils of terrestrial strife and darkness and faithless misunderstanding that well-nigh overpowered him at times and made bitter burdens for us all to bear. . . .

"At length brought to earth by old age and a broken limb, he was yet youthful and enthusiastic to the end, his mind active and glowing like a fire beneath all his burden of years and pains."[48]

On November 20 Sarah shared her feelings with her brother, now back home in California, about their father's death.

"Yes, John, we were all glad and thankful that so many of the family could be with Father these last days of his life. It must be a great satisfaction to all. When your telegram reached us mother said at once that she could not come. I told her I thought it would be a great satisfaction to her in after days to be together once more, but she said she felt that the journey and all connected with it would be too much for her, that if she should go she did not think she would ever come back again. Of course I could say no more. . . ."[49]

John was disappointed that every member of the family could not be there at the end. "Then the entire family would be gathered together once more and how gladly we would bring that about! for in all our devious ways and wanderings we have loved one another."[50]

# XIII

# A HELPING HAND

*John's coming was a great help and comfort to us
all. He cheered us beyond what seemed possible
under the circumstances. I don't know what
we would have done without him.*
                                                    —Annie Muir

After his father's funeral, John returned to Martinez, accompanied by his sister Annie. Although he worried whether she were well enough to withstand the arduous railroad journey from Kansas City, he knew a long stay in California would be beneficial to her health. Under the protective wing of John and Louie, Annie soon began to thrive in the warmer climate amid the beauty of the Alhambra Valley hills.

In a letter to his brother David shortly after his return to the ranch John recalled the time he spent as a visiting celebrity at the Parry & Muir store in Portage. He said he didn't know half the people who claimed to know him.

"Remember me to your boys and girls and to Mr. Parry and your bookkeeper and clerks for whose benefit I so assiduously smoked."[1]

Then he inquired about the syndicate business. When the Muir brothers were in Kansas City, they discussed speculation in Kansas lands. They were interested in taking part in the Kansas land boom, buying cheap and expecting to sell at a profit. Walter Brown had recently invested in vast tracts of land as well as some acreage in his own Kansas City neighborhood. In December John sent his brother-in-law $2,000 to invest in Kansas City property. An entrepreneur, Walter later attempted to persuade David to raise $10,000 from what he termed David's banks and capitalists to speculate in large Kansas real estate ventures with the promise of high profits. Evidently, David did not do this.

Annie probably stayed with John and Louie about three years. An autograph book later carried a rather creditable amateur poem by her friend Susie A. Waters about the Alhambra Valley surroundings. The page was dated February 18, 1888, Alhambra Ranch. One stanza described a walk she and Annie had taken among the hills:

> After reaching the lofty green hilltops
> What a lovely scene met our view
> The grand & majestic Diablo
> With its surroundings of every hue
> Now as we gaze down the valley
> What beautiful scenery we find
> The hills, the bay & the village
> With towering blue mountains behind.[2]

"I am very glad to know that your health has improved so much since you left Portage," Anne Muir wrote her daughter January 21, 1886. "You must feel quite encouraged and what a comfort it must be to spend the winter among fruits and flowers."[3]

Anne Muir described an entirely different winter in Portage—snow as high as the garden fences and temperatures twenty-five degrees below zero. It took a lot of effort to keep the house warm.

Ten days later she wrote again, this time to congratulate John and Louie on the birth of their second daughter, Helen, on January 23, 1886. She was happy that Wanda would have a little sister to play with.

Within six months there was another death in the family. On June 15, 1886, David Muir's son John drowned in Silver Lake in Portage at the age of eighteen years and nine months. It was seven years almost to the day after his nineteen-year-old cousin George Galloway lost his life to the Fox River.

Almost a year passed and in the spring of 1887 Sarah and her mother moved to another home in Portage.

Anne described it for John: "We are a little nearer town, just two streets up from the river. I have a beautiful view of the river from my window. The street is a pleasant one with large trees on both sides."[4]

Anne used only two rooms of the west Cook Street house, but she liked them better than the ones she had left. She was pleased, too, with the gentle horse and new carriage David Muir had just bought. "I rode in it yesterday. His daughter Annie and I rode up to Prospect Hill and many other places. Portage grows. [There are many] new homes."[5]

David, as usual, was spending long hours at the Parry & Muir store. It had been two years since he lost his beloved wife Katie, and he was lonely. On July 11, 1887, he married his faithful bookkeeper and friend, Juliaette Williams Treadway.

The wedding took place in the Presbyterian Church in Portage where David, an active member, sang in the choir. Pastor J. H. Ritchey conducted the ecclesiastical service. David's brother-in-law Willis T. Hand and his partner William T. Parry attended the couple, as did Juliaette's sister, Ida Westlake, and D. C. Treadway.

John wished David and Juliaette much happiness in his congratulatory letter and noted that the wedding was not unexpected. He said that his mother and all the family were pleased with his domestic arrangements.

In Crete, Nebraska, John Reid and his longtime partner, John Foster, were engaged in large-scale stock operations. For years in Portage the Reid and Foster partnership had dealt in sheep and other livestock. At one time they were known as the largest wool dealers in Wisconsin. Now they were engaged in a large feedlot operation in Crete and raising mustang horses at Spring Valley Ranch near Collyer, Kansas.

Reid explained to John Muir August 24, 1887, that problems had arisen when the partners took in 700 or 800 horses at the Crete feedlots over the preceding winter. Since the mustang owners did not have enough money to pay for the feed, they were in debt to Reid and Foster for $20,000. They gave Reid a bill of sale for this amount, and he attempted to sell three carloads of horses in Kansas City to make up some of the loss. To his dismay, Reid then learned that Foster had signed a note in behalf of the partnership without his knowledge. Other tactics involved the partnership in a threatened lawsuit that cost them $2,500. Reid tried to buy out his partner, but Foster would neither sell his interest nor buy Reid's. To make matters worse, Reid owed money on his land deals. As time went on, John and Maggie's financial situation became more and more precarious.

At Mound Hill, Sarah was in a reminiscent mood when she wrote to her brother John in February of 1888. She was thinking about California poppies. "We had so many of them growing at our first home, Fountain Lake—the old house where we as an unbroken family spent so many of our first years in this country, and afterwards, David and I with our band of little folks made our home so long. Of all this for us there are only memories left."[6]

By September of that year, Annie Muir had returned to Portage from her extended California stay. At the end of the month she wrote to Wanda and Helen.

"Grandma's home in Portage looks very pretty to me for there is a green lawn all around the house except at the back door and some large oak trees in it and beautiful flowers for there has been plenty of rain all summer. Auntie."[7]

In October Sarah shared more reminiscences with John. "I went out to the cemetery in Buffalo where beside our own dear ones, so many of our neighbors of long ago are laid to rest. The greater part of the place looks sadly neglected.

"We had a very pleasant visit with John Gray sometime since. He had been in Buffalo visiting the old home and some of the neighbors. He said that writing up David [Gray's] early life had created a strong desire to visit some of the scenes connected with it, but like yourself was disappointed with the appearance of everything."[8]

The Muir family had been saddened by the death of David Gray, one of the twa Davies who had inspired John Muir so long ago. Gray, who was very ill, died after suffering the trauma of a dramatic train wreck in the state of New York in 1888. His illustrious public career as editor of the Buffalo (New York) Courier and writer of travel books spanned many years.

"I have been reading David Gray's books aloud in the evenings this winter," Sarah commented the following April, "and have enjoyed them very much. It has been a great pleasure to Mother to have so many of the happenings of those years brought to mind again."[9]

Davie Taylor, the other of the twa Davies, was still living on the original Town of Buffalo farm. Alone now, he spent a great deal of his time writing. His highly imaginative stories and his well-thought-out speeches given at the old settlers' picnics were published in the *Marquette County Tribune*. He also wrote poetry. A Town of Buffalo neighbor whose life went back to the time of Davie Taylor once said, "Taylor was odd. He wrote poetry at night and then tore it up the next morning."[10]

During this time, John was exploring the wilderness and penning articles in behalf of wild nature. He would always remember the inspiration David Gray and David Taylor gave him that day so long ago when they all worked on the corduroy road together. He still remembered the excitement he felt as he listened to the twa Davies reciting Dickens.

In January, 1889, Reid and Foster finally ended their partnership. Maggie explained that the horses were mortgaged for more than they were worth and the banks were involved. She and John were placed in a financial bind reminiscent of the time they lost their farm just after their marriage, only this time there was vastly more at stake. They had just enough money to feed the horses. It was very hard.

For some time now John and David Muir had been corresponding about their brother-in-law's financial problems. On April 20, 1889, John informed David he had just sent John Reid $1,000.

"It seems strange," he added, "that so practical a stockman should have been so easily imposed on as he was in the matter of those mustang colts."[11] He questioned his brother as to how their Nebraska "syndicate" investments with Dan were going and about their Kansas City investments.

He said he offered Maggie and John's son Willie a job on the Alhambra Valley ranch. He told Willie that it would be "careful, painstaking work, hard though not half as hard as we had to work at Fountain Lake and Hickory Hill in the grim and Gad-grind early days."[12]

In her April 5, 1889, letter to John, Sarah said that John Reid's Kansas affairs were still in bad condition, and she didn't know how the lands he bought for her were faring. Since this property was in her name and the deeds not yet recorded, she didn't think Reid's creditors could touch it.

On April 21, 1889, John celebrated another birthday. His mother enclosed pressed flowers in her birthday note. "I have been spared to see your 51st year. I went off this afternoon to the woods across the railroad track to look for a spring flower to send you, but I only found these. . . ."[13]

In California John continued his travels and writing, as well as bearing the heavy burden of farm work. In September he described his responsibilities for his old university friend, Professor James Davie Butler. "All the year I have from fifteen to forty men to look after on the ranch, besides the selling of the fruit, and the editing of 'Picturesque California,' and the writing of half of the work or more. This fall I have to contribute some articles to the 'Century Magazine', so you will easily see that I am laden. . . .

"In a year or two I hope to find a capable foreman to look after this ranch work, with its hundreds of tons of grapes, pears, cherries, etc., and find time for book-writing and old time wanderings in the wilderness. . . ."[14]

For about ten years Muir had regularly contributed mountain articles to *Scribner's Monthly*, and he continued to do so when it became the *Century Magazine*. During the summer of 1889, *Century* editor Robert Underwood Johnson traveled from the eastern editorial offices to San Francisco to work on a series of western articles. When Muir met him at his hotel, the two men struck up an immediate friendship, an association that would have a profound effect on the national park movement. Muir planned a comprehensive Yosemite and Sierra mountain trip to show Johnson firsthand some of the wonders he had so well described in his articles.

Johnson was impressed with the magnificent Douglas and Silver firs, and the incomparable Sequoia gigantea trees. He marveled at the mountain panorama stretched out before him at Inspiration Point. With three burros, and accompanied by an attendant-cook, Muir and Johnson journeyed into the Sierra high country. There they set up camp by Soda Springs at Tuolumne Meadows. The two men roamed the region and shared their conservation views around the evening campfire. Muir bemoaned the fact that the sheepmen's "hoofed locusts" had destroyed the mountain meadows where earlier a profusion of flowers had grown "breast high to a horse."

Johnson felt that the lands around the state-protected Yosemite Valley should become a national park and to that end he proposed that John write two articles for *Century Magazine*. One would be called "The Treasures of Yosemite," and the other "The Proposed Yosemite National Park." Johnson would then take the information therein to his influential friends in Congress. Muir wrote the articles as scheduled and Underwood used them to get the park lobby effort rolling. The following year, October 1, 1890, Yosemite National Park became a reality.

In the meantime, in Portage, Sarah was in financial difficulty since no money had ever materialized from her Kansas land investments. To make ends meet, she turned her home into a boarding house. When Joanna came to Portage in December, 1889, she stayed with Sarah while her husband, Walter Brown, now president of the Railroad and Trust Co. of Philadelphia, was in that city on business. She remained in Portage for about a year.

It helped Sarah to have Joanna and her three children room and board with her. She explained to John how they would arrange it. Joanna could have her parlor and whatever rooms she needed upstairs. As they had been doing for her mother and Annie, Sarah and her daughter Grace would get the meals for everyone. By being careful they would all live comfortably.

Sarah answered John's inquiries about their mother's affairs.

"You ask about Mother. David knows better what Mother has than I do, but she always looks nice and comfortable and no matter what stir or hurry may be going on in other parts of the house nothing of the kind enters there.

"She reads her papers and books and receives her company. If she wishes the children in awhile she enjoys them. (She just loves the baby) and if she gets tired she has quiet again. She keeps her rooms in order with help from Annie sometimes. If anything extra is required she gets other help.

"Then her expenses for living are small, so if there is no great income neither is there any great outlay.

"I think Mother enjoys unusually good health for a person of her age. She has a little of her old trouble once in a while but her simple remedy always helps. I am so glad that she can go out and enjoy her friends. It just cheers her up and does her good."[15]

Anne Muir was paying Sarah five dollars a month now, and helping her daughter Annie to buy things she needed.

As financial problems continued to plague the Reids, John was concerned about his sister Maggie's welfare. She was discouraged and he wanted to help. Consequently, he invited his brother-in-law to come to California to work on the ranch. He explained to David that he knew it would be hard for Reid to leave his land and begin a new business at his time of life.

Sarah's February 10, 1891, letter to John underscored her brother's need for help on the ranch. "I'm sorry the business drives you so unmercifully. I hope that matters are so arranged that you will be able to take things more moderately."

She finished by explaining her own circumstances:

". . . all belonging to [David's] estate now is invested in that Kansas land. I haven't received anything from it for over 3 years." She said that there were two unpaid notes due her from people in Fort Winnebago Township for approximately $250.

"From that source I have received some money, my wood for fires, also butter and eggs I have needed and all the vegetables I could use in gardening."[16] Of course, Sarah received money from her boarders.

The Portage branch of the family managed to keep going, but John and Maggie finally could hold on no longer. Reid had not been able to sell any of his sections of land and he had already given up his sheep. He was afraid they would die from scab; he had dipped then twice, but it did no good.

On February 3, 1891, John Reid wrote to his brother-in-law from Crete.

"I have made up my mind to leave this place for awhile. What would be the prospect of getting work from you for awhile till we see how things go. The fact is, John, I have got to work to support my family."[17]

Once again John came to the aid of a family member. With great relief Maggie and John Reid accepted his immediate offer to give them a place on the ranch.

"We received your surprising letter Fri. . . . Your letter has worked wonders. You have fairly converted us over to thinking that it is the best thing for us to do is to come to California, and accept your kind offers and a chance to get on our feet financially. . . . We received the three hundred dollars yesterday. Maggie.

"Bro John, Will start in about two weeks. 4 of us—John, Maggie, May, Johnnie. Harry will have to stay and take care of the place and the horses. Jno. Reid."[18]

So the Reids were rescued and continued the trek west they had begun eleven years before. With their coming, Muir would gain some needed time to write, lobby, and travel in behalf of wilderness.

For months both John and David Muir had been doing everything they could to help their sister Maggie. On March 4, 1891, David informed John, "You wrote me to send [them] money last year. We were hard pushed ourselves last year for money—the hardest I ever was.

"Ever since Jno Reid left Portage I have paid his life insurance for Maggie's sake which with other things amt's to about $1,000. [Another time] I borrowed $500 and sent it. I couldn't decide whether to charge you for this because you wrote me not to send the money for the land, but for Maggie's necessities . . . so you decide."

David was also helping his mother and sisters in Portage. He summed up the family fortunes there for John.

"Mother's health is good, very much better than last winter. She goes out considerably and seems to be contented and happy and has plenty.

"Sarah's health improved last year. [She] has no money except what she earns. She boards Mother, Annie, Joanna and her three children and a young lady who attends school. . . . Gets a living & her clothes."

David said he had persuaded Joanna to live with Sarah for the sake of helping her.

"They all live in my house for which I charge no rent. Annie's money is all used. She makes considerable money by selling fish tail jewelry to the ladies, manufactured by a Miss Moore. [Annie's] health fair. Mother helps her when she is in need.

"Joanna is all right. Walter sends her plenty of money so she pays her way in no stinted manner. Walter and his bank have passed the crisis and are making money with a bright prospect." According to Brown's latest letterhead, his bank was now the Continental Trust and Finance Bank of Philadelphia.

As for his own living pattern, David said "[We] rented our house to Mrs. Muir's cousin. We board with them and have all the room we want and Mrs. Muir works in the store with me." Parry & Muir was getting along "okay, but paying interest on a large sum retards us."[19]

David Muir had been in the retail business in Portage for thirty years, three as a clerk for Forbes store and the last twenty-seven as a partner in the Parry & Muir firm. William Parry had also previously clerked at Forbes. Carrying a good line of dry goods and men and women's clothing, Parry & Muir enjoyed a fine reputation in Portage and the surrounding countryside.

When William Parry became an assemblyman in the Wisconsin State Legislature, he spent much time in Madison, leaving David with most of the responsibility for managing the firm. David weathered many a lean time, yet somehow succeeded in keeping the business afloat.

In 1892 a crisis developed. Although, Parry received $2,000 a year for his state duties, he continued to drain the store of its operating capital. The final blow was the store's inability to sell its winter inventory. Although collapse was imminent, the firm advertised heavily in February and part of March in a desperate effort to move their goods.

The local newspaper carried large ads about the Grand Special Sale held during February: "All winter goods must go to make room for spring goods." On March 7 the firm advertised the arrival of its "large spring stock of ready-made clothing and the beautiful spring dress goods." The store went further into debt, until, finally, it was no longer able to survive.

On Saturday, March 19, 1892, area people were shocked to read the *Portage Daily Register's* account of Parry & Muir's demise. There had been no warning.

"MADE A VOLUNTARY ASSIGNMENT" the headlines proclaimed. "Parry & Muir Decided to Close—Assets Equal Liabilities.

"It was with much regretful astonishment that the citizens of Portage learned today of the failure of Parry & Muir, dealers in drygoods and clothing. Last evening they made an assignment to Ll[ewellen] Breese and today the store is closed. It is stated by their attorney, J. H. Rogers, that the liabilities and assets are each about $35,000. He explains that the mildness of the past few winters has hurt business, leaving on hand a surplus of seasonable goods that with ordinary weather would have been sold. That is one of the causes.

"The firm of Parry, Bebb & Muir was organized in 1865. Four years later Mr. Bebb retired and since then the business has been carried on under the firm name of Parry & Muir. The partners are William T. Parry and David G. Muir. For several years previous to engaging in business of themselves, they were clerks in Portage. The firm has always enjoyed a large share of public patronage, and not a business house in Portage has been more familiarly or favorably known in the surrounding tributary country."[20]

It was a stressful time for David and Juliaette. He wrote John the particulars:

"We made an assignment of everything for the benefit of our creditors last night. We had Mother's money in the store so I deeded my home (where she lives) to her which makes her good I hope. She won't worry too much over my misfortune. Really, I've had such a hard time in the store, such hard pulling to get through after so much worry, that I feel relieved, although I have nothing.

"Mr. Parry is entirely to blame. He owes the store $9,522, i.e., he has drawn out that much more than I have. He had a state office at $2000 per annum. He agreed to put it all in, but he drew out more than he put in and last year was a bad one for us and we lost money.

"I've just been to Mother's and told her all about it. She says she is glad I am out of it for my own sake, and takes it philosophically.

"Well, I'm in want of a job. I don't want to stay here. Ette wants work also. Do you know of anything I can go into and make money without capital? Are there any big chances in Alaska? Any offers or suggestions will be acceptable."[21]

The next month was a difficult one for David and Juliaette. After working so long to make a success of the business, it was a crushing blow to see it dismantled and the merchandise sold.

On April 6, 1892, the *Daily Register* carried a small item: "Julius Simon of Chicago is in the city to bid on the Parry & Muir stock." The April 8 issue stated: "Notice is hereby given that all persons owing the late Parry & Muir are requested to call at once at the store of Breese, Loomis & Co. and pay their accounts. Ll. Breese, Assignee."

On April 14 a prominently placed news story carried a detailed account of the Parry & Muir auction.

"The center of interest for our city's street corner philosophers, and curbstone chroniclers this afternoon, has been the Parry & Muir store on Cook street.

"The stock of the firm was put up at auction to be sold to the highest bidder at 2 o'clock, and there being a goodly number of prospective purchasers in attendance, the bidding was free, and the bids, comparatively high. J. D. Simon of Chicago, made the first bid for the stock."

There followed a detailed account of the bidding. The final bid by Atty. Stroud for Simon was $13,550.

"The stock was then knocked down to Mr. Stroud, who handed Mr. Breese, the assignee, a check for that amount.

"Mr. Simon, the purchaser, is a young man of good business ability and comes to this city with the best of references."

On April 15th the Portage paper noted that "John Muir, the famous Alaskan traveler, is visiting his brother today. He resides in California."

John evidently arrived too late for the merchandise sale. He had been prepared to put a large amount of money into salvaging what he could. He found not only David to be in a bad plight, but also the rest of the family. He described the situation to Louie a few days later.

"I reached here Thursday night. The store is sold and guided by advice from David's friends we did not buy fearing trouble from creditors.

"David is greatly worn and distressed and is threatened with inflammation of the brain. I will get him away from here as soon as I can. Mother, Sarah, and Annie were I fear hard up when I sent the first fifty dollars. I gave them fifty apiece more when I arrived and the next day your fifty arrived but I will not need to invest the large sum proposed in the goods or any part of it. I'll be glad when the end of this miserable business is reached and I can get David away from here to anywhere."[22]

Despite the serious situation, John, as usual, found satisfaction in nature. On April 18 he wrote to his daughter Helen.

"It is pretty cold this morning and no flowers or leaves are to be seen yet, but I saw a robin gathering strings and bits of cloth to make a nest and that shows that spring will soon be here. I saw a very pretty blue jay in the yard this morning, far prettier than the California jay but his voice is not good. . . . The maple buds are just beginning to swell."[23]

To Wanda he wrote:

"Yesterday I went to church with Mother and many of the old acquaintances came up and spoke to me. This country seems cold and flat compared to California."[24]

On April 19 a small item in the Portage paper noted: "D. G. and John Muir left for Lincoln, Nebraska this morning to visit Dr. Daniel Muir, a brother."

So David Muir's thirty-year business career had come to an end. He and Juliaette did not know what the future would bring. John urged them to come to Martinez. He knew David would make an excellent ranch manager and that both David and Ette, as he called his sister-in-law, would make a fine addition to the ranch. He really needed them.

Wednesday, April 20, found John in Kearney, Nebraska with his sister Mary and her husband Willis. He wrote to Louie on Willis's stationery that showed Willis L. Hand to be president of the Central Nebraska Land and Immigration Co., with capital stock of $1,000.

"David does not yet know whether he will come out to California or stay in Lincoln. Ette will help him make a decision.

"He is much better now and sleeps better.

"Dan is hard up, but by close economy makes out to hold all the land he bought during the boom. I have not yet made any arrangements as to our claim."[25]

A few days later John was in Lincoln at the home of Dan and Emma.

"I arrived here last evening from Indianapolis," he informed Louie, "and after a short visit will push on to Kearney to see Mary once more.

"I left everybody well in Portage and greatly cheered by the little assistance we gave in time of need. At Indianapolis three days. . . .

"When I left Portage, Dave came with me, he going to Lincoln, I to Indiana. Looking over town with Dan with view to settling here.

"Ette was left behind to settle up some business affairs. She will join Dave here in a few days and I suppose aid him in forming a decision. She is an excellent housekeeper and therefore I wish she could see good grounds for deciding for California when she is so much needed."[26]

On April 28, Annie Muir recounted the unhappy affair for Louie.

"[It is] already ten days since 'the boys' John and David left us, and amid most depressing circumstances. You could not, I think, without being here, comprehend the feeling which has been aroused in our little city and the surrounding country by the failure of the firm of Parry and Muir. People who have known David nearly all of their lives, and had perfect confidence in him are now ready to listen to any sort of a report even to reports which would prove positive rascality on his part. You will, however, hear enough of this when they reach California. . . .

"Perhaps you can imagine something of the pain and mortification it has brought with crushing weight on David's honest heart, and through him, in less degree, upon us all. I need add nothing more on this sad subject. It is all before you with the deep sense of loneliness which we feel in losing our last Brother from among us.

"John's coming was a great help and a comfort to us all. He cheered us up beyond what seemed possible under the circumstances. I don't know what we would have done without him for it was hard enough even then.

"I was glad to see John looking so well. He is certainly much better than when I left California.

"Ette has just been in to say goodbye to us. She leaves from Madison. Expects to be in Lincoln by Sat."

Like her brother John, Annie found solace in nature.

"The blue birds have just returned from the South with their sweet soft voices and bright dainty coloring and we know that Spring is again at hand with its glorious resurrection beauty."[27]

On May 5, 1892, David wrote to John from Dan's home in Lincoln.

"Still here. Juliaette arrived 7 hours after you left. Brought your laundry. Dan trying to get us to stay. If you needed me as much as you seem to it would not be so difficult for us to decide. . . .

"I wish I knew more about that village of yours. I am feeling a little better but haven't much 'sand.' It seems hard to get my spirits and hope revived. Thanx [sic] for kind acts and intentions. . . ."[28]

David and Ette finally decided to move on to California where John and Louie eagerly awaited them. The newcomers soon settled into ranch life. David learned the fruit business and Ette did her part by occasionally boarding some of John's workmen. After the anxious months in Portage, David's spirits began to lift. He and Ette enjoyed eleven-year-old Wanda and six-year-old Helen and renewed bonds with Maggie and John Reid. That year John and Louie celebrated David's fifty-second birthday with a fine turkey dinner. Once again John had come to the rescue of his family.

David missed the store after all his years in business there, but it felt good to return to farming, especially in the Alhambra Valley hills. All in all he felt he had made the best choice. The arrangement was of mutual benefit to both the Muir brothers. David's coming proved a boon to John, for he had found the capable manager he needed. With the weight of day to day management of the ranchlands lifted from his shoulders, he became more fully absorbed in his writing and working for wilderness.

Although Anne Muir had relied on her son David, she was pleased to think that he and Ette had found such a pleasant home in California. Three of her eight children now lived in the Alhambra Valley near Martinez.

For about a month longer, Parry & Muir advertisements continued to dominate the Portage newspaper. Julius Simon ran large front page ads in a dozen editions of the *Daily Register* for the sale of Parry & Muir bankrupt stock. Pins, hooks and eyes, and thread sold for a penny, "Ladies and Mens shoes" for a dollar, and suits for two and five dollars.

In the final days, there was a flurry of ads announcing auctions at Mike Huber's Stand beginning Saturday, May 7, at 2:00 P.M. under the hammer of Steve Turner, auctioneer. Several such sales were held until the last of the goods was sold. The Parry & Muir era had come to a close.

# XIV

# PRESERVATION CAUSES AND FAMILY AFFAIRS

*So now John has no ranch to look after and can*
*stick to his books. He is well pleased with the way*
*I managed his vineyards and orchards last year.*
—David Muir

For more than ten years after his 1880 marriage to Louisiana Strentzel, John Muir operated the Alhambra Valley ranch—both the Strentzel lands and his own. He had found it increasingly hard to balance the needs of the ranch with his writing and travels.

When Dr. Strentzel died in 1890, John and Louie moved from the original ranch house near the creek to the Strentzel mansion on the hill. In 1892, when David and Ette were well settled in the old house, and David began to manage the orchards, John was able to turn his attention to pressing conservation issues. There were causes on all fronts to address.

One cause was working for the recession of the Yosemite Valley from the State of California to the United States Government. In 1864 President Lincoln had granted the valley to the state. Muir believed the state mismanaged it and thought the lands would be more secure under federal supervision as part of the surrounding Yosemite National Park.

Another project was bringing together the many people who wanted to save the western wilderness, including Yosemite Valley. To that end Muir, Robert Underwood Johnson, and others organized the Sierra Club, which became a reality June 4, 1892. Its purposes were "to explore, enjoy, and render accessible the mountain regions of the Pacific Coast . . . to publish authentic information concerning them," and "to enlist the support and cooperation of the people and government in pre-serving the forests and other features of the Sierra Nevada Mountains."[1] Muir was elected president and served in that capacity for the remain-der of his life. Under his leadership, with the dedication of the people around him, the Sierra Club proved effective in accomplishing its goals. Yosemite Valley was eventually receded to the federal government and became a part of Yosemite National Park.

The following year, Muir headed east to set sail for Europe. En route he stopped at Portage and Chicago. In Chicago, New York, and Boston he was treated as a celebrity and was guest of honor at numerous func-tions. Hosted by local dignitaries, he saw famous sites that were special to him, including Emerson's home and grave at Concord and Thoreau's Walden Pond. In New York he visited his publishing house and was well looked after by the Robert Underwood Johnsons.

Then it was on to Europe and Scotland to visit "the auld lang syne," a special part of his extensive European travels. On the afternoon of July 5, 1893, he boarded the train at Edinburgh bound for the seacoast town of Dunbar. It had been forty-four years since Muir had walked the streets of his early childhood.

The Muir home on High Street was now the Lorne Hotel. He stayed at the Lorne "if for nothing else [than] to take a look at that dormer window I climbed in my nightgown, to see what kind of an adventure it really was."[2] In *The Story of My Boyhood and Youth* he told of the time he and David climbed out the upper story window onto the steep roof. When David was unable to climb back into the room, John grabbed his brother by the heels and pulled him in to safety.

Muir sauntered around Dunbar and renewed old acquaintances. He visited early childhood scenes—the school where he had studied and been whipped, and the places where he played, including the ruins of ancient Dunbar castle on the North Sea. He roamed the countryside, observing from an adult perspective the towns, castles, and farms.

"Dunbar is an interesting place . . . ," he wrote to Louie, "beauti-fully located on a plateau above the sea and with a background of beau-tiful hills and dales, green fields in the very highest state of cultivation, and many belts and blocks of woods. . . . the modulation of the ground stretching away from the rocky, foamy coast to the green Lammermoor Hills is charming."[3]

As they had done so many times throughout the years, John's brothers and sisters followed his travels in their imagination. They had always looked forward to his letters with their vivid descriptions and read with keen interest his later published writings wherein he further developed his ideas. As well, they tried to understand the scientific aspect of his message.

Muir's *The Mountains of California* was published in 1894, the year after his European trip. Based on his early articles, it gave a fine overview of the Sierra Nevada. There were many printings of this popular book that "contains much of Muir's finest writing between 1875 and 1882 and is considered by many Muir admirers to be his finest book."[4] Treasured in homes across America, his books and articles created public awareness and interest in preserving significant portions of the national landscape.

At each Christmas, John sent his relatives generous gifts of money. He did the same in 1894. In her thank-you letter of January 9, 1895, Sarah said she had distributed the Portage gifts to the others. Joanna, who had been staying with her for some months, was especially grateful for hers, for Walter was not successful in business. The year before John had heard of Walter's reverses and sent Joanna $25 to help tide her over.

When she described how she used her Christmas gift, Sarah's thoughts went back to the Fountain Lake years.

"Do you remember the old clock that you and I bought together more than thirty years ago? Well the shelf it stood upon I put up myself. The screws at the upper part of the brackets proved to be too short, and unnoticed, worked loose, and so some weeks ago, the old clock that had served us so well came down to the floor with a crash and is in such a broken condition I have not tried to get it mended. When I feel able to go downtown I will use your gift toward putting another in its place, and as I take note of the hours and the minutes I will often think of your kindness."[5]

Sarah and John had shared so much over time and were always devoted to one another. When Sarah needed him most, he was there to help, and John counted on her constant interest and encouragement in all his endeavors.

While John was turning out more articles and books, the ranch was in the competent hands of his brother David. On January 5, 1896, David wrote to his mother.

"Well, Mother, I (or rather we) are able to pay our interest in the ranch and reduce the principal considerably. . . . I have also paid the interest on Mr. Rogers' mortgage on your house and reduced the principal to $400.00, so we will pound away the best we know how for another year and hope to do still better.

"So now John has no ranch to look after and can stick to his books. He is well pleased with the way I managed his orchards and vineyards last year. I know I made more money out of it than he could have done, for I am with the men every day all day while he was only with them perhaps half an hour per day. . . .

"We are beginning to feel at home here, and Ette and myself like it very much. Joined the Congregational Church in Martinez."[6]

David said he felt sorry that the crops around Portage had been so poor that year and the prices so low. Remembering how much farm economics had affected the financial health of Parry & Muir, he sympathized with the merchants also.

David and John's relationship continued to be successful. In a letter to his mother, February 24, 1896, John said that David was making headway in his new business.

"I see David quite often. I saw him yesterday. He is looking quite well & is now making money & fast recovering from his business reverses. Ette also is well & very hopeful since she sees that she will soon have a beautiful home all paid for.

"Maggie comes over to our house quite often & Helen & I often go to see her in our walks for exercise. She is better than she was a year ago, though her daughter May is now keeping house about a quarter of a mile from her house and so now Maggie's family is reduced to John & Johnnie.

"I am so glad to think that your Wisconsin spring will soon come to bring warm weather to you all so that you can take walks in fresh air instead of being held prisoner around the stove. . . .

"I do hope Annie will have better health when she can be out in the reviving spring & summer air & Joanna & Sarah also.

"I was very glad to hear that Dan has been paying you a visit. It must have been a great pleasure after so long being without a sight of your three boys. I wish Dave & I could also have been with you.

"Anyhow that our Heavenly Father may continue to bless us & lead us in the way that is best I firmly believe. Ever your affectionate son John."[7]

John had not been home to see his mother since the 1893 stopover. In 1896, when Harvard University offered him an honory degree, he decided to attend the June commencement exercises at Cambridge to receive it. On the way he planned to visit his family at Portage.

As he wrote to his daughter Helen afterward:

"Everything done seems to be done for the best and I believe God has been guiding us. If I had not decided to go to Harvard I would have gone to Alaska and would never more have seen my Mother.

"Then if I had not compelled Mary to come to Portage, she would not have had her help. And had I not been in Portage probably Dan would not have come either, so all was for the best."[8]

Twenty-five years earlier, when Professor James Davie Butler passed by Yosemite's El Capitan, John, on the rocks above, received a telepathic message that his old professor was below him in the valley. In 1885, he had a premonition about his father and arrived at Daniel's bedside only days before his death. Now, in June, 1896, he had another premonition.

"As in the case of my father's death, while seated at work in my library in California, I was suddenly possessed with the idea that I ought to go back to Portage . . . to see my mother once more, as she was not likely to live long, though I had not heard that she was failing. I had not sent word that I was coming."[9]

Acting on this feeling, John soon headed east by train. At John's urging, Mary boarded the train at Kearney, Nebraska, where she and her family lived.

"I got here yesterday at 2:00 P.M.," John wrote Louie the day after his arrival. "When I was within 2 hours of Kearney I telegraphed ahead to Mary and she and Willis and all the children met me at the station. The train stopped only 2 or 3 minutes and I barely had time to rush out and drag Mary and Helen aboard before Willis could say boo.

"We found Mother very sick and low and Sarah and Annie said, 'God sent you.'

"But this morning Mother is much better and ate a good breakfast and asked me all about you and Grandma and Wanda and Helen. She has been confined to bed only a day or two and seems quite bright and hopeful. Of course, she was very glad to see Mary and me—'her ain bairns' as she said.

"The doctor tells me that she is likely to recover from this last illness (biliousness) and live comfortably through the summer. But she is now 83 years old and liable to leave us anytime.

"I feel sleepy and benumbed from so much carbonic acid in the sleeping car and the natural care that comes with Mother's condition.

"Sarah & Joanna & Annie were extremely glad to see Mary—a surprise. I'll stop here until I see whether Mother is going to get well."[10]

At the same time he wrote a note to Wanda and Helen:

"This is a charming summer day. So many trees, oaks, elms, maples are planted in Portage it looks like a forest and the sunbeams are pouring through the green and yellow leaves and the birds are singing, it is all delightful.

"I saw two scarlet tanagers this morning, red as coals of fire, and more robins than I could count getting breakfast on a mulberry tree before the door. They are tame because they are not disturbed by cats or dogs or guns. Four robins on the lawn were within 5 steps of my feet as I sat on the veranda. The tanagers are so red I think they would frighten California cats.

"It is just noon and the bells and whistles are making a jangling noise ridiculously big for so little a town."[11]

The first day he was in Portage, John sent a telegram to Martinez about his mother's condition, following it up the next day with a more cheerful one. Louie went immediately to tell Maggie Reid who had been worrying about her mother.

"We stayed quite awhile walking in the garden, and she soon began to look better," Louie wrote her husband. "I have sent Ah Tin with a note to David.

"The rivers and lakes near Portage must be beautiful now, and I hope the pond lilies are in bloom. If the ferns and mosses are still fresh please send us some."[12]

During the days with his mother John walked out to the old home farm at Fountain Lake. There he relived his boyhood adventures around the lake and the wonderful years of youthful discovery.

As he walked along present County Highway F, he spotted a boy plowing in the field by the lake. It was young Sam McGwin who later recounted the incident to his daughter Bessie Eggleston, who now owns a portion of the original Muir farm. Mrs. Eggleston said that her father and his three brothers were born in the house that stood on the site where the John Muir Memorial Park marker is now located. Her father grew up there and later lived across the road from the present park. She related the story her father told her about his experience with John Muir.

"When he was sixteen years old, he went to the field to plow. A man came along the road. He had long hair and a flowing white beard. He said he was John Muir. He told my father he came to the area wanting to buy some of the land by the lake where he had lived when he was a boy and first came from Scotland. He had traveled on foot from Portage to the lake.

"He said he had talked to Mr. McReath about buying land from him on the south end of the lake by the land that the Muirs had owned. He wanted to preserve and study the many beautiful plants near where the creek flowed. Muir told my father that McReath wouldn't sell him the land."[13]

Consequently, Muir failed for a third time in his effort to preserve a treasured piece of Wisconsin landscape.

John daily sent news of his mother to the California family. "I have been sitting by her bedside telling her Scotch stories, stirring up old memories and made her laugh many times as she has not laughed for many a day so they tell me."[14]

He said he telegraphed for Dan to come, "but he could not come for want of money to buy a ticket. I sent it yesterday."[15]

Since Anne Muir's condition seemed somewhat improved, John decided to take the train for Cambridge to receive Harvard's honorary MA degree. He was still in the east when she died on the evening of June 22. He returned to Portage for the funeral.

For several years, David Muir had been keeping a small diary.[16] For June 10, 1896, he entered the brief, poignant entry: "John and Mary arrived in Portage in time, praise God." And for June 22, 1896: "Mother died at 6 o'clock p.m. Dan arrived at 2 o'clock p.m." It turned out that Dan arrived at his mother's bedside just four hours before her death.

John wrote of the final days. "On Friday at noon we lay our blessed Mother's remains in the kind ground. In the coffin she seemed to be in calm sleep, beautiful as an angel.

"Mother seemed to suffer scarce at all. Natural weary sleep gradually deepened into the sleep of death. She was conscious and spoke clearly to within an hour of the last. She greatly enjoyed and was comforted by my week's visit at her bedside. We talked over all the old days and the coming change, and I am glad I was brought to her in her hour of need—of loneliness. . . . Dan arrived the last day and his coming completed her joy. Just before the last sleep she saw her husband and threw up her arms as if to embrace him and said joyfully,

"'It's dawn father. Now I see you all. It's all right. It's all well.'"[17]

Although John and the others interpreted Anne's vision to be that of her husband Daniel, it would be more likely that she referred to her own father, David Gilrye, when she said, "It's dawn, Father." She had not seen her parents for forty-seven years, but they had often been in her thoughts.

And when she said, "Now I see you all," it would be more natural that she meant the Dunbar family she had left behind in the churchyard—not her present family clustered around her. In years past when she spoke of the Gilryes she had emphasized how many of them there were. She had always held the belief that she would be reunited with them some day.

On June 25 Louie wrote to her husband with great compassion.

"How strange and sad and lonesome everything will seem to you all without the beloved Mother. . . . Kind fate led you home in time for that last happy visit with her, a blessed week to be remembered all your life."[18]

For many years, Anne Muir had been the mainstay of her widely-scattered sons and daughters, especially after Daniel left the family to preach in Canada. They would all miss her enduring support and encouragement.

John was named executor of his mother's estate.

"Mother's will gave all she had—the house and lot, furniture, etc. and about $1,000 worth of notes to Annie.

"Sarah has nothing but the $10 per month I got John Reid to send her. I think we might offer her a home with Maggie or ourselves though she might not be able to leave her children."[19]

It was rather odd that Anne Muir willed everything to her daughter Annie and nothing to Sarah. For some years Sarah had taken the primary responsibility for looking after her mother. Perhaps Anne thought Sarah was more independent and Annie, who had suffered so much illness, needed more assistance.

Anne Muir's estate also involved the trust set up for her by her father, David Gilrye, in October, 1851. This trust was administered by a Dunbar firm.

John received a communication dated July 30, 1896, from the Town Clerk's Office, Dunbar, Scotland, written by Charles Notman, "trustee for David Gilrye, your grandfather, who died at Dunbar in Dec. 1852."

Notman informed him of the "1260 lbs. invested for your mother in life and children 'in revision.' The interest or dividend had been regularly remitted by Combes, late candlemaker, as trustee to your late Mother."[20]

Notman went on to say that some money was invested in the Glasgo [sic] and Southwestern Railway Company, August 19, 1871. It was the duty of the trustee to divide the fund, now amounting to over 2000 pounds, among the heirs.

It took almost a year to settle the trust and the rest of the estate. On May 22, 1897, John informed his sister Annie:

"I take pleasure in sending today your share of Grandfather's money. The trustees sent the whole sum L1903,S10.D8 to me to distribute & I have just returned from the city with the drafts.

"I had a long letter from Mr. Notman explaining the delay. It was caused by Mr. Combes who refused to sell the R. R. stock until he was [threatened with] prosecution & shown my letter exposing the fraud before he would yield. He has already been overpaid. He still holds our half year's interest, which we will never get.

"Now you will have to send to each of us one eighth of the interest Combes sent you. David is lifting the mortgage from your house. Hope you'll take good care of your money. Your brother John."[21]

In years to come after leaving the University of Wisconsin for the university of the wilderness, Muir was well remembered by his professors and fellow students alike. They followed the career of this unique alumnus with interest.

One classmate wrote an article, "Concerning An Old Student," appearing in the *Wisconin Free Press* in 1881, and signed with the initials, I. N. He commented, ". . . John now has the reputation of knowing more of Yosemite Valley and the [Sierra] Nevada mountains than any other living man."[22]

At the university, this student lived opposite Muir's room on the first floor of the North Dormitory and had firsthand knowledge of Muir's genius in whittling inventions. I. N's roommate was Milton Griswold who had given Muir his first lesson in botany.

In 1896 John Muir had received the honorary MA degree from Harvard and had traveled to Concord to be duly honored. The following year the University of Wisconsin conferred the Doctor of Laws degree upon him. On June 7, 1897, the faculty voted to recommend that the university regents confer the degree on Muir and three others. On the afternoon of June 23, the day before graduation, the regents voted to do so.

The 1897 Regents Records Book stated that "specific action was taken at this time upon the conferring of honorary degrees upon four persons, all requirements having been fulfilled and by vote taken separately." Inasmuch as the action was taken at the time of graduation, there was no accompanying ceremony and the honor was bestowed by mail.[23]

On July 17 Muir sent his one sentence reply from Martinez: "I have the honor to acknowledge the receipt of a diploma sent by you, attesting the fact that the Regents of the University of Wisconsin have conferred upon me the degree of Doctor of Laws."[24]

Sarah stayed in Portage for three years after her mother died. Then, her children grown, she too journeyed westward. David's diary gives some indication of her travels and affairs: On September 23, 1899, he noted that "Sarah went to Nebraska to visit." November 20, 1899, "Sarah reached California." The entry for November 23 that same year read, "Mary Zamzow moved into Sarah's [Portage] rooms." According to the diary, Sarah's rooms were then occupied by Dr. and Mrs. West from October 21, 1900, till March 28, 1901, when a Mrs. Owen moved into them. Finally, in March, 1902, Sarah "Decided not to return to P[ortage]."

In California, Sarah found a far different life from her years of toil on the Wisconsin farms: raising her family, running the Portage boarding house, and looking after her mother. After all the years apart, Sarah renewed fellowship with her family. She was especially pleased to get together with her older sister Maggie. Four of the eight brothers and sisters now lived near each other. For a time the extensive ranch nurtured them all.

David's management of the orchards left John a much freer hand to pursue his life work, allowing him to write prolifically in behalf of the preservation of forest lands and parks. His powerful pen and oral persuasion abilities were instrumental to the movement's success.

*Our National Parks,* published in 1901, with a number of subsequent printings, created awareness and interest in the national park movement.

Muir stated in the preface:

"In this book, made up of sketches first published in the *Atlantic Monthly,* I have done the best I could to show forth the beauty, grandeur, and all-embracing usefulness of our wild mountain forest reservations and parks, with a view to inciting the people to come and enjoy them, and get them into their hearts, that so at length their preservation and right use might be made sure. Martinez, California September 1901."[25] One of Muir's most famous quotes is found on page one of the volume: ". . . going to the mountains is going home."

*Our National Parks* truly emphasized "the growing interest in the care and preservation of forests and wild places in general. . . ."[26] The 1909 edition listed total national park acreage at over three and a half million acres, with an additional one and a half million set aside for national monuments. Almost 168,000 acres were set aside for national forests.

Louie's letter to her daughter Wanda, in July, 1902, gave pleasant glimpses of home life on the ranch. John was away at the time and Sarah was staying with Louie in the mansion on the hill. David was busy building his new home, now nearing completion.

"Aunt Ette tel. this morning to come move the jasmine as the carpenters will come tomorrow to begin to move the old house, so I drove up there at once, and Lun took up the precious old vine with tolerably good roots and I brought it to her to plant in the shade of the libocedrus.

"Uncle David showed me where a perfectly lovely view of the old house could be taken from near the olive tree as they cut out an olive branch that hid the house before. This gives a view of both the north and west porces [sic], the masses of shining ivy and the rose wreathed chimney. David then telephoned to Mr. Wilson to come and take the picture but he said he could not come for his camera was out of order. . . .

"I feel almost wild about it, for this could be even a finer view of our old home than the one we have, but seems that nothing can be done as the carpenters are in a great hurry with another job waiting for them.

"Keenie is all right. I let him go with me this morning and I chained him under a tree at Uncle David's and he was greatly pleased. Aunt Sarah lets him loose in the morning, very early to walk around the garden."[27]

Louie hastily closed her letter. Sarah had just come from Maggie's to say that the postman was almost there, and Louie wanted to give him the letter. Although Louie was not successful in getting someone to take a photograph of her old home in time, she did paint a fine word picture of it.

Two months after Louie's letter to Wanda, the Muirs were shocked to learn of Dan's unhappy situation. He was still practicing medicine in Lincoln, Nebraska. On September 29, 1902, the Lincoln newspaper carried the item: "Emma Muir secured a divorce from Dr. D. H. Muir, a leading local physician. The cause given was incompatibility of temper. By agreement the wife secured a title to the home property and $50 a month alimony. The couple have moved in the highest society circles here."

In a letter to her mother, Maggie Reid, Jessie Reid described a talk she had with her Uncle Dan. Before his divorce became public, Dan said he did not have "the courage or the will" to confide in his brothers and sisters the trouble he had lived with for so many years.

Dan told his niece that Emma and her two sisters were considered mentally ill, and that Emma's sisters were well known to the Lincoln police for their strange behaviour. Emma was by far the "best of the three, but she was just enough off to make her think *everything* was wrong."[28]

Jessie related the rest of the dismal story. "She wasn't satisfied with anything he would do or with himself; that it was a continual nagging & making things so hot that he simply couldn't stand it any longer; . . . he couldn't get any peace in the house day or night. That he was glad to escape to the furthest corner of the house to try to get in a little nap before the door would open & it would begin again. That many a time he had stood it until 1 or 2 in the morning & then gone down to the office & spent the rest of the night on the lounge."

Dan told Jessie that Emma had strange ideas. If anyone outside the family were in the house overnight she was afraid they were trying to take possession of the house. Emma told a reporter that her husband refused her daughters medical attention when they needed it. Dan said on one occasion he asked a doctor friend to come in to look after his daughter Mabel. He cautioned his friend not to say who sent him, "or the medicine would go anywhere but to Mable as Aunt Emma was too spiteful to give it to her if she knew where it came from." This episode was also written up in the paper.

"I know Zeph took care of him that night when he was so sick," Jessie continued. "When it was the coldest winter weather, he was in the hired girls' room a little bare cold room, with no way of heating it. Zeph told us he couldn't understand it . . . how they could let him be in that cold room & he so sick. He said Aunt Emma made some excuse when he spoke to her about it but it didn't explain anything. He kept his overcoat on all night & nearly froze tho he was busy all the time doing something for Uncle Dan. He said Uncle Dan kept saying that night over & over again that life wasn't worth anything."[29]

David's diary entry for December 6, 1901, referred to this illness: "Brother Dan *very ill* with pneumonia with complications." The family was worried about Dan. They knew he was at a low physical ebb, but they did not know the depth of his depression.

At the time of the divorce Jessie said many people came to express sympathy and tell Dan of their friendship. "We are very sorry about it. He never said a word to anybody about his trouble until the time really came but he had them for a long time."[30] As they always did with each other, his brothers and sisters supported Dan during his time of stress.

When Sarah left for California, Annie was the only member of the Muir family still living in Portage. Although she no longer had her own family about her, she had many friends and led a full life. She found her greatest satisfaction in her church. Later, her obituary stated that Miss

Muir was one of the most prominent members of the First Baptist Church of Portage.

"For many years she was clerk of the church and although her labors were arduous, her work was always done efficiently. She could always be found working with all her might toward the advancement of God's word and made every sacrifice possible for the poor. As a missionary worker she had no equal, and her charitable deeds will always be remembered by countless people who have benefitted through her good offices."[31]

Annie kept in close touch with her family. On October 18, 1902, she wrote to John about his early inventions.

"I write to say . . . that I shipped a box for you, by freight, yesterday, containing the parts of your wooden clock and other things whittled long ago. I am not at all sure that you will find them satisfactory as they had become so scattered and mixed and possibly broken that it was a very difficult matter for me to know what to send and what to leave here, such as the brass wheels, and iron bars, etc. Most of the things sent were found upstairs in the barn loft. They were left in Sarah's care and she knew better about them. However, I have done the best I could with them, washing off the dust of years and packing them with all sorts of things to keep them from getting broken on their journey westward . . . it has taken me a month at least to get everything together and packed to my mind . . . I also enclosed the buffalo horns and in each horn you will find one of Sarah's little ink cases which I wanted her to have. There are also two packages of pressed plants, which she used to prize very highly which were left here. I have sent them also."[32]

Annie had never been physically strong. All her adult life she had suffered much illness associated with her lungs. She had tried so often to regain her health, including the time Dan tried to help her in Nebraska and the time John took her to California in 1885. Recently, John believed his sister to be feeling much better.

In November, 1902, when Annie was fifty-six years old, she became ill in her beloved Baptist Church and was taken home. She seemed to be on the way to recovery and wrote cheerful letters to her family.

On Christmas night the temperature registered below zero and high winds were blowing. That evening, seventy-three year old Mrs. Owen, who lived in the house with Annie, ventured out to a Christmas entertainment with her family. While they were gone, Annie wrote a letter to John. She had been shut in for over a month. She told him she had decided to send him "the old family Bible containing the Family Record, much of which is written by father and mother themselves. It includes the grandchildren's names also—nearly all of them. You are the eldest son and I think it belongs to you. So I shall send it as soon as I am able to go down to the express office and attend to it. Inside the cover you will find a clipping just as it left Mother's hands on 'Old Dunbar Characters' . . . ."

She ended her letter with these lines: "I dreamed one night last week that I saw you coming in the gate and ran to meet you on the steps, and what a glad meeting we had. When will it be?"[33] Later, John placed the precious letter in a folder and marked it "Sister Annie's last letter."

During the week after Christmas Annie felt well enough to visit her friends and attend a Bible class at the church. She even went on a "merry sleigh ride." Soon thereafter she went to the express office to send her brother the family Bible as she promised.

"On the evening of [January] 8th she was stricken with Apoplexy," John wrote to a Dunbar cousin, "and Dan was telegraphed for."[34]

Annie was lonesome for her sisters. She said to Mrs. Edwards, her friend who attended her, "I love my sisters and I wish Mary and Joanna were here. O! I wish they were here. I am glad Dan is coming. He loves me, and he will take me in his big strong arms and make me so comfortable."[35]

Dan arrived from Lincoln in time to care for his sister during her last few days. He did everything he could to help her, but Annie died on January 15, 1903. "I am sure we are inexpressibly thankful that Dan, the one who could do the most, *was not too late*,"[36] Joanna said.

True to Annie's selfless nature, "her last thoughts were of others' comfort and happiness . . . she gave directions to the nurse to have $5 paid for wood and other necessities she felt must be lacking in a poverty stricken household."[37]

The California family was shocked at Annie's death, since they thought her well on the way to recovery. From a distance Sarah reasoned that Mary must not have realized how seriously ill Annie was, for she only reached Portage from Kearney in time for her twin's funeral.

Annie was buried beside her mother in Silver Lake Cemetery in Portage. Joanna well expressed the sentiment felt by them all. "I feel greatly saddened that our family circle of brothers and sisters has at last been broken. Who will be next? Annie was a power for good in her own way and there will be great mourning amidst the poor and friendless of Portage that she has been taken from them. Maybe she has done more than any of us, considering her strength and means."[38]

One obituary stated:

"Miss Muir leaves behind a life-record of noble work—work in the church, work in missionary societies, work in temperance organizations, work in relieving the poor and afflicted of all denominations and none at all. She was a devout member of the local Baptist church, and had served many years as its clerk, but in deeds of charity she made no distinctions of creed or antecedents. . . . those who knew of the bright ness thus infused into many darksome lives became accustomed to send her money for distribution. Late years she had handled in this way considerable sums."[39]

Dr. Byron Meacher, who lived next door to the Muir home, attended Annie. He listed the cause on her death certificate as cerebral meningitis.

The Meachers were a pioneer family who came to America a few years before the Muirs and settled in the general area of Hickory Hill. Byron's grandfather William once indignantly chided Daniel Muir for cutting trees on the government land adjacent to Hickory Hill. Without formal schooling, William attended to the community's medical needs. He was known in the neighborhood as the bonesetter, and as his nickname implied, he set many a broken bone around the countryside. Byron's father, also named William, was an early Pardeeville, Wisconsin,

doctor. Continuing the family medical tradition, Byron became a prominent doctor who practiced in Portage for many years. His office was
located over the Graham Drug Store.

It was Mary's sad duty to dispose of Annie's belongings, as well as
their mother's few remaining things. After giving the family the items
they wanted, and selling some things, she reported to John what she
did with the rest. She took home the organ, a chair, the [spinning] wheel,
two little stands, and a trunk filled with many trifles.

"The two little rooms were emptied, or nearly emptied, and when
stopping to think how cheap and almost valueless everything is that
made the rooms seem somewhat cosy, I say again to myself, that only
the fact that they so long belonged to dear Mother and twin sister, and
were in a way precious to them and gave them comfort, makes it seem
at all wise to ask for them or care to pay expense in getting them to our
homes. We hardly would consent to sell them for little or nothing and
let them all be scattered among strangers.

"The Dunbar chest containing some things I did not know what
to do with remains in a storeroom upstairs, for whoever may ask for it.
Mother's old, old wooden rocking-chair I left in care of Mrs. Owen.
Mother always liked it and never set it aside."[40]

When Mary completed her task, virtually all the vestiges of the Muir
family were gone from Portage. Annie was the last.

John administered Annie's estate, and David helped with the settlement as well. In his petition for administration to the Columbia
County Court, dated February 25, 1903, John listed Annie's personal
estate at less than one thousand dollars and stated that she owned no
real estate except for her home.

There was a problem with the estate. Years before, when David was
looking after his mother's affairs, he had invested her interest from her
father's trust in Parry & Muir. He owned the home his mother and the
others lived in. At the time of the store's bankruptcy in 1892, he deeded
the home to her, and continued to pay the mortgage. When he finally
"lifted" the mortgage, he had, in effect, paid back the "Scotch money"
invested in the store.

Upon their mother's death, the sisters and brothers felt that the "Scotch money" represented by the value of the home should have been divided among them all, and not have gone only to Annie.

Annie died intestate, but years before she had written a memorandum giving her property to Joanna. It was not a legal document. As Mary put it, "We may agree that money in the home was Scotch money that never was divided and should be,"[41] but she thought that at least Annie's portion of it should now be given to Joanna.

After consultation and agreement with the others, John administered the estate under existing probate laws in "the regular way all the heirs sharing lawfully alike, and then dividing as they thought best under present circumstances instead of trying to make legal the memorandum written years ago."[42]

John, for one, did not wish to keep any of the estate money. On February 27, 1907, he wrote to Joanna, "Here is some of poor Annie's money, with none of which, as I think I told you, will I have anything to do except helping to distribute it in accordance with her will, which though technically imperfect, should have been lovingly respected."[43]

Joanna was completely surprised by her brother's generous action. She recalled "that you did not want any share in the money from the family estate, yet I had never thought of your turning it over to me . . ." Joanna hesitated to accept the money, but she did so "considering dear Annie's expressed wishes."[44] As far as John was concerned, he had handled the matter well, both legally and morally.

At the time of Annie's death the remaining brothers and sisters were scattered across the country. Joanna Brown lived in Norfolk, Virginia. Dan Muir lived in Lincoln, Nebraska, while Mary Hand's home was in Kearney, Nebraska. The other four were at the Martinez ranch—John and David Muir, Margaret Reid, and Sarah Galloway. Annie was gone from them, but they still felt close to each other.

As John expressed it, ". . . We have much as a family to be thankful for. Few families as old as ours are is so whole."[45]

# XV

# THE SHINING LIGHT

*John Muir and God are friends. Muir fraternized
with the birds of the fields and forest and
chummed with the squirrel and the bear. He
rhapsodized over the beauty and sweetness of
flowers and communed with God through the
redwoods and pines. His life was a glorification
of God's original handiwork.*
— Charles L. Edson

In May of 1903, John Muir took on the task of guiding President Theodore Roosevelt through Yosemite in the hope of gaining his support for preserving that valley as well as thousands of acres of western forests. Roosevelt and Muir escaped the official planned events and, instead, camped out in the midst of Yosemite grandeur. Tramping around the wilderness with Muir for four days, and talking around the evening campfire, made such an indelible impression on Roosevelt that he became committed to the conservation effort and later signed a law protecting thousands of acres of forest lands.

Shortly thereafter, on May 24th, Muir left on an extensive year-long world tour, in large part to study world trees with Charles S. Sargent.

Earlier in the year Muir had stood ready to offer the Martinez ranch as a haven to his niece, Anna Galloway Eastman, after the death of her husband Hiram in December, 1902. Anna faced raising her two small children, Kenneth and Marjorie, alone. Her mother, Sarah Galloway, was now living in California.

In the fall of 1902 the Eastman family had moved from Portage to Scappoose, Oregon. A few days before they left Portage, Anna and Hiram were at the Muir house—then Annie Muir's—selling what they could of the things Sarah had left there and packing others to bring out west with them. Hiram was suffering severe complications from a spider bite he had received seven years before while working in a hay meadow.

Dr. Frank Paulin, married to Sarah's daughter Grace, urged Hiram to come to him in Chicago immediately for treatment, but Hiram delayed going until he first settled his family in their Oregon home. Then he left for Chicago on December 4, leaving Sarah to stay with Anna and the children while he was away. However, he died in Chicago before Christmas as the result of the cancerous growth that had developed. His death occurred three weeks before the death of Annie Muir. Although she could have moved to Martinez, Anna decided to remain in Oregon for the present, and Sarah stayed on to help her daughter and grandchildren through a difficult time.

Eventually, Anna and her children left Scappoose to locate in Pacific Grove on California's beautiful Monterey Peninsula, while Sarah moved there from Martinez.

A half dozen of the Muir clan were now clustered in Pacific Grove. David and Ette Muir were living there enjoying the leisure of retirement. After his years of toil on Marquette County farms, in the Portage store, and on the Martinez ranch, David was ready for more relaxed living along the Pacific shore.

"We all ate our Thanksgiving dinner with David and Ette and went out to the beach in the afternoon," Sarah wrote to John December 28, 1904. "Yes, we felt that we had much to be thankful for in many ways."[1]

John explained to their Dunbar cousin, Margaret Lunam, that Sarah "is now living with her daughter Anna in Pacific Grove, on the seacoast, about a hundred miles from here. She enjoys her grandchildren and her walks along the seashore gathering shells and sea weeds. She says the waves with their briny breath make her think of old Dunbar when she was a little child."[2] Sarah planted flowers around her home and took pleasure in the beauty of her surroundings as she always did wherever she lived.

John told their cousin that "David has built a house there. He was tired of farming and is enjoying life by the sea, fishing and going to church, etc."[3]

As for John, upon his return from his world tour, he plunged into the midst of the Yosemite recession fight. When the bill to recede Yosemite Valley to the federal government finally passed the California legislature on February 24, 1905, the battle was only half over. Now it was up to the federal government to accept the lands.

At the same time Muir was very anxious about his daughter Helen's recurring health problems. In late May, 1905, he and Wanda took her to the Arizona desert to recuperate in the dry desert air from an earlier bout with pneumonia.

But Louie was not well herself. The following month she wrote bravely to her family that she had been ill but was all right now. She was far from it for she was suffering from a tumor on her lung. A June 24 telegram called John home.

Sarah worried about her sister-in-law's serious illness. She wrote to John that she knew Louie would find comfort in *having you all back and about her*.

Her family was deeply saddened when Louisiana Strentzel Muir died August 6, 1905. Muir was shocked. "Up to her last day my noble wife was not aware of the hopelessness of recovery," he informed his Dunbar cousin, "nor indeed were any of us, though warned by the doctors a month before. She suffered but little pain, was cheerful, and at last simply fell asleep . . ."[4]

John buried his beloved wife near the old ranch house in the tiny cemetery by the creek. Her grave was located close to those of her parents, John and Louisiana Strentzel, and her young brother John, and small sister Lottie who preceded her in death.

Despite the fact that John had been away from home so very much of the time during their twenty-five year marriage, Louie had been indispensable to him. She had done much of the ranch supervision during earlier years when John was away on his mountain and Alaskan journeys. She kept ranch life flowing during his absence and welcomed him warmly upon his return. She maintained the beauty of her smooth-running home and tended the profusion of flowers, shrubs, and trees she had planted everywhere.

Louie understood her husband's need to be close to nature, to continually explore and learn; she understood his drive to work unceasingly for wilderness preservation. John and Louie's letters to each other over the years showed the deep bond and caring between them. Muir's grief lasted a very long time.

He was still anxious about Helen, who continued to live in the desert in an effort to recover her health. Six months after Louie's death he wrote a doleful letter to Joanna from Adamana, Arizona.

"Helen, who had pneumonia two years ago is getting well in this dry Arizona air, but is still a source of great anxiety. I suppose she will have to remain here at least another year before she can return to the desolate California home. Wanda, fortunately, is always well, and takes care of Helen when I have to go back to California. Most of the time we are both with her.

"As for my ordinary literary work, I have not been able to do anything since the beginning of the last trouble-ful summer, but hope to try soon again. In the meantime I am making some headway in my studies of the wonderful fossil forests hereabouts. David, I suppose you know, has left his Martinez farm and gone to the seaside at Pacific Grove. At last accounts he is well and satisfied with the change. Sarah is there too, and is growing younger and happier with her daughter and grandchildren. Dear Maggie is very frail and thin, but is able nevertheless to be up every day, and looks after her house affairs about as usual."⁵ John and his sister Maggie were now the only ones of the Muir clan left in Martinez.

In the summer of 1906 Muir celebrated a special victory. The United States Congress accepted the Yosemite Valley in June, and it became a part of Yosemite National Park. On July 16, John wrote to his friend and editor, Robert Underwood Johnson.

"Let every Yosemite tree and stream rejoice. The fight you planned by that famous Tuolumne campfire 17 years ago is at last fairly, gloriously won, every enemy derry down."⁶

Referring to Arizona's petrified forest, he said "I am absorbed in these enchanted carboniferous forests." Muir closed his letter with the good news that Wanda was married the month before to engineer Thomas Rae Hanna, and that Helen was feeling better.

Wanda and her husband set up housekeeping in the old adobe house across the orchard from the mansion on the hill. In August, when Helen returned from the desert and joined her father at the ranch, Muir's life seemed to assume a measure of normality.

Helen, however, again became ill in Martinez, so in December, 1907, her father took her to Daggett, California, over the mountains from San Bernardino. There in the desert he built a cabin for her. Then he returned to the Martinez ranch where he plunged into new conservation fights.

In April, 1908, John was cheered by a visit from his old Marquette County, Wisconsin, friend, Bradley Brown. Upon receiving word that his chum from log school days planned to visit him, he hastened to send directions from San Francisco to Muir Station via the Santa Fe Railway.

"I'll be delighted to see you coming so far out of the auld lang syne . . . Yesterday I was three score years and ten years young. I don't feel a bit older to-day than I did when first I made your acquaintance at the Log Schoolhouse drawing wisdom from George Branch."[7]

After the two old friends had a good visit on the ranch, sharing many a reminiscence, John wrote to Bradley again. "Old friends on the three-score-and-ten boundary should make the most of each other before dark."[8] John's capacity to keep lifelong friendships was a trademark.

In 1908 Muir became active in the disheartening, losing fight to save the magnificent Hetch Valley—a valley likened to Yosemite—from being dammed as a source for San Francisco's water supply.

Also that year, while he was the guest of railroad magnate, E. H. Harriman, at his Pelican Bay lodge in Oregon, Muir dictated to his host's secretary his autobiography about his boyhood years.

In December, 1909, Sarah noted from Pacific Grove that "We of the clan here are all well and enjoying bright days. . . . I hope you are well, and I'm sure you will be busy, writing as usual in that room of yours upstairs and bringing out something more to make people glad to read and learn."[9] Sarah was referring to Muir's famous scribble den on the mansion's second floor overlooking the ranch lands where her brother spent so many hours writing his articles and books and keeping up with his voluminous correspondence. She noted too how fine it was that Wanda lived nearby and what a comfort her little boy Strentzel must be to them all.

The following year, the circle of Muir brothers and sisters was broken for a second time when Maggie died on June 11, 1910. The oldest of the family, she was almost seventy-six years old. There was an increased sense of desolation at the ranch for both John Reid and John Muir.

In June, 1911, Muir's *My First Summer in the Sierra* was published. Earlier in the year *The Atlantic Monthly* carried four selections from the forthcoming book as a series of articles. Sarah, who still eagerly followed her brother's career, commented:

"We read your articles in the Atlantic Monthly entitled 'My First Summer in the Sierra.' It was very interesting and brought back old times when you wrote home so much of it in the early days and all was so eagerly looked for and enjoyed by each one of us. I have so many of the old letters still."[10]

1911 and 1912 saw John Muir on another extensive trip, this time in South America and Africa. As she had done on his first trip in 1867 when he tramped to the Gulf of Mexico, Sarah closely followed her brother's travels.

"How eagerly we have watched for any notice of your whereabouts during your long absence," she wrote May 3, 1912, "and of your success in discovering the three varieties of trees which you were so anxiously looking for, make us glad also.

"This morning I see a notice of your new book 'The Yosemite,' which I suppose will soon be published. . . . Wanda will now be at home and you will have still another grandson to welcome."[11]

*The Story of My Boyhood and Youth* was published in March, 1913.

Before the volume came out, Sarah wrote, "Your Autobiography will bring up many remembrances of old times and the people we met in those early days as well as much that was wonderful in the new country. The birds were so different from those we knew in Scotland and the wild flowers so fine and how we wandered about and enjoyed them."[12] She remembered, too, how they planted seeds in their early garden at Fountain Lake that a friend brought from Scotland.

In writing about his own experiences, Muir portrayed the life of the family as well. When she read the published work, Sarah vividly relived the early days on the first farm. ". . . how it all brings back to me the memories of long ago. The home life with its pleasures and difficulties that had in some measure passed from my mind."

Sarah remembered John's problems at home. "You had much to struggle against and overcome, but generally those who have made the most of their life have been those who have had many difficulties and perplexities to over come that others knew nothing of.

"As I looked at the old Fountain Lake House I remember your patient careful work in penciling it so that every minute detail should be brought out perfectly, and how well you succeeded.

"The Lake and Meadow view is fine, and brings to mind our admiring and gathering the beautiful wild flowers that grew so plentifully, and the walks we took about the lake and the hills on the other side and oh, the beauty of the sunsets over the Lake. All those things were a source of never failing pleasure.

"The Hickory Hill farm I never was as fully acquainted with, though I have racked and bound wheat after the cradle there too.

"It is fine that you have your clocks and other inventions illustrated and brought out so well. They were all so wonderful. Your desk with the wonderful machinery that did the work required so well seems one of the greatest. I have a copy of it that you penciled and gave me in those early days.

"Though you did so much of that and other work under difficulties that seemed stern, later on Father saw the mistake and urged Mary and Joanna to govern their children by love and not by fear. . . ."[13]

Joanna reacted with great sentimentality when she read her brother's book. "It is a charming bit of natural history, and with the sketches of the two old homes, the one in which I was born, and Hickory Hill, every nook and corner of which is engraven on my memory, it is to me a great treasure.

"The portion relating to yourself and the family was read in tears, and I wished with all my heart it had not been so true. In other words, that the hard things had never occurred so they would not have been there to record."[14]

In May, 1913, Sarah's grandson Kenneth graduated from the Polytechnic school in Los Angeles while her granddaughter Marjorie graduated from the Pacific Grove high school. When Marjorie went on to attend the normal school in Los Angeles that fall, Anna moved to that city as well. She said she could look after her son and daughter while they were busy with school or work. Sarah was left alone in her Pacific Grove home.

David explained the arrangement to John: "Mr. Guidinger will build a small house on his land for them and Kenneth will earn the money to pay the bills. He gets $50 a month or more. He graduated from the Polytechnic last June. Sarah is real well and brave, and I will look after her what I can."[15] The latter sentiment was an echo of earlier years in Portage when David did so much for his mother and sisters.

Four months later David commented, "Sister Sarah is a wonder. 78 years old and as smart as a girl, lives alone and is brave, and enjoys housekeeping like a new married woman."[16]

February, 1914, brought a great deal of concern for John's health. "I have just heard to-day that you have been quite ill with Grippe," Sarah wrote. "Ette brought in a Martinez paper this morning with the item, also telling that you were now much improved, for which I am very glad. I have been thinking so much about you lately and wondering how you could be."[17]

Muir was not at all well, but he continued to write in his scribble den, currently on his travels to Alaska. He had been working on this manuscript for two years.

On December 4, 1914, Cecelia Galloway wrote her uncle from the Metropolitan Hotel in Fort Worth, Texas.

"Dear Uncle John,

"I am sending you under separate cover a little picture I came across when I was in Denver. It is a picture of the dear little wind flowers I remember so well when I was a child in Wisconsin. I have never seen them anywhere else, and they looked so natural that I could almost smell their delicate fragrance. My memory of them is that they were the very earliest of all the spring flowers, and I was delighted when I found my first wind flower, every spring.

". . . I know you are fond of them for I notice you mention them specially in your book about your boyhood in Wisconsin.

"Wisconsin is a lovely state, and I remember many beautiful flowers that were familiar to me in my childhood, that I have never seen anywhere else."

When Cecelia closed her letter "With my love, and best wishes for the approaching Christmas season, and all the New Year,"[18] she could not know her uncle would not live the few short weeks until Christmas. For him there would be no new year.

Just after the middle of December, Muir boarded the train at Martinez to spend the holiday with Helen, who was married and living at Daggett, California.

Helen's husband, Buel Funk, later explained to the newspapers that his father-in-law had contracted a heavy cold and went to Daggett on the advice of friends who thought the desert would be beneficial to his health. But during the week pneumonia developed.

On December 24, the *Chicago Tribune* recounted that "A physician and a nurse were summoned from Los Angeles, but the condition of the naturalist steadily grew worse and it was decided to remove him to Los Angeles. Accompanied by his son-in-law, the physician, and the nurse, Mr. Muir arrived at the California Hospital last night."[19] They journeyed by train.

Throughout his lifetime explorations he had survived many a brush with death, but this time there was no escape. John Muir died at 10 o'clock in the morning the day before Christmas, 1914. His manuscript on his travels to Alaska was spread out before him on the bed.

Afterward, Dan Muir wrote of his shock at his brother's unexpected death. From a doctor's perspective he added, "I could hardly think why an inflamitory [sic] attack could terminate his life so suddenly till I remembered that he had La Grippe earlier in the year and that La Grippe leaves the system greatly weakened for a long time and especially the heart and lungs. . . ."[20]

News of Muir's death sent shock waves through his family and friends and people throughout the country. Newspapers all over the nation and abroad carried the death notice, many with accompanying features about the great naturalist's lifetime accomplishments.

The *Kansas City* (Missouri) *Times* stated:

"As all the Nation was aglow with holiday merriment last week the flame of life was snuffed out in one of its noblest men. John Muir was dead.

"If trees had tongues, if brooks wrote books, if stones could preach, the forests, fields and mountains of America would now be joining tongue and pen in a most solemn memorial. John Muir was their friend."

On December 26, John Muir's body was placed aboard the 5:15 P.M. train at Los Angeles for the final journey to Martinez. His funeral took place on the afternoon of December 27.

The San Francisco Chronicle carried this account:

"MUIR LAID TO REST ACROSS THE BAY

"Nature Smiles as the Famous Naturalist Is Gathered Into Her Bosom

"Nature, dry-eyed after a night of weeping, looked her prettiest yesterday when friends and neighbors of John Muir tenderly laid him to rest in an entrancing little beauty spot in the Contra Costa hills. . . .

"The remains of John Muir, naturalist, scientist and writer, were placed beside those of his wife, Louise [Louisiana] in the family plot at Muir. Boughs of the Sequoia gigantea, whose beauties he made known to the world, lined the grave.

"Tributes were paid to the departed by the Sierra Club, of which he was president, the Wisconsin Society and old friends and neighbors. The funeral ceremonies were conducted under the joint direction of them all. . . .

"Over one hundred members of the Sierra Club and the Wisconsin Society went to Muir [Station] from San Francisco and Bay Cities in a special train. Through fields that were the playground of Muir they trudged to his former home on the heights, whence, after simple but beautiful services, they walked to the grave a winding mile away.

"There were many Sierra Club members in the cortege who had followed John Muir over tortuous trails, had climbed mountains with him and revered him as a leader. And as they tramped behind him in other days, . . . so they went with him on his final journey yesterday.

"Through fields and orchards that were vibrant with the songs of happy birds, . . . the friends and neighbors . . . wended their way.

"As the beloved body was being lowered into the grave, quail on the side hills called out their farewells and overhead in the trees Muir himself planted forty years ago. . . .Robins and larks sang in the vineyards and orchards.

"Near by, his hat in his hand, and sad-faced, waited Wong, for twenty-five years the faithful servant of Muir. He stood a little apart from the others. He was motionless, but there was that in his eyes that made you turn away from him with a strange gripping at your throat."

Many people had a special memory of John Muir. Tributes came in from unexpected places. One touching reminiscence, written in a poor hand and with poor spelling, came from George Gray, son of Alexander Gray who helped the Muirs get settled in their new homeland in 1849. George now lived in East Los Angeles. The words belong to George Gray, but the difficult-to-read letter has been edited in order to clarify his heartfelt sentiment. It brings Muir's life full circle.
"Dear Friend,

I take this opportunity to write you of sorrow and sad heart . . . [on] the death of your good father and my dear old Sunday School teacher when I was a mere boy. The State of California has lost one of the greats. I was raised along side of your good father when we were all boys together. . . . It seems too bad to think such a man as he had to die.

"Mr. Muir, Johns father was terribly religious. Also a hard parent to his family. John Muir, also Sarah, Margaret and David done some awful hard work on their father's farm in early days of Wisconsin. John was always full of his share of fun but we all liked John all the same. John Muir never had an enemy among us boys. Every one of his associates loved John Muir.

"Your father early left home on account of his father always going after him. So John came over to our place and I can well remember how bad he felt over the actions of his father.

"My father was a good kind hearted man and he hired John for 12 dollars a month to drive a breaking team . . . of cattle. I used to ride the head ox [and] throw the grubs when John handled the plow. My dear old Aunt Sally used to bring us out lunches in the field. Your father worked a few months for my father and then he left and went to school doing chores for his board.

"One time John went home and his father and mother went to Portage on a trip. While they were gone John took down the old wooden clock and put it together again. So then John went to work and made a clock with his jacknife and my mother has the pieces of it. It stands about 5 feet high the clock did. John wanted to put it up on his father's barn and make it strike a large bell so all the neighbors would know the time of day. My father thought it would be a grand thing for the neighborhood. John's father thought it would interfere with the Lord and would not allow it to be put up. Also John made a bed to throw out the man at any hour of the night and keep the woman in or throw them both out. I have laid on that bed when I was a boy. We all thought it was fun.

"Your father than went to Madison College and served a term or two under the teaching of Dr. Carr. Mr. Carr and Mrs. Carr died here in Pasadena. I furnished them their wool for years since I came to California.

"I called on your father some 5 years ago and spent a few hours of happy life here in Los Angeles at Mr. Hooker's fine home. I tell you I never will forget that happy happy meeting for it was over 45 years since we shook hands together. When we were talking over old times it was good.

When I shook hands goodbye with your good father at Mr. Hooker's that night we promised each other we would meet again. Oh, how sad I feel that we did not meet again.

"So now I will close. Bidding you goodbye with sorrow and grief. . . ."[21]

John's sisters and brothers were crushed at losing their older brother. He had so often been their protector over the years. They were all proud of him and had taken great pleasure in his career.

". . . his work is done, now he is resting," Sarah wrote from Pacific Grove, "but how many will miss him through the days and the years."[22]

Joanna well expressed her feelings and those of the others when she wrote to Wanda from Richmond, Virginia.

"You and Helen are constantly in my mind for in the death of your father we have sustained a common loss. Your telegram which came at midnight, Christmas Eve, was a great blow to me, . . . hard indeed to realize that the great life had gone so suddenly.

"As I have just written Helen I have always had a treasured hope in my heart that being the youngest of our large family I might have the honor of ministering in some degree to his wants and his comfort in the trying years of old age; and so suddenly to know that he has gone from our love and all possibility of even seeing his well-known hand-writing in an occasional letter is difficult to bear. . . .

"I know by the experience of the care of my own father just how glad you will be to the end of your days that you could do so much for him. Perhaps you remember that Grandpa Muir was with me in Kansas City, Mo. when he died.

"The first letter I ever wrote was to my well beloved brother John and when he came home the first time from the university well do I remember how he picked me up in his strong arms and carried me into the house kissing me the while.

"We early learned to recognize the great fire of genius which burned in his soul and to give him honor. And thank God the flame will never die out for he has been as consecrated to his mission of expounding the great book of Nature as any minister of the gospel in expounding the written word."[23]

Later, when Wanda sent Joanna sheets of public tributes to her father, Joanna commented, ". . . this bereavement will be very hard to heal for he was the one I always felt I would turn to and depend upon if any great trouble should overtake us."[24]

Mary wrote to Wanda from Kearney, Nebraska:

"The printed sheet you inclosed is wonderful—a wonderful page. . . . And I would read and weep—read again and weep and think and think—thus passing the time until office hours closed and Willis appeared for dinner a little later than five o'clock.

"Just a week ago when Mr.Hand was at church a good friend of ours handed him a copy of Collier's containing the following lines written by Charles L. Edson of the New York *Evening Mail*. Rather peculiar though fascinating. . . .

"Collier's remarks are these: 'John Muir and God are friends. Muir fraternized with the birds of the fields and forest and chummed with the squirrel and the bear. He rhapsodized over the beauty and sweetness of flowers and communed with God through the redwoods and pines. His life was a glorification of God's original handiwork.'"[25]

Muir left succeeding generations of Americans a tremendous natural heritage, most notably in the national park system. His love for the native landscape was passed on to future generations of his own family as well. Sarah Galloway had shared her brother's love of nature since Fountain Lake days and taking care of his herbarium during the early trips increased her knowledge and love of plants. Throughout his life she followed him in her imagination along his many pathways. Cecelia Galloway's last letter to her Uncle John showed the passage of the legacy.

As they grew up in the lovely Alhambra Valley, Wanda and Helen attained an intimate knowledge and understanding of their father's life work. With their mother, they too loved beauty in nature.

The manuscript sheets spread before him on his hospital bed that morning of December 24th were testimony to the fact that Muir worked to share his love and knowledge of nature to the end. He had begun the book on his Alaskan odysseys in 1912.

"The work on this book was the chief pleasure and recreation of Mr. Muir's last days," wrote Marion Parsons, who had worked on the manuscript with him, "for through it he lived again many of the most glorious experiences of his life."[26]

When Muir was ill with pneumonia at Helen's, and as he lay dying in California Hospital, his mind was on the wonderful Alaskan trips he had made over the past thirty-five years. The *Travels in Alaska* manuscript was almost finished, and he was absorbed in the 1890 trip to Glacier Bay and his exploration of the magnificent Muir Glacier.

The manuscript described one foot journey he took on the Muir Glacier. On a July, 1890, morning, pulling a sled and a few supplies, he left his camp to head out to the main glacier. It was ". . . one of the loveliest mornings I ever saw in Alaska; not a cloud . . . in all the wide sky. There is a yellowish haze in the east, white in the west, mild and mellow as a Wisconsin Indian Summer, but finer, more ethereal, God's holy light making all divine."[27]

A few days later he lay between two boulders "gazing into the starry sky and across the sparkling bay." He was watching a spectacular display of the aurora borealis with its bright prismatic colors.

"Once long ago in Wisconsin I saw the heavens draped in rich purple auroral clouds fringed and folded in most magnificent form. . ."[28] As Muir's life ebbed away, his spirit may have been immersed in the glories of the glaciers and the brilliance of the aurora.

Many years had passed since John Muir climbed as a youth onto the rhyolite outcrop of Marquette County's Observatory Hill and beheld the rolling glacial landscape before him. His work in unlocking the icy secrets of the Sierra Nevada and Alaska was only a promise then.

Over his lifetime he had preached nature's gospel and brought his own bright light to preserving the national landscape. Through the success of his efforts, John Muir's light continued to shine through the generations. It shines today.

# Abbreviations

BADÉ    William Frederic Badé, *The Life and Letters of John Muir*, Manuscript Edition, (Boston and New York: Houghton Mifflin Company, 1923).

BT    Badé transcription, John Muir Papers.

GULF    John Muir, *A Thousand Mile Walk to the Gulf*, (Boston and New York: Houghton Mifflin Co., The Riverside Press, 1916).

HUN    Reproduced by permission of The Huntington Library, San Marino, California.

JMP    John Muir Papers, Holt-Atherton Department of Special Collections, University of the Pacific Libraries. Copyright 1984 Muir-Hanna Trust.

LF    John Muir, *Letters to a Friend*, Copyright 1915, by Wanda Muir Hanna, by arrangement with Houghton Mifflin Co.

MBY    John Muir, *The Story of My Boyhood and Youth* (Boston and New York: Houghton Mifflin Company, March, 1913), Copyright 1912 and 1913, by the Atlantic Monthly Company. Copyright 1913 by John Muir. (Madison: The University of Wisconsin Press, 1965)

MFS    John Muir, *My First Summer in the Sierra* (Boston: Houghton Mifflin, 1916).

NEW    Newman collection, John Muir Historic Site, Martinez, California.

SHSW    State Historical Society of Wisconsin archives, Madison, Wisconsin.

# Chapter Notes

## CHAPTER ONE

1. Badé, 9: 209-210.
2. John Muir, MBY, 63-64. Several incidents of the Fountain Lake period are taken from this autobiography.
3. MFS, 211.
4. Daniel Muir's obituary written by John Muir, *Wisconsin State Register*, Portage, October 31, 1885.
5. John Muir to his sister Mary, April 22, [1867], JM Papers.
6. Daniel Muir's obituary.
7. Ibid.
8. Anne Muir to her son Dan, Feb. 15, 1878, Hun.
9. Gulf, 177.
10. Background information on Alexander Gray and the mile of countyline road where he and others of the family had their homes, provided by an unpublished manuscript by Lila Brown Jerred, 1951, "My Homes and Travels and the Persons who Shared Them by the Little Brass Teakettle from Scotland." Through the courtesy of her sister, Barbara Brown Sommers, grandniece of Alexander Gray. Further details furnished by Mrs. Sommers in an interview by the author, Dec. 19, 1972.
11. Anne Muir to her son John, November 11, 1869, JM Papers.
12. John to his brother David, [May, 1870], JM Papers.
13. John to Mary, April 22, [1867], JM Papers.
14. James Whitehead to John, March 31, 1913, SHSW.
15. Newspaper collections, SHSW.
16. MBY, 214-217.
17. MBY, 1913, 1st printing run, 217.
18. James Whitehead to John, March 10, 1913, SHSW.
19. Whitehead to John, Jan. 30, 1913, SHSW.
20. Whitehead to John, March 31, 1913, SHSW.
21. John to Whitehead, Feb. 13, 1913, SHSW.
22. MBY, second 1913 printing run, 217.
23. John Gray, *Letters, Poems and Selected Prose Writings of David Gray*, Edinburgh, Scotland, 1836—Buffalo, New York, 1888, (Buffalo: The Courier Company, Printers, 1888). The story of the Gray family and the friendship of the twa Davies is taken from this volume.
24. George B. Mair, article, *Montello* (Wisconsin) *Express*, March 12, 1900, SHSW.
25. Interview with Harry Kearns by the author, Oct. 14, 1982.

26. John Gray, *Letters, Poems and Selected Prose Writings of David Gray.*
27. James Whitehead letter to *Montello Express*, April 7, 1900.
28. Ibid.
29. Ibid.
30. Ibid.
31. Interview with Allen McReath by the author, 1978.
32. Interview with Ben and Mary Hull by the author, 1971.
33. Badé, 10: 213.
34. SHSW archives.

## CHAPTER TWO
1. Daniel Muir's obituary, written by John Muir, *Wisconsin State Register*, Portage, Oct. 31, 1885.
2. Information on Fox-Wisconsin river history was gathered from *Early Days at the Fox-Wisconsin Portage* by Portage historian, Ina Curtis. Copyright, 1974, printing by the Times Publishing Co., Pardeeville, Wis.
3. Information on the work of sub-Indian agent John Kinzie and his wife Juliette at Fort Winnebago and the agency house was provided by Rita Fredrick, curator of the Old Indian Agency House historic site operated by the National Society of the Colonial Dames of the State of Wisconsin.
4. Background information on the canal was obtained from the booklet, *Portage Canal History*, compiled and written by Frederica Kleist for the Portage Canal Society, Inc., 1983.
5. Galloway family background provided by a letter from Sarah Muir Galloway's granddaughter, Marjorie Eastman Shone, to Eva Johnston, Jan. 23, 1961; and *Genealogical Compilations* by Ruth J. Merrihew Lofgren, through the courtesy of Lura Johnston Krouscup.
6. MBY, 230-232.
7. Interview with Harry Kearns by the author, early 1970s.
8. Interview with Eva Turner by the author, Jan. 4, 1973.
9. Interview with Annie Duncan Waite and Frank Waite by the author, Dec. 19, 1972.
10. Alfred Bradley Brown to John, undated, [1858], JM Papers.
11. Charles Reid to John, Feb. 22, 1858, JM Papers.
12. Alfred Bradley Brown to John, undated, [1858], JM Papers.
13. Alfred Bradley Brown to John, March 18, 1859, JM Papers.
14. Charles Reid to John, Feb. 9, 1858, JM Papers.
15. Charles Reid to John, March 10, 1858, JM Papers.
16. William Reid to John, April, 1858, JM Papers.
17. William Reid to John, May 5, 1858, JM Papers.

18. Interview with Eva Turner by the author, Jan. 4, 1973.
19. Badé, 9: 156.
20. Letter from Marjorie Eastman Shone to Eva Johnston, Jan. 23, 1961.
21. John to Mrs. Edward Pelton, fall, 1862, SHSW.

## CHAPTER THREE

1. Quotations on Muir leaving home, his overnight stay in Pardeeville, and his train ride to Madison are from MBY, 230-232.
2. John to Mary, [Nov. 29, 1860], New.
3. Madison *Evening Patriot*, Sept. 25, 1860, SHSW.
4. Madison *Wisconsin State Journal*, Sept. 26, 1860, SHSW.
5. MBY, 216.
6. Mr. Hinkley's speech is from the *Wisconsin State Journal*, Sept. 26, 1860.
7. *Evening Patriot*, Sept. 26, 1860, SHSW.
8. *Evening Patriot* ad, Sept., 1860, SHSW.
9. *Evening Patriot*, Sept. 26, 1860, SHSW.
10. Ibid.
11. *Wisconsin State Journal*, Sept. 25, 1860, SHSW.
12. *Evening Patriot*, Sept. 25, 1860, SHSW.
13. *Evening Patriot*, Sept. 26, 1860, SHSW.
14. *Wisconsin State Journal*, Sept 26, 1860, SHSW.
15. Background information on the ice boat from William J. Petersen's article, "Wiard and His Ice Boat," The *Palimpsest*, Vol. 25 (April, 1944): 106, Reprinted as XLIV, No. 2 (Feb., 1963): 65, William J. Petersen, Editor, The State Historical Society of Iowa.
16. The *Palimpsest* (April, 1944): 108, (Feb., 1963): 67.
17. The Prairie du Chien *Leader*, May 10, 1860, SHSW.
18. John to his sister Sarah Galloway, [Sept., 1860], JM Papers, BT.
19. Ibid.
20. An 1986 interview by the author with Mary Antoine de Julio, researcher at the Villa Louis, SHSW historic site, Prairie du Chien, Wis., provided background material on the area. Also, her article, "Great Council Was Vain Attempt to Keep Peace," *Prairie du Chien Shopping News*, Oct., 1986.
21. Prairie du Chien *Leader*, May 10, 1860, SHSW.
22. Ibid.
23. Regular ads appeared in the Prairie du Chien *Courier* during the summer and fall of 1860 and the winter of 1860-61. SHSW.
24. Ibid.
25. *History of Crawford and Richland Counties 1884* (Springfield, Ill.: Union Publishing Co.).

26. Ibid.
27. Prairie du Chien *Leader*, June 15, 1860 and other issues, SHSW.
28. J. M. Pelton, *Genealogy of the Pelton Family in America*. (Albany, New York: Joe Munsells' sons, Publishers, "Entered acc. to act of Congress, 1892, by J. M. Pelton"), 110.
29. Ibid.
30. Ibid., 117-118.
31. Ibid., 109.
32. Ibid., 117-118.
33. John Muir to Emily Pelton, Jan. 29, [1870], SHSW. Year supplied by SHSW.
34. John to Emily Pelton, Feb. 19, [1872], SHSW. Year supplied by SHSW.
35. John to Emily Pelton, Jan. 11, 1902, SHSW.
36. Early descriptions of the Mississipi River valley are from Ellison Orr, "Reminiscences of a Pioneer Boy," undated, unpublished manuscript, Effigy Mounds National Monument archives, Harpers Ferry, Iowa.
37. Ibid.
38. John to Emily Pelton, May 23, 1865, SHSW.
39. Sarah to her brother John, [Dec., 1860], JM Papers.
40. Anne Muir to her son John, Oct. 21, 1860, JM Papers.
41. Daniel Muir to his son John, Oct. 14, 1860, JM Papers.
42. David Muir to his brother John, Oct. 14, 1860, JM Papers.
43. Sarah to her brother John, Oct. 14, 1860, JM Papers.
44. Maggie to her brother John, Oct. 14, 1860, JM Papers.
45. David Galloway to his brother-in-law John, Dec. 21, 1860, JM Papers.
46. Maggie to John, Dec. 8, 1860, JM Papers.
47. David Galloway to John, Dec. 21, 1860, JM Papers.
48. David Muir to John, Dec. 21, 1860, JM Papers.
49. Prairie du Chien *Courier*, Jan 24, 1861, SHSW.

## CHAPTER FOUR

1. Information on entering the university, MBY, 274-275.
2. MBY, 276.
3. John to Sarah and David Galloway, [March 20, 1861]
4. Anne Muir to John, March 30, 1861, JM Papers.
5. Daniel Muir to his son John, April 17, 1861, JM Papers.
6. James Whitehead article, "Recollections of John Muir," *Emporia* (Kansas) *Weekly Gazette*, Jan. 21, 1915.
7. John to Sarah and David, [March 20, 1861], JM Papers.
8. Ibid.
9. John to his family at Hickory Hill, [June, 1861], JM Papers.

## CHAPTER FIVE

1. John to Sarah and David, [Aug. or Sept., 1861], JM Papers.
2. Ibid.
3. John to Mrs. Edward Pelton, [fall, 1861], JM Papers.
4. Maggie Muir Reid to John and David Muir, [Oct. 5, 1861], JM Papers.
5. Carolyn J. Mattern, *Soldiers When They Go. The Story of Camp Randall, 1861-1865,* (Madison: Published by the State Historical Society of Wisconsin, 1981, Logmark Editions), 2.
6. Ibid., IX, X.
7. Ibid., 3, 4.
8. Anne Muir to John, May 12, 1862, JM Papers.
9. John to Emily Pelton, fall, 1861, SHSW.
10. John to Sarah and David, Feb. 9, [1862] JM Papers.
11. Anne Muir to John, Dec. 1, 1861, JM Papers.
12. Anne Muir to David, Dec. 1, 1861, JM Papers.
13. Anne Muir to John, Dec. 1, 1861, JM Papers.
14. Anne Muir to John, Jan. 10, 1862, JM Papers.
15. Mary to John, Feb. 19, 1861, JM Papers.
16. John Muir, Daniel Muir's obituary, *Wisconsin State Register,* Portage, Oct. 31, 1885.
17. Charles E. Vroman, "John Muir at the University," *Wisconsin Alumni,* June, 1915, 557-562.
18. Muir's study clock is on display at the State Historical Society of Wisconsin, Madison.
19. Sarah to John, May 23, 1862, JM Papers.
20. MBY, 280-283.
21. Milton Griswold to John, Feb. 17, 1909, JM Papers, BT.
22. MBY, 279-280.

## CHAPTER SIX

1. Anne Muir to David Muir, Dec. 1, 1861, JM Papers.
2. Anne Muir to John, May 12, 1862, JM Papers.
3. Maggie Muir Reid to John, Oct. 8, 1862, JM Papers.
4. David Muir to John, Nov. 15, 1862, JM Papers.
5. *The History of Columbia County,* 1880, 559.
6. John Reid to John Muir, Nov. 5, 1862, JM Papers.
7. David Muir to John Muir, Dec. 31, 1862, JM Papers.
8. Ibid.
9. Badé: 92-94.

10. James Davie Butler, "The Early Decade of Wisconsin University," *The Badger*, 1890, SHSW.

11. *Circular of the Wisconsin State University for the Year 1861*, 65, University of Wisconsin archives.

12. *Record A, Regents of University of Wisconsin*, p. 305, University of Wisconsin archives.

13. Ibid.

14. Ezra Slocum Carr, undated article, SHSW.

15. LF, 13, John to Jeanne Carr, Sept. 13, [1866].

16. LF, 12, John to Jeanne Carr, Sept. 13, [1866].

17. Ibid.

18. Carr article.

19. Carr article.

20. LF, 13, John to Jeanne Carr, Sept. 13, [1866].

21. *Wisconsin State Journal*, Madison, Dec. 2, 1858, SHSW.

22. Reuben Gold Thwaites, "Memorial Address: James Davie Butler," reprinted from Vol. XV, Part II of the *Transactions of the Wisconsin Academy of Sciences, Arts and Letters*, (Issued December, 1907).

23. Butler, "The Early Decade of Wisconsin University," *The Badger*, 1890, SHSW.

24. Ibid.

25. William H. Brown to John, Nov. [9], 1862, JM Papers.

26. Annie Muir to John, Nov., 1862, JM Papers.

27. Draft of March 31, 1913 letter, James Whitehead to John, SHSW.

28. Anne Muir to John, March 1, 1863, JM Papers.

29. Anne Muir to John, May 16, 1863, JM Papers.

30. David Galloway to John, March 1, 1863, JM Papers.

31. Sarah to John, April 29, [1863], JM Papers.

32. John to Sarah and David Galloway, June 1, 1863, JM Papers.

33. John to Mr. and Mrs. Ambrose Newton, Aug. 2, 1863, SHSW.

34. Charles E. Vroman, "John Muir at the University," *The Wisconsin Alumni Magazine*, June, 1915.

35. Sarah to John, April 29, [1863], JM Papers.

36. Ibid.

37. John to Sarah and David, June 1, 1863, JM Papers.

38. John to Sarah and David, June 8, 1863, JM Papers.

39. Sarah and David to John, June 13, 1863, JM Papers.

40. Background information on the town of McGregor, Iowa, provided by *MacGregor and His Town*, by Lena D. Myers (McGregor, Iowa: McGregor Public Library, May, 1971.) Mrs. Mae Huebsch of the McGregor Historical Society provided pertinent information from the society archives.

41. John to Emily Pelton, backdated letters, July 7, 8, and 9, 1863, SHSW.
42. Badé, 9:111-112.

CHAPTER SEVEN
1. David Muir to John, April 17, 1863, JM Papers.
2. David Muir to John, June 9, 1863, JM Papers.
3. John to Dan, Dec. 20, 1863, Hun.
4. Ibid.
5. Ibid.
6. Badé, 9: 114.
7. John to Bradley Brown, Jan. 17, 1864, JM Papers.
8. John Muir's address before the Sierra Club, *Sierra Club Bulletin*: 1, 1893-1896, (San Francisco, Calif.: The Sierra Club 1950) 276-277. Printed in the United States of America by the New York Lithographic Corp. and bound by the Chas. H. Bohn & Co., Inc.
9. John to Emily Pelton, Feb. 27, 1864, SHSW, and Badé, 9: 116.
10. John to Emily Pelton, March 1, 1864, SHSW, and Badé, 9: 116.
11. Badé, 9: 119-120.
12. Badé, 9: 120-121.
13. John to Annie, Oct. 23, [1864], JM Papers, BT.
14. W.H. Trout, *Trout Family History*, (Milwaukee, Wis., 1916). Quotations and information for Dan and John's sojourn at the Trout Mill is gleaned from pp. 121-128.
15. Badé, 9: 128-129.
16. Badé, 9: 135, John to Emily Pelton, May 23, 1865.
17. John to Emily Pelton, May 23, 1865, SHSW.
18. Annie to Dan, Sept. 9, 1865, Hun.
19. Dan to John, [Nov., 1865], JM Papers.
20. Badé, 9: John to Mary, Annie, and Joanna, Dec. 24, 1865.
21. Joanna to John, Jan. 7, 1866, JM Papers.
22. Anne to Dan, Jan. 1, 1866, Hun.
23. *Trout Family History*, 121-128.
24. Ibid.
25. Badé, 9: 153-154.
26. Badé, 9: 152, John to Sarah, May, 1866.
27. This portion of John's May, 1866 letter to Sarah is quoted from the JM Papers.
28. Anne to Dan, July 2, 1866, Hun.
29. Badé, 9: 153.
30. Joanna to Dan, Dec. 25. 1866, Hun.
31. John to Mary and Annie Feb. 11, [1867], New.

32. John to Mary, April 22, [1867] Yosemite National Park Research Library.
33. John to Anna Galloway, Jan., 1867, JM Papers.
34. The three original charts are on file at the State Historical Society of Wis. Department of Iconography.
35. Badé, 9: 154.
36. LF, 15, John to Jeanne Carr, April 3, [1867].
37. LF, 19, John to Jeanne Carr, April 6, [1867].
38. John to Sarah and David Galloway, April 12, 1867, JM Papers.
39. Mary to John, April 14, 1867, JM Papers.
40. LF, 22-23, John to Jeanne Carr, May 2, 1867.
41. John to Sarah and David Galloway, June 7, 1867, JM Papers.
42. LF, 24, John to Jeanne Carr, June 9, 1867.
43. John to Janet and Chris Moores, July 12, 1867, JM Papers.
44. Badé, 9: 161, John to Catherine Merrill, Aug. 12, 1867.
45. LF, 25, John to Jeanne Carr, [1867].
46. Anna Galloway to Dan, Aug. 9, 1867, Hun.
47. Sarah to Dan, Aug. 8, 1867, Hun.
48. Linnie Marsh Wolfe, *Son of The Wilderness, The Life of John Muir*, 144, (Madison, Wis.: Reprinted by the University of Wisconsin Press Inc., 1978, by arrangement with Alfred A. Knopf, Inc.). Copyright 1945 by Alfred A. Knopf, copyright renewed 1973 by Howard T. Wolfe.

## CHAPTER EIGHT

1. John to Dan, Sept. 1, 1867, Hun.
2. Gulf, 2.
3. Gulf, 14.
4. Gulf, 16.
5. Gulf, 30.
6. Gulf, 32.
7. Gulf, 47.
8. Ibid.
9. Gulf, 69.
10. Gulf, 123.
11. John to David Muir, March 3, [1868], JM Papers.
12. Sarah to John, March 17, 1868, JM Papers.
13. John to David Muir, Oct. 15, 1867, JM Papers.
14. Sarah to John, March 17, 1868, JM Papers.
15. Gulf, 187.
16. Badé, 9: 180.

17. Badé, 9: 182.
18. Badé, 9: 189.
19. Anne Muir to John, July 10, 1868, JM Papers.
20. Sarah to Dan, July 12, 1868, Hun.
21. Anne Muir to Dan, Oct. 18, 1868, Hun.
22. LF, 50-51, John to Jeanne Carr, Feb. 24, 1869.
23. Mary to John, April 4, 1869, JM Papers.
24. John to Mary, May 20, 1869, New.
25. John to Dan, April 17, 1869, Hun.
26. Cecelia Galloway to John, April 4, [1869], JM Papers.
27. Badé, 9: 195.
28. John to Mrs. James Davie Butler, Aug. 7, 1869, SHSW.
29. MFS, 154-155.
30. MFS, 240.
31. MFS, 239-240.
32. John to Mrs. James Davie Butler, Aug. 7, 1869, SHSW.
33. Ibid.
34. Ibid.
35. Badé, 9: 200.
36. MFS, 354.

## CHAPTER NINE

1. Sarah to Dan, Oct. 3, 1869, Hun.
2. Anne Muir to John, Nov. 8, 1869, JM Papers.
3. Ibid.
4. Anne Muir to John, Nov. 11, 1869, JM Papers.
5. Badé, 9: 207-208.
6. Badé, 9: 208, 210, John to David Muir, March 20, [1870].
7. John to Mary Muir, March 24, [1870], New.
8. John to David Muir, [May, 1870], JM Papers.
9. Anna Galloway to John, May 8, 1870, JM Papers.
10. Sarah to John, May 17, 1870, JM Papers.
11. Anne Muir to Dan, June 29, 1870, Hun.
12. Sarah to Dan, Sept. 4, 1870, Hun.
13. Sarah to Dan, Sept. 18, 1870, Hun.
14. John to David Muir, Dec. 1, [1871], JM Papers.
15. John to Anna Galloway, the new year, 1869 or 1870, JM Papers.
16. Sarah to John, Jan. 15, 1871, JM Papers.
17. Sarah to John, May 30, 1871, JM Papers.

18. John to David Galloway, Sept. 8, [1871], JM Papers.
19. Sarah to John, Nov. 9, 1871, JM Papers.
20. Anne Muir to John, Nov. 9, 1871, JM Papers.
21. Badé, 9: 314-316, John to Anne Muir, Nov. 16., [1871].

CHAPTER TEN

1. Anne Muir to Dan, Feb. 26, 1872, HUN.
2. Anne Muir to John, Feb. 26, 1872, JM Papers.
3. John to David, Feb. 20, 1872, JM Papers.
4. Anne Muir to Dan, April 4, 1872, HUN.
5. John to Dan, March 5, [1872], HUN.
6. John to Sarah and David Galloway, April 25, 1872, JM Papers.
7. David Muir to John, April 25, 1872, JM Papers.
8. Anne Muir to Dan, May 30, 1872, HUN.
9. Anne Muir to Dan and Emma, Sept. 22, 1872, HUN.
10. John to Sarah, July 16, 1872, JM Papers.
11. Sarah to John, Oct. 27, 1872, JM Papers.
12. John to Emily Pelton, (Jan. or Feb., 1861), SHSW.
13. John to David, March 1, 1873, JM Papers.
14. Anne Muir to Dan, April 18, 1873, HUN.
15. John to Sarah, Sept. 3, 1873, JM Papers, BT.
16. Anne Muir to Dan, Oct. 27, 1873, HUN.
17. Joanna to Mary, Nov. 16, 1873, NEW.
18. Joanna to Mary, Nov. 30, 1873, NEW.
19. Daniel Muir to John, March 19, 1874, JM Papers.
20. Interview with Harry Kearns by the author, June, 1979.
21. Joanna to Dan and Emma, May 16, 1874, HUN.
22. Joanna to Mary, June 3, 1874, NEW.
23. Anne Muir to Dan, June 29, 1874, HUN.
24. Sarah to John, Aug. 30, 1874, JM Papers.
25. John to Sarah, Sept. 7, 1874, JM Papers.
26. Joanna to Mary, Sept. 8, 1874, NEW.
27. Anne Muir to Dan, Sept. 25, 1874, HUN.
28. Anne Muir to John, Nov. 21, 1874, JM Papers, BT.
29. Anne Muir to Dan, June 29, 1875, HUN.
30. John to Sarah, Nov. 2, 1875, JM Papers.
31. Sarah to John, undated letter, written sometime before Grandma Galloway's death in Dec., 1876, JM Papers.
32. John to Sarah, Jan. 12, [1877], JM Papers.

33. Anne Muir to John, Feb. 22, 1877, JM Papers.

34. Anne Muir to Dan, Aug. 8, 1877, HUN.

35. Joanna to John, March 6, 1878, JM Papers.

CHAPTER ELEVEN

1. Joanna to Mary, Feb. 11, 1878, New.

2. David to John, April 2, 1878, JM Papers.

3. Anne Muir to John, March 23, 1878, JM Papers.

4. Anne Muir to John, May 16, 1878, JM Papers.

5. Anne Muir to John, Oct. 20, 1878, JM Papers.

6. Mary to John, May 27, 1878, JM Papers.

7. Sarah to John, Feb. 16, 1879, JM Papers.

8. John Muir, "A Windstorm in the Forests of the Yuba," *Scribner's Monthly:* XXII, Nov., 1878, 55-59.

9. Ibid., 57-58.

10. Ibid, 59.

11. Mary to John, May 27, 1878, JM Papers.

12. John Muir, Daniel Muir obituary, Oct. 31, 1885, *Wisconsin State Register*, Portage.

13. Anne Muir to Dan, March 8, 1879, Hun.

14. Anne Muir to John, Oct. 18, 1879, JM Papers.

15. Joanna to John, May 31, 1879, JM Papers.

16. S. Hall Young, *Alaska Days With John Muir*, (New York, Chicago, Toronto, London, and Edinburgh: Fleming H. Revell Company, 1915), 113-117.

17. Maggie to John, Feb. 11, 1880, JM Papers.

18. Anne Muir to Dan, July 21, 1878, Hun.

19. Anne Muir to John, March 21, 1880, JM Papers.

20. *Contra Costa Gazette*, Martinez, Calif., undated clipping, courtesy of Sherry Hanna.

21. Anne Muir to John, May 2, 1880, JM Papers.

22. Louisiana Erwin Strentzel's unpublished journal, 1868-1869, courtesy of Sherry Hanna.

23. David to John, June 26, 1880, JM Papers.

24. Joanna to John, July 1, 1880, JM Papers.

25. Anne Muir to John, Sept. 20, 1880, JM Papers.

26. Anne Muir to John, Oct. 6, 1880, JM Papers.

27. Joanna to John and Louie, Oct. 25, 1880, JM Papers.

28. Annie Muir to her brother Dan, Dec. 22, 1880, Hun.

29. Sarah to John, Dec. 3, 1880, JM Papers.

30. *Wisconsin State Register*, Portage, Jan. 17, 1880, courtesy of Portage Public Library.

31. Sarah to John, Dec. 3, 1880, JM Papers.

CHAPTER TWELVE

1. Annie to Dan, Dec. 22, 1880, Hun.
2. Sarah to John, Dec. 3, 1880, JM Papers.
3. Anne Muir to John, April 5, 1881, JM Papers.
4. Anne Muir to John, April 8, 1881, JM Papers.
5. Sarah to John, Sept. 14, 1881, JM Papers.
6. Information for this paragraph gathered from John Muir, *Travels In Alaska*, (Boston and New York: Houghton Mifflin Company, The Riverside Press Cambridge, Copyright 1915).
7. *Wisconsin State Journal*, Portage, Courtesy of Portage Public Library.
8. Louie Muir to Anne Muir, Sept. 29, 1881, JM Papers.
9. Anne Muir to John, Nov. 14, 1881, JM Papers.
10. Anne Muir to John, Feb. 21, 1882, JM Papers.
11. Ibid.
12. Joanna to John, April 22, 1882, JM Papers.
13. Joanna to Mary, April 25, 1882, New.
14. Joanna to Mary, June 7, 1882.
15. Anne Muir to John, Aug. 16, 1882, JM Papers.
16. Anne Muir to John, May 7, 1882, JM Papers.
17. David Muir to Maggie, Sarah, Louie, and John, Dec. 17, 1882, JM Papers.
18. John to Mary and Willis Hand, Jan. 1, 1883, New.
19. Sarah to John and Louie, Oct. 19, 1883, JM Papers, BT.
20. Sarah to John and Louie, June 2, 1883, JM Papers.
21. Sarah to John and Louie, Oct. 19, 1883, JM Papers, BT.
22. Joanna to John and Louie, Nov. 16, 1883, JM Papers.
23. Anne Muir to John, Dec. 4, 1883, JM Papers, BT.
24. Joanna to John, Jan. 26, 1884, JM Papers.
25. David Muir to John Muir, Feb. 6, 1884, JM Papers, BT.
26. Sarah to John, Feb. 10, 1884, JM Papers.
27. Anne Muir to John, March 6, 1884, JM Papers.
28. Anne Muir to John, April 21, 1884, JM Papers.
29. Annie Muir to John, May 5, 1884, JM Papers, BT.
30. Ibid.
31. Anne Muir to Dan, June 28, 1884, Hun.
32. Anne Muir to John, Sept. 3, 1884, Hun.
33. David Muir to John, Sept. 28, 1884, JM Papers.
34. David Muir to John, March 28, 1885, JM Papers.
35. John to David, April 20, 1885, JM Papers.
36. Anne Muir to John, April 21, 1885, JM Papers.

37. Anne Muir to John, June 15, 1885, JM Papers.
38. John to Louie, Aug. 30, 1885, JM Papers.
39. John to Louie, Sept. 10, 1885, JM Papers.
40. John to Louie, Aug. 30, 1885, JM Papers.
41. John to Wanda, Sept. 9 and 10, 1885, JM Papers.
42. John to Louie, Sept. 10, 1885, JM Papers.
43. John to Louie, Sept. 19, 1885, JM Papers.
44. John to Louie, Sept. 26, 1885, JM Papers, BT.
45. Anne Muir to Louie, Sept. 30, 1885, JM Papers.
46. John to Louie, Oct. 4, 1885, JM Papers, BT.
47. John to Louie, Oct. 5, 1885, JM Papers, BT.
48. John to Louie, Oct. 6, 1885, JM Papers, BT.
49. Sarah to John, Nov. 20, 1885, JM Papers, BT.
50. John to Louie, Oct. 6, 1885, JM Papers, BT.

## CHAPTER THIRTEEN
1. John to David, Oct. 30, 1885, JM Papers.
2. This autograph book is in the archives of the John Muir National Historic Site, Martinez, Calif.
3. Anne Muir to Annie Muir, Jan. 21, 1886, JM Papers.
4. Anne Muir to John, May 8, 1887, JM Papers.
5. Anne Muir to Dan, April 28, 1887, Hun.
6. Sarah to John, Feb. 3, 1888, JM Papers.
7. Annie Muir to her nieces, Wanda and Helen, Sept. 28, 1888, JM Papers.
8. Sarah to John, Oct. 18, 1888, JM Papers.
9. Sarah to John, April 5, 1889, JM Papers.
10. Interview with Harry Kearns by the author, Oct. 14, 1982.
11. John to David, April 20, 1889, John Muir Papers.
12. Ibid.
13. Anne Muir to John, April 23, 1889, JM Papers.
14. Badé, 10: 231-232, John to James Davie Butler, Sept. 1, 1889.
15. Sarah to John, undated, 1890, JM Papers.
16. Sarah to John, Feb. 10, 1891, JM Papers.
17. John Reid to John Muir, Feb. 3, 1891, JM Papers.
18. John and Maggie Reid to John Muir, Feb. 15, 1891, JM Papers.
19. David Muir to John, March 4, 1891, JM Papers.
20. The March 19, 1892 edition of the Portage Daily Register and other issues quoted are from the collections of the Portage Public Library, Portage, Wis.
21. David to John, March 19, 1892, JM Papers.

22. John to Louie, April 18, 1892, JM Papers.

23. John to Helen, April 18, 1892, JM Papers.

24. John to Wanda, April 18, 1892, JM Papers.

25. John to Louie, April 20, 1892, JM Papers.

26. John to Louie, April 25, 1892, JM Papers.

27. Annie Muir to Louie, April 27, 1892, JM Papers.

28. David to John, May 5, 1892, JM Papers.


CHAPTER FOURTEEN

1. Badé, 10: 256.

2. Badé, 10: 273, John to Louie, July 6, 1893.

3. Badé, 10: 276-278, John to Louie, July 12, 1893.

4. William F. and Maymie B. Kimes, *John Muir A Reading Bibliography* (Fresno, California: Panorama West Books, 1986), 54.

5. Sarah to John, Jan. 9, 1895, JM Papers.

6. David to Anne Muir, Jan. 5, 1896, JM Papers.

7. John to Anne Muir, Feb. 24, 1896, JM Papers.

8. John to Helen, July 3, 1896, JM Papers.

9. Badé, 10: 296.

10. John to Louie, June 11, 1896, JM Papers.

11. John to Wanda and Helen, June 11, 1896, JM Papers.

12. Louie to John, June 12, 1896, JM Papers.

13. Interview with Bessie Eggleston of Marquette County, by the author, July 4, 1983.

14. John to Louie, June 12, 1896, JM Papers.

15. John to Louie, June 17, 1896, JM Papers.

16. This tiny diary kept by David Muir is in the archives of the John Muir National Historic Site, Martinez, Calif.

17. John to Louie, June 28, 1896, JM Papers.

18. Louie to John, June 25, 1896, JM Papers.

19. John to Louie, June 28, 1896, JM Papers.

20. Town clerk's communication to John, July 30, 1896, JM Papers.

21. John to Annie Muir, May 22, 1897, JM Papers, BT.

22. University of Wisconsin archives.

23. Ibid.

24. Ibid.

25. John Muir, *Our National Parks*, (Boston and New York: Houghton Mifflin and Company, November, 1901), preface.

26. *Our National Parks*, 2.

27. Louie to Wanda, July 14, 1902, Courtesy of Sherry Hanna.

28. Jessie Reid to her mother, Maggie Reid, Oct. 28, 1902, courtesy of John Muir National Historic Site, Martinez, California.
29. Ibid.
30. Ibid.
31. Undated obituary clipping.
32. Annie to John, Oct. 18, 1902, JM Papers, BT.
33. Annie to John, Dec. 25, [1902], JM Papers, BT.
34. John to his Dunbar cousin, Margaret Lunam, Jan. 26, 1903, JM Papers, BT.
35. Joanna to John, Feb. 1, 1903, JM Papers, BT.
36. Ibid.
37. Undated obituary clipping.
38. Joanna to John, Jan. 22, 1903, JM Papers, BT.
39. Undated obituary clipping.
40. Mary to John, March 4, 1903, JM Papers, BT.
41. Mary to John, March 4, 1903, JM Papers, BT.
42. John to Sarah, undated, [1903], JM Papers, BT.
43. John to Joanna, Feb. 27, 1907, JM Papers, BT.
44. Joanna to John, March 8, 1907, JM Papers, BT.
45. John to Mary, April 3, 1903, JM Papers, BT.

## CHAPTER FIFTEEN

1. Sarah to John, Dec. 28, 1904, JM Papers, BT.
2. John to Margaret Lunam, April 17, 1905, JM Papers, BT.
3. John to Margaret Lunam, May 13, 1906, JM Papers, BT.
4. John to Margaret Lunam, Oct. 13, 1905, JM Papers, BT.
5. John to Joanna, Feb. 14, 1906, JM Papers, BT.
6. John to Robert Underwood Johnson, July 16, 1906, Badé, 10: 357.
7. John to Alfred Bradley Brown, April 22, 1908, JM Papers, BT.
8. John to Alfred Bradley Brown, June 22, 1908, JM Papers, BT.
9. Sarah to John, Dec. 14, 1909, JM Papers, BT.
10. Sarah to John, July 3, 1911, JM Papers, BT.
11. Sarah to John, May 3, 1912, JM Papers, BT.
12. Sarah to John, Dec. 7, 1912, JM Papers, BT.
13. Sarah to John, April 9, 1913, JM Papers, BT.
14. Joanna to John, Oct. 7, 1913, JM Papers, BT.
15. David to John, Sept. 6, 1913, JM Papers, BT.
16. David to John, Jan. 3, 1914, JM Papers, BT.
17. Sarah to John, Feb. 7, 1914, JM Papers, BT.
18. Cecelia Galloway to John, Dec. 4, 1914, JM Papers, BT.

19. The newspaper accounts of Muir's death—obituaries and features—are from the collection of Sherry Hanna and are used through her courtesy.
20. Dan Muir to Wanda, Jan. 13, 1915, courtesy of Sherry Hanna.
21. George Gray to Wanda, Jan. 31, 1915, courtesy of Sherry Hanna.
22. Sarah to Wanda, Jan. 1, 1915, courtesy of Sherry Hanna.
23. Joanna to Wanda, Dec. 29, 1914, courtesy of Sherry Hanna.
24. Joanna to Wanda, Feb. 9, 1915, courtesy of Sherry Hanna.
25. Mary to Wanda, undated, 1915, courtesy of Sherry Hanna.
26. Kimes, 97.
27. John Muir, *Travels In Alaska*, (Boston and New York) Houghton Mifflin Company, The Riverside Press, Cambridge, Fifth Impression, February, 1916), 301.
28. Ibid., 314.